Fodor's

FOURTH
New
EDITION

Nova Scotia, New Brunswick, Prince Edward Island

The complete guide, thoroughly up-to-date

Packed with details that will make your trip

The must-see sights, off and on the beaten path

What to see, what to skip

Mix-and-match vacation itineraries

City strolls, countryside adventures

Smart lodging and dining options

Essential local do's and taboos

Transportation tips, distances and directions

Key contacts, savvy travel tips

When to go, what to pack

Clear, accurate, easy-to-use maps

Reprinted from *Fodor's Canada* and *New England*.

Fodor's Travel Publications, Inc.
New York • Toronto • London • Sydney • Auckland
www.fodors.com/

Fodor's Nova Scotia, New Brunswick, Prince Edward Island

EDITOR: Linda Cabasin

Editorial Contributors: Robert Andrews, Robert Blake, David Brown, Susan Brown, Audra Epstein, Ed Kirby, Hilary M. Nangle, Heidi Sarna, Helayne Schiff, M.T. Schwartzman (Gold Guide editor), Dinah Spritzer, Julie Watson, Ana Watts

Editorial Production: Linda K. Schmidt

Maps: David Lindroth, *cartographer*; Robert Blake, *map editor*

Design: Fabrizio La Rocca, *creative director*; Guido Caroti, *associate art director*; Jolie Novak, *photo editor*

Production/Manufacturing: Mike Costa

Cover Photograph: Greig Cranna

Copyright

Fourth Edition

ISBN 0–679–03514–1

Special Sales

Fodor's Travel Publications are available at special discounts for bulk purchases for sales promotions or premiums. Special editions, including personalized covers, excerpts of existing guides, and corporate imprints, can be created in large quantities for special needs. For more information, contact your local bookseller or write to Special Markets, Fodor's Travel Publications, 201 East 50th Street, New York, NY 10022. Inquiries from Canada should be directed to your local Canadian bookseller or sent to Random House of Canada, Ltd., Marketing Department, 1265 Aerowood Drive, Mississauga, Ontario L4W 1B9. Inquiries from the United Kingdom should be sent to Fodor's Travel Publications, 20 Vauxhall Bridge Road, London, England SW1V 2SA.

PRINTED IN THE UNITED STATES OF AMERICA

10 9 8 7 6 5 4 3 2 1

CONTENTS

ON THE ROAD WITH FODOR'S

WE'RE ALWAYS THRILLED to get letters from readers, especially one like this:

It took us an hour to decide what book to buy and we now know we picked the best one. Your book was wonderful, easy to follow, very accurate, and good on pointing out eating places, informal as well as formal. When we saw other people using your book, we would look at each other and smile.

Our editors and writers are committed to making every Fodor's guide "the best one"—not only accurate but always charming, brimming with sound recommendations and ideas, right on the mark in describing restaurants and hotels, and full of facts that make you view what you've traveled to see in a rich new light.

About Our Writers

Our success in achieving our goals—and in helping to make your trip the best of all possible vacations—is a credit to the hard work of our extraordinary writers.

Award-winning Fredericton columnist **Ana Watts** updated the chapter on her province, New Brunswick, providing fresh material on new attractions and adventures. **Ed Kirby,** a Newfoundland and Labrador tourism writer who lives in St. John's, carefully combed through his chapter. Food and travel writer **Julie Watson,** who updated Nova Scotia and Prince Edward Island, lives on Prince Edward Island and tours the region researching articles and books such as her latest: *Ship Wrecks and Seafaring Tales* and *A Fine Catch Seafood Cookbook.* Writer **Susan Brown,** based in Washington State, updated the Gold Guide material.

New This Year

We're proud to announce that the American Society of Travel Agents has endorsed Fodor's as its guidebook of choice. ASTA is the world's largest and most influential travel trade association, operating in more than 170 countries, with 27,000 members pledged to adhere to a strict code of ethics reflecting the Society's motto, "Integrity in Travel." ASTA shares Fodor's devotion to providing smart, honest travel information and advice to travelers, and we've long recommended that our readers consult ASTA member agents for the experience and professionalism they bring to the table.

On the Web, check out Fodor's site (www.fodors.com/) for information on major destinations around the world and travel-savvy interactive features. The Web site also lists the 85-plus stations nationwide that carry the *Fodor's Travel Show,* a live call-in program that airs every weekend. Tune in to hear guests discuss their adventures—or call in to get answers to your questions.

How to Use This Book

Organization

Up front is the **Gold Guide,** an easy-to-use section divided alphabetically by topic. Under each listing you'll find tips and information that will help you accomplish what you need to in Nova Scotia, New Brunswick, and Prince Edward Island. You'll also find addresses and telephone numbers of organizations and companies that offer destination-related services and detailed information and publications.

The first chapter in the guide, Destination: Nova Scotia, New Brunswick, Prince Edward Island, helps get you in the mood for your trip. New and Noteworthy cues you in on trends and happenings, What's Where gets you oriented, Pleasures and Pastimes describes the activities and sights that really make the region unique, Fodor's Choice showcases our top picks, and Festivals and Seasonal Events alerts you to special events you'll want to seek out.

Chapters in *Nova Scotia, New Brunswick, Prince Edward Island* are divided by geographical area; within each area, towns are covered in logical geographical order, and points of interest between them are indicated by the designation *En Route.* Throughout, Off the Beaten Path sights appear after the places from which they are most easily accessible. And within town sections, all restaurants and lodgings are grouped together.

To help you decide what to visit in the time you have, all chapters begin with recommended itineraries; you can mix and match those from several chapters to create a complete vacation. The A to Z section that ends all chapters covers getting there and getting around. It also provides helpful contacts and resources.

Icons and Symbols

★   Our special recommendations
✕   Restaurant
⊡   Lodging establishment
✕⊡   Lodging establishment whose restaurant warrants a special trip
⚕   Campgrounds
☺   Good for kids (rubber duckie)
☞   Sends you to another section of the guide for more information
⊠   Address
☎   Telephone number
☉   Opening and closing times
⊠   Admission prices (those we give apply to adults; substantially reduced fees are almost always available for children, students, and senior citizens)

Currency

Unless otherwise stated, prices are quoted in Canadian dollars.

Dining and Lodging

The restaurants and lodgings we list are the cream of the crop in each price range. Price charts appear in the Pleasures and Pastimes section that follows the chapter introduction.

Hotel Facilities

We always list the facilities that are available—but we don't specify whether they cost extra: When pricing accommodations, always ask what's included. In addition, assume that all rooms have private baths unless otherwise noted.

Assume that hotels operate on the **European Plan** (EP, with no meals) unless we note that they use the **American Plan** (AP, with all meals), the **Modified American Plan** (MAP, with breakfast and dinner daily), or the **Continental Plan** (CP, with a Continental breakfast daily).

Restaurant Reservations and Dress Codes

Reservations are always a good idea; we note only when they're essential or when they are not accepted. Book as far ahead as you can, and reconfirm when you get to town. Unless otherwise noted, the restaurants listed are open daily for lunch and dinner. We mention dress only when men are required to wear a jacket or a jacket and tie.

Credit Cards

The following abbreviations are used: **AE,** American Express; **D,** Discover; **DC,** Diners Club; **MC,** MasterCard; and **V,** Visa.

Don't Forget to Write

You can use this book in the confidence that all prices and opening times are based on information supplied to us at press time; Fodor's cannot accept responsibility for any errors. Time inevitably brings changes, so always confirm information when it matters—especially if you're making a detour to visit a specific place. In addition, when making reservations be sure to mention if you have a disability or are traveling with children or if you have specific dietary needs or other concerns.

Were the restaurants we recommended as described? Did our hotel picks exceed your expectations? Did you find a museum we recommended a waste of time? If you have complaints, we'll look into them and revise our entries when the facts warrant it. If you've discovered a special place that we haven't included, we'll pass the information along to our correspondents and have them check it out. So send us your feedback, positive *and* negative: E-mail us at editors@fodors.com (specifying the name of the book on the subject line) or write the *Nova Scotia, New Brunswick, Prince Edward Island* editor at Fodor's, 201 East 50th Street, New York, New York 10022. Have a wonderful trip!

Karen Cure

Karen Cure
Editorial Director

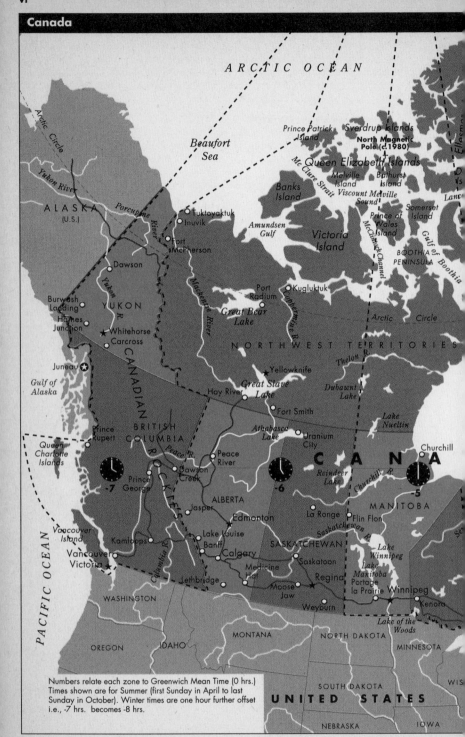

ARCTIC OCEAN

Arctic Circle

Beaufort Sea

Prince Patrick Island

Sverdrup Islands

North Magnetic Pole (c.1980)

Queen Elizabeth Islands

Yukon River

Porcupine

ALASKA (U.S.)

Tuktoyaktuk

Inuvik

Fort McPherson

Dawson

Burwash Landing

Haines Junction

YUKON

Whitehorse

Carcross

Juneau

Gulf of Alaska

Mackenzie River

McClure Strait

Banks Island

Amundsen Gulf

Victoria Island

Melville Island

Bathurst Island

Viscount Melville Sound

Prince of Wales Island

McClintock Channel

Somerset Island

Gulf of Boothia

BOOTHIA PENINSULA

Ellesmere Is

Lanc

Port Radium

Great Bear Lake

Kugluktuk

Coppermine R.

Arctic Circle

NORTHWEST TERRITORIES

Thelon R.

Yellowknife

Great Slave Lake

Hay River

Fort Smith

Dubawnt Lake

Lake Nueltin

Queen Charlotte Islands

Prince Rupert

BRITISH COLUMBIA

CANADIAN

Athabasca Lake

Uranium City

Churchill

Churchill R.

Prince George

Dawson Creek

Peace R.

Peace River

Reindeer Lake

-7

-6

-5

CANA A

Jasper

ALBERTA

Edmonton

La Ronge

Flin Flon

Saskatchewan R.

MANITOBA

Vancouver Island

Kamloops

Columbia R.

Lake Louise

Banff

Calgary

Jasper

SASKATCHEWAN

Saskatoon

Lake Winnipeg

Lake Manitoba

Vancouver

Victoria

Medicine Hat

Regina

Portage la Prairie

Winnipeg

Kenora

WASHINGTON

Lethbridge

Moose Jaw

Weyburn

Lake of the Woods

PACIFIC OCEAN

OREGON

IDAHO

MONTANA

NORTH DAKOTA

MINNESOTA

Numbers relate each zone to Greenwich Mean Time (0 hrs.)
Times shown are for Summer (first Sunday in April to last
Sunday in October). Winter times are one hour further offset
i.e., -7 hrs. becomes -8 hrs.

SOUTH DAKOTA

UNITED STATES

WIS

NEBRASKA

IOWA

ICELAND

GREENLAND
(Denmark)

Denmark Strait

Ellesmere Island

Devon
Island

Lancaster Sound

Baffin
Bay

Baffin Island

Davis Strait

Prince
Charles
Island

Foxe
Basin

Lake Amadjuak
Iqaluit

Lake Harbour

Hudson Strait

Cape Chidley

Labrador
Sea

Southampton
Island

Coats
Island

Mansel
Island

Ivujivik

Ungava
Bay

Nain

Hudson
Bay

D   A

Belcher
Islands

Scefferville

LABRADOR

Goose Bay

Labrador City

Battle
Harbour

2:30

-4

Fort Severn

Fort George

QUEBEC

Sept-Îles

Anticosti Island

Gander

St. John's

James
Bay

Lake
Mistassini

GASPÉ
PENINSULA

-3

ONTARIO

Moosonee

Rimouski

Chicoutimi

PRINCE
EDWARD
ISLAND

ST. PIERRE AND
MIQUELON
(France)

Lake
Nipigon

Cochrane

Ste-Agathe-
Des-Monts

Québec
City

Trois-
Rivières

NEW
BRUNSWICK

Fredericton

Sydney

Charlottetown

NOVA
SCOTIA

Thunder
Bay

Timmins

Saint John

Halifax

Lake Superior

Sudbury

North
Bay

Montréal

Bay of
Fundy

MAINE

ATLANTIC
OCEAN

Sault
Ste. Marie

Ottawa

St. Lawrence

Toronto

Lake
Huron

Lake Michigan

Niagara
Falls

Lake
Ontario

VT

N.H.

WISCONSIN

MICHIGAN

Lake Erie

NEW YORK

MASSACHUSETTS

R.I.

CONN.

WISCONSIN

ILLINOIS

INDIANA

OHIO

PENNSYLVANIA

N.J.

Severn R.

NEWFOUNDLAND

0   400 miles

0   600 km

World Time Zones

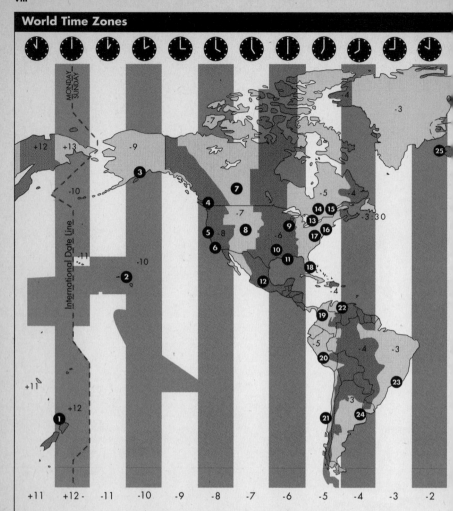

Numbers below vertical bands relate each zone to Greenwich Mean Time (0 hrs.).
Local times frequently differ from these general indications,
as indicated by light-face numbers on map.

Algiers, **29**
Anchorage, **3**
Athens, **41**
Auckland, **1**
Baghdad, **46**
Bangkok, **50**
Beijing, **54**

Berlin, **34**
Bogotá, **19**
Budapest, **37**
Buenos Aires, **24**
Caracas, **22**
Chicago, **9**
Copenhagen, **33**
Dallas, **10**

Delhi, **48**
Denver, **8**
Djakarta, **53**
Dublin, **26**
Edmonton, **7**
Hong Kong, **56**
Honolulu, **2**

Istanbul, **40**
Jerusalem, **42**
Johannesburg, **44**
Lima, **20**
Lisbon, **28**
London
(Greenwich), **27**
Los Angeles, **6**
Madrid, **38**
Manila, **57**

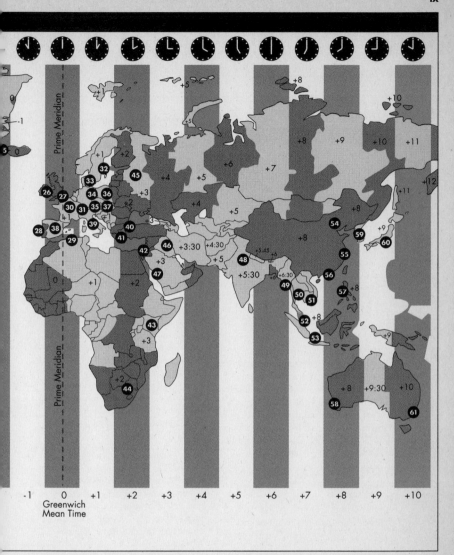

SMART TRAVEL TIPS A TO Z

Basic Information on Traveling in the Maritimes,
Savvy Tips to Make Your Trip a Breeze,
and Companies and Organizations to Contact

A

AIR TRAVEL

MAJOR AIRLINE OR LOW-COST CARRIER?

Most people choose a flight based on price. Yet there are other issues to consider. Major airlines offer the greatest number of departures; smaller airlines—including regional, low-cost and no-frill airlines—usually have a more limited number of flights daily. Major airlines have frequent-flyer partners, which allow you to credit mileage earned on one airline to your account with another. Low-cost airlines offer a definite price advantage and fewer restrictions, such as advance-purchase requirements. Safety-wise, low-cost carriers as a group have a good history, but **check the safety record before booking** any low-cost carrier; call the Federal Aviation Administration's Consumer Hotline (☞ Airline Complaints, *below*).

With the liberalizing of bilateral air agreements between the United States and Canada, there are now more regular flights from many American cities to Canadian cities including Saint John, Halifax, and Yarmouth.

➤ MAJOR AIRLINES: **Air Canada** (☎ 800/776–3000). **Northwest** (☎ 800/225–2525).

➤ SMALLER AIRLINES: **Air Atlantic** (☎ 800/426–7000). **Air Nova** (☎ 800/776–3000). **Canadian** (☎ 800/426–7000).

➤ FROM THE U.K.: **Air Canada** (☎ 0990/247–226) from London Heathrow. **British Airways** (☎ 0345/222–111) and **Canadian Airlines International** (☎ 0181/577–7722) via Toronto.

➤ AIRPORT: **Halifax International Airport** (☎ 902/873–1223 for information) is the major gateway to the Atlantic provinces.

GET THE LOWEST FARE

The least-expensive airfares to Nova Scotia are priced for round-trip travel. Major airlines usually require that you **book far in advance and stay at least seven days** and no more than 30 to get the lowest fares. Ask about "ultrasaver" fares, which are the cheapest; they must be booked 90 days in advance and are nonrefundable. A little more expensive are "supersaver" fares, which require only a 30-day advance purchase. Remember that penalties for refunds or scheduling changes are stiffer for international tickets, usually about $150. International flights are also sensitive to the season: **plan to fly in the off season** for the cheapest fares. If your destination or home city has more than one gateway, **compare prices to and from different airports.** Also price flights scheduled for off-peak hours, which may be significantly less expensive.

To save money on flights from the United Kingdom and back, **look into an APEX or Super-PEX ticket.** APEX tickets must be booked in advance and have certain restrictions. Super-PEX tickets can be purchased at the airport on the day of departure—subject to availability.

DON'T STOP UNLESS YOU MUST

When you book, **look for nonstop flights** and **remember that "direct" flights stop at least once.** International flights on a country's flag carrier are almost always nonstop; U.S. airlines often fly direct. Try to **avoid connecting flights,** which require a change of plane. Two airlines may jointly operate a connecting flight, so ask if your airline operates every segment—you may find that your preferred carrier flies you only part of the way.

USE AN AGENT

Travel agents, especially those who specialize in finding the lowest fares (☞ Discounts & Deals, *below*), can be especially helpful when booking a plane ticket. When you're quoted a price, **ask your agent if the price is likely to get any lower.** Good agents know the seasonal fluctuations of airfares and can usually anticipate a sale or fare war. However, waiting can be risky: The fare could go *up* as seats become scarce, and you may wait so long that your preferred flight sells out. A wait-and-see strategy works best if your plans are flexible, but if you must arrive and depart on certain dates, don't delay.

CHECK WITH CONSOLIDATORS

Consolidators buy tickets for scheduled flights at reduced rates from the airlines then sell them at prices that beat the best fare available directly from the airlines, usually without advance restrictions. Sometimes you can even get your money back if you need to return the ticket. Carefully read the fine print detailing penalties for changes and cancellations, and **confirm your consolidator reservation with the airline.**

➤ CONSOLIDATORS: **United States Air Consolidators Association** (✉ 925 L St., Suite 220, Sacramento, CA 95814, ☎ 916/441–4166, ℻ 916/441–3520).

Airlines routinely overbook planes, knowing that not everyone with a ticket will show up, but sometimes everyone does. When that happens, airlines ask for volunteers to give up their seats. In return these volunteers usually get a certificate for a free flight and are rebooked on the next flight out. If there are not enough volunteers the airline must choose who will be denied boarding. The first to get bumped are passengers who checked in late and those flying on discounted tickets, **so get to the gate and check in as early as possible,** especially during peak periods.

Always **bring a photo ID to the airport.** You may be asked to show it before you are allowed to check in.

ENJOY THE FLIGHT

For better service, **fly smaller or regional carriers,** which often have higher passenger-satisfaction ratings. Sometimes you'll find leather seats, more legroom, and better food.

For more legroom, **request an emergency-aisle seat;** don't, however, sit in the row in front of the emergency aisle or in front of a bulkhead, where seats may not recline.

If you don't like airline food, **ask for special meals when booking.** These can be vegetarian, low-cholesterol, or kosher, for example.

COMPLAIN IF NECESSARY

If your baggage goes astray or your flight goes awry, complain right away. Most carriers require that you file a claim immediately.

➤ AIRLINE COMPLAINTS: U.S. Department of Transportation **Aviation Consumer Protection Division** (✉ C-75, Room 4107, Washington, DC 20590, ☎ 202/366–2220). **Federal Aviation Administration (FAA) Consumer Hotline** (☎ 800/322–7873).

B

BUS TRAVEL

The bus is an essential form of transportation in Canada, especially if you want to visit out-of-the-way towns that do not have airports or rail lines.

➤ BUS COMPANIES: **Greyhound** (✉ 222 1st Ave. SW, Calgary, Alberta, T2P 0A6, ☎ 403/265–9111 or 800/231–2222) and **Voyageur** (✉ 505 E Boulevard Maisonneuve H2L 1Y4, Montréal, ☎ 514/843–4231), offer interprovincial service. In the United Kingdom, contact **Greyhound International** (✉ Sussex House, London Road, E. Grinstead, East Sussex, RHI9 1LD, ☎ 01342/317317).

➤ FROM THE U.S.: **Greyhound** (☎ 800/231–2222).

BUSINESS HOURS

Stores, shops, and supermarkets are usually open Monday through Saturday from 9 to 6—although in major cities, supermarkets are often open from 7:30 AM until 9 PM. Blue laws are in effect in much of Canada, but a growing number of provinces have stores with limited Sunday hours, usually from noon to 5 (shops in areas highly frequented by tourists are usually open on Sunday). Retail stores are generally open on Thursday and Friday evenings, most shopping malls until 9 PM. Most banks in Canada are open Monday through Thursday from 10 to 3, and from 10 to 5 or 6 on Friday. Some banks are open longer hours and also on Saturday morning. All banks are closed on national holidays. Drugstores in major cities are often open until 11 PM, and convenience stores are often open 24 hours a day, seven days a week.

C

CAMERAS, CAMCORDERS, & COMPUTERS

Always **keep your film, tape, or computer disks out of the sun.** Carry an extra supply of batteries, and **be prepared to turn on your camera, camcorder, or laptop** to prove to security personnel that the device is real. Always **ask for hand inspection of film,** which becomes clouded after successive exposure to airport x-ray machines, and **keep videotapes and computer disks away from metal detectors.**

➤ PHOTO HELP: Kodak Information Center (☎ 800/242–2424). *Kodak Guide to Shooting Great Travel Pictures,* available in bookstores or from Fodor's Travel Publications (☎ 800/533–6478; $16.50 plus $4 shipping).

CAR RENTAL

Rates in Nova Scotia begin at $32 a day and $165 a week for an economy car with air conditioning, an automatic transmission, and 150 free miles. This does not include tax on car rentals, which is 15%.

➤ MAJOR AGENCIES: Avis (☎ 800/331–1084, ☎ 800/879–2847 in Canada). Budget (☎ 800/527–0700, 0800/181181 in the U.K.). Hertz (☎ 800/654–3001, 800/263–0600 in Canada, 0345/555888 in the U.K.). National InterRent (☎ 800/227–3876; 0345/222525 in the U.K., where it is known as Europcar Inter-Rent).

CUT COSTS

To get the best deal, **book through a travel agent who is willing to shop around.**

Also **ask your travel agent about a company's customer-service record.**

How has it responded to late plane arrivals and vehicle mishaps? Are there often lines at the rental counter, and, if you're traveling during a holiday period, does a confirmed reservation guarantee you a car?

Be sure to **look into wholesalers,** companies that do not own fleets but rent in bulk from those that do and often offer better rates than traditional car-rental operations. Prices are best during off-peak periods. Rentals booked through wholesalers must be paid for before you leave the United States.

➤ RENTAL WHOLESALERS: **Auto Europe** (☎ 207/842–2000 or 800/223–5555, FAX 800/235–6321). The **Kemwel Group** (☎ 914/835–5555 or 800/678–0678, FAX 914/835–5126).

NEED INSURANCE?

When driving a rented car you are generally responsible for any damage to or loss of the vehicle. You also are liable for any property damage or personal injury that you may cause while driving. Before you rent, **see what coverage you already have** under the terms of your personal auto-insurance policy and credit cards.

BEWARE SURCHARGES

Before you pick up a car in one city and leave it in another, **ask about drop-off charges or one-way service fees,** which can be substantial. Note, too, that some rental agencies charge extra if you return the car before the time specified on your contract. To avoid a hefty refueling fee, **fill the tank just before you turn in the car,** but be aware that gas stations near the rental outlet may overcharge.

MEET THE REQUIREMENTS

In Canada your own driver's license is acceptable.

CHILDREN & TRAVEL

CHILDREN IN CANADA

Both Canadian and U.S. Customs and Immigration are cooperating with measures to reduce parental and other kinds of child abduction. Travelers crossing the border with children should carry identification for them similar to that required by adults (i.e., passport or birth certificate). Children traveling with one parent or other adult should have a letter of permission from the other parent, parents, or legal guardian. Divorced parents with shared custody rights should carry legal documents establishing their status.

Be sure to plan ahead and **involve your youngsters** as you outline your trip. When packing, include things to keep them busy en route. On sightseeing days try to schedule activities of special interest to your children. If you are renting a car don't forget to **arrange for a car seat** when you reserve. Most hotels in Nova Scotia allow children under a certain age to stay in their parents' room at no extra charge, but others charge them as extra adults; be sure to **ask about the cutoff age for children's discounts.**

FLYING

As a general rule, infants under two not occupying a seat fly at greatly reduced fares and occasionally for free. If your children are two or older **ask about children's airfares.**

In general the adult baggage allowance applies to children paying half or more of the adult fare. When booking, **ask about carry-on allowances for those traveling with infants.** In general, for babies charged 10% of the adult fare you are allowed one carry-on bag and a collapsible stroller, which may have to be checked; you may be limited to less if the flight is full.

According to the FAA it's a good idea to use safety seats aloft for children weighing less than 40 pounds. Airlines, however, can set their own policies: U.S. carriers allow FAA-approved models but usually require that you buy a ticket, even if your child would otherwise ride free, since the seats must be strapped into regular seats. Airline rules vary regarding their use, so it's important to **check your airline's policy about using safety seats during takeoff and landing.** Safety seats cannot obstruct any of the other passengers in the row, so get an appropriate seat assignment as early as possible.

When making your reservation, **request children's meals or a free-standing bassinet** if you need them; the latter are available only to those seated at the bulkhead, where there's enough legroom. Remember, however, that bulkhead seats may not have their own overhead bins, and there's no storage space in front of you—a major inconvenience.

GROUP TRAVEL

If you're planning to take your kids on a tour, look for companies that specialize in family travel.

➤ FAMILY-FRIENDLY TOUR OPERATORS: **Grandtravel** (✉ 6900 Wisconsin Ave., Suite 706, Chevy Chase, MD 20815, ☎ 301/986–0790 or 800/247–7651) for people traveling with grandchildren ages 7–17.

CONSUMER PROTECTION

Whenever possible, **pay with a major credit card** so you can cancel payment if there's a problem, provided that you can provide documentation. This is a good practice whether you're buying travel arrangements before your trip or shopping at your destination.

If you're doing business with a particular company for the first time, **contact your local Better Business Bureau and the attorney general's offices** in your state and the company's home state, as well. Have any complaints been filed?

Finally, if you're buying a package or tour, always **consider travel insurance** that includes default coverage (☞ Insurance, *above*).

➤ LOCAL BBBs: **Council of Better Business Bureaus** (✉ 4200 Wilson Blvd., Suite 800, Arlington, VA 22203, ☎ 703/276–0100, 703/525–8277).

CUSTOMS & DUTIES

When shopping, **keep receipts** for all of your purchases. Upon reentering the country, **be ready to show customs officials what you've bought.** If you feel a duty is incorrect, appeal the assessment. If you object to the way your clearance was handled, get the inspector's badge number. In either case, first ask to see a supervisor, then write to the port director at the address listed on your receipt. Send a copy of the receipt and other appropriate documentation. If you still don't get satisfaction you can take your case to customs headquarters in Washington.

ENTERING CANADA

American and British visitors may bring in the following items duty-free: 200 cigarettes, 50 cigars, and 14 ounces of tobacco; 1 bottle (1.1 liters or 40 imperial ounces) of liquor or wine, or 24 355-milliliter (12-ounce) bottles or cans of beer for personal consumption. Any alcohol and tobacco products in excess of these amounts is subject to duty, provincial fees, and taxes. A deposit is sometimes required for trailers (refunded upon return). Cats and dogs must have a certificate issued by a licensed veterinarian that clearly identifies the animal and certifies that it has been vaccinated against rabies during the preceding 36 months. Seeing-eye dogs are allowed into Canada without restriction. Plant material must be declared and inspected. With certain restrictions (some fruits and vegetables), visitors may bring food with them for their own use, providing the quantity is consistent with the duration of the visit.

Canada's firearms laws are significantly stricter than the U.S.'s. All handguns, semi-automatic, and fully automatic weapons are prohibited and cannot be brought into the country. Sporting rifles and shotguns may be imported provided they are to be used for sporting, hunting, or competition while in Canada. All firearms must be declared to Canada Customs at the first point of entry. Failure to declare firearms will result in their seizure, and criminal charges may be made.

Legislation has been passed requiring the registration of all firearms in Canada. This will mean that visitors with permitted firearms will also be required to have them registered and temporarily licensed when crossing the border. Details of how this will be done have not yet been announced.

ENTERING THE U.S.

You may bring home $400 worth of foreign goods duty-free if you've been out of the country for at least 48 hours and haven't already used the $400 allowance or any part of it in the past 30 days.

Travelers 21 and older may bring back 1 liter of alcohol duty-free. In addition, regardless of your age, you are allowed 200 cigarettes and 100 non-Cuban cigars. (At press time, a federal rule restricting tobacco access to persons 18 years and older did not apply to importation.) Antiques, which the U.S. Customs Service defines as objects more than 100 years old, enter duty-free, as do original works of art done entirely by hand, including paintings, drawings, and sculptures.

You may also send packages home duty-free: up to $200 worth of goods for personal use, with a limit of one parcel per addressee per day (and no alcohol or tobacco products or perfume worth more than $5); label the package PERSONAL USE, and attach a list of its contents and their retail value. Do not label the package UNSOLICITED GIFT, or your duty-free exemption will drop to $100. Mailed items do not affect your duty-free allowance on your return.

➤ INFORMATION: **U.S. Customs Service** (Inquiries, ✉ Box 7407, Washington, DC 20044, ☎ 202/927–6724; complaints, Office of Regulations and Rulings, 1301 Constitution Ave. NW, Washington, DC 20229; registration of equipment, ✉ Resource Management, 1301 Constitution Ave. NW, Washington DC, 20229, ☎ 202/927–0540).

ENTERING THE U.K.

From countries outside the EU, including Canada, you may import, duty-free, 200 cigarettes or 50 cigars; 1 liter of spirits or 2 liters of fortified or sparkling wine or liqueurs; 2 liters of still table wine; 60 milliliters of perfume; 250 milliliters of toilet water; plus £136 worth of other goods, including gifts and souvenirs.

➤ INFORMATION: **HM Customs and Excise** (✉ Dorset House, Stamford St., London SE1 9NG, ☎ 0171/202–4227).

D

DISABILITIES & ACCESSIBILITY

ACCESS IN CANADA

➤ LOCAL RESOURCES: **Canadian Paraplegic Association National Office** (✉ 1101 Prince of Wales Dr., Ottawa, ON K2C 3W7, ☎ 613/723–1033) provides information about touring in Canada.

TIPS AND HINTS

When discussing accessibility with an operator or reservationist, **ask hard questions.** Are there any stairs, inside *or* out? Are there grab bars next to the toilet *and* in the shower/tub? How wide is the doorway to the room? To the bathroom? For the most extensive facilities meeting the latest legal specifications, **opt for newer accommodations,** which are more likely to have been designed with access in mind. Older buildings or ships may offer more limited facilities. Be sure to **discuss your needs before booking.**

➤ COMPLAINTS: **Disability Rights Section** (✉ U.S. Department of Justice, Box 66738, Washington, DC 20035–6738, ☎ 202/514–0301 or 800/514–0301, FAX 202/307–1198, TTY 202/514–0383 or 800/514–0383) for general complaints. **Aviation Consumer Protection Division** (☞ Air Travel, *above*) for airline-related problems. **Civil Rights Office** (✉ U.S. Department of Transportation, Departmental Office of Civil Rights, S-30, 400 7th St. SW, Room 10215, Washington, DC, 20590, ☎ 202/366–4648) for problems with surface transportation.

TRAVEL AGENCIES & TOUR OPERATORS

The Americans with Disabilities Act requires that travel firms serve the needs of all travelers. That said, you should note that some agencies and operators specialize in making travel arrangements for individuals and groups with disabilities.

➤ TRAVELERS WITH MOBILITY PROBLEMS: **Access Adventures** (✉ 206 Chestnut Ridge Rd., Rochester, NY 14624, ☎ 716/889–9096), run by a former physical-rehabilitation counselor. **CareVacations** (✉ 5019 49th Ave., Suite 102, Leduc, Alberta T9E 6T5, ☎ 403/986–6404, 800/648–1116 in Canada) has group tours and is especially helpful with cruise vacations. **Hinsdale Travel Service** (✉ 201 E. Ogden Ave., Suite 100, Hinsdale, IL 60521, ☎ 630/325–1335), a travel agency that benefits from the advice of wheelchair traveler Janice Perkins. **Wheelchair Journeys** (✉ 16979 Redmond Way, Redmond, WA 98052, ☎ 206/885–2210 or 800/313–4751), for general travel arrangements.

DISCOUNTS & DEALS

Be a smart shopper and **compare all your options before making a choice.** A plane ticket bought with a promotional coupon may not be cheaper than the least expensive fare from a discount ticket agency. For high-price travel purchases, such as packages or tours, keep in mind that what you get is just as important as what you save. Just because something is cheap doesn't mean it's a bargain.

LOOK IN YOUR WALLET

When you use your credit card to make travel purchases you may get free travel-accident insurance, collision-damage insurance, and medical or legal assistance, depending on the card and the bank that issued it. American Express, MasterCard, and Visa provide one or more of these services, so **get a copy of your credit card's travel-benefits policy.** If you are a member of the American Automobile Association (AAA) or an oil-company-sponsored road-assistance plan, always **ask hotel or car-rental reservationists about auto-club discounts.** Some clubs offer additional discounts on tours, cruises, or admission to attractions. And don't forget that auto-club membership entitles you to free maps and trip-planning services.

DIAL FOR DOLLARS

To save money, **look into "1-800" discount reservations services,** which use their buying power to get a better price on hotels, airline tickets, even car rentals. When booking a room, always **call the hotel's local toll-free number** (if one is available) rather than the central reservations number—you'll often get a better price. Always ask about special packages or corporate rates.

When shopping for the best deal on hotels and car rentals **look for guaranteed exchange rates,** which protect you against a falling dollar. With your rate locked in you won't pay more even if the price goes up in the local currency.

➤ AIRLINE TICKETS: ☎ 800/FLY–4–LESS. ☎ 800/FLY–ASAP.

SAVE ON COMBOS

Packages and guided tours can both save you money, but don't confuse the two. When you buy a package your travel remains independent, just as though you had planned and booked the trip yourself. Fly/drive packages, which combine airfare and car rental, are often a good deal.

JOIN A CLUB?

Many companies sell discounts in the form of travel clubs and coupon books, but these cost money. You must use participating advertisers to get a deal, and only after you recoup the initial membership cost or book price do you begin to save. If you plan to use the club or coupons frequently you may save considerably. Before signing up, find out what discounts you get for free.

➤ DISCOUNT CLUBS: **Entertainment Travel Editions** (✉ 2125 Butterfield Rd., Troy, MI 48084, ☎ 800/445–4137; $23–$48, depending on destination). **Great American Traveler** (✉ Box 27965, Salt Lake City, UT 84127, ☎ 800/548–2812; $49.95 per year). **Moment's Notice Discount Travel Club** (✉ 7301 New Utrecht Ave., Brooklyn, NY 11204, ☎ 718/234–6295; $25 per year, single or family). **Privilege Card International** (✉ 237 E. Front St., Youngstown, OH 44503, ☎ 330/746–5211 or 800/236–9732; $74.95 per year). **Sears's Mature Outlook** (✉ Box 9390, Des Moines, IA 50306, ☎ 800/336–6330; $14.95 per year). **Travelers Advantage** (✉ CUC Travel Service, 3033 S. Parker Rd., Suite 1000, Aurora, CO 80014, ☎ 800/548–1116 or 800/648–4037; $49 per year, single or family). **Worldwide Discount Travel Club** (✉ 1674 Meridian Ave., Miami Beach, FL 33139, ☎ 305/534–2082; $50 per year family, $40 single).

DRIVING

Canada's highway system is excellent. It includes the Trans-Canada Highway, the longest highway in the world, which runs about 8,000 km (5,000 mi) from Victoria, British Columbia, to St. John's, Newfoundland, using ferries to bridge coastal waters at each end.

By law, you are required to **wear seat belts** (and use infant seats). Some provinces have a statutory requirement to drive with vehicle headlights on for extended periods after dawn

and before sunset. Right turns are permitted on red signals in all provinces except Quebec.

Speed limits vary from province to province, but they are usually within the 90–100 kph (50–60 mph) range outside the cities. The price of gasoline costs from 44¢ to 63¢ a liter. (There are 3.8 liters in a U.S. gallon.) Distances are always shown in kilometers, and gasoline is always sold in liters.

AUTO CLUBS

Members of the Automobile Association of America (AAA) can contact the **Canadian Automobile Association** (for emergency road service check locally since each regional- or provincial-affiliated auto club has its own telephone number). Members of the Automobile Association of Great Britain, the Royal Automobile Club, the Royal Scottish Automobile Club, the Royal Irish Automobile Club, and the automobile clubs of the Alliance Internationale de Tourisme (AIT) and Fédération Internationale de l'Automobile (FIA) are entitled to all the services of the CAA on presentation of a membership card.

➤ AUTO CLUBS: In the U.S., **American Automobile Association** (☎ 800/564–6222). In the U.K., **Automobile Association** (AA, ☎ 0990/500–600), **Royal Automobile Club** (RAC, membership ☎ 0990/722–722; insurance 0345/121–345).

FROM THE U.S.

Drivers must have proper owner registration and proof of insurance coverage, which is compulsory in Canada. The Canadian Non-Resident Inter-Provincial Motor Vehicle Liability Insurance Card, available from any U.S. insurance company, is accepted as evidence of financial responsibility anywhere in Canada. The minimum liability coverage in Canada is $200,000 except in Québec, where the minimum is $50,000. If you are driving a car that is not registered in your name, carry a letter from the owner that authorizes your use of the vehicle.

The U.S. Interstate Highway System leads directly into Canada: I–95 from Maine to New Brunswick; I–91 and I–89 from Vermont to Québec; I–87 from New York to Québec; I–81 and a spur off I–90 from New York to Ontario; I–94, I–96, and I–75 from Michigan to Ontario; I–29 from North Dakota to Manitoba; I–15 from Montana to Alberta; and I–5 from Washington state to British Columbia. Most of these connections hook up with the Trans-Canada Highway within a few miles.

F

FERRIES

Car ferries provide essential transportation on both the east and west coasts of Canada. **Marine Atlantic** (⊠ Box 250, North Sydney, NS B2A 3M3, ☎ 902/794–5700 or 800/341–7981 in the U.S. only) operates ferries between Nova Scotia and Newfoundland; New Brunswick and Prince Edward Island; New Brunswick and Nova Scotia; and also between Portland, Maine, and Nova Scotia.

G

GAY & LESBIAN TRAVEL

➤ GAY- AND LESBIAN-FRIENDLY TRAVEL AGENCIES: **Advance Damron** (⊠ 1 Greenway Plaza, Suite 800, Houston, TX 77046, ☎ 713/850–1140 or 800/695–0880, FAX 713/888–1010). **Club Travel** (⊠ 8739 Santa Monica Blvd., West Hollywood, CA 90069, ☎ 310/358–2200 or 800/429–8747, FAX 310/358–2222). **Islanders/Kennedy Travel** (⊠ 183 W. 10th St., New York, NY 10014, ☎ 212/242–3222 or 800/988–1181, FAX 212/929–8530). **Now Voyager** (⊠ 4406 18th St., San Francisco, CA 94114, ☎ 415/626–1169 or 800/255–6951, FAX 415/626–8626). **Yellowbrick Road** (⊠ 1500 W. Balmoral Ave., Chicago, IL 60640, ☎ 773/561–1800 or 800/642–2488, FAX 773/561–4497). **Skylink Women's Travel** (⊠ 3577 Moorland Ave., Santa Rosa, CA 95407, ☎ 707/585–8355 or 800/225–5759, FAX 707/584–5637), serving lesbian travelers.

H

HEALTH

MEDICAL PLANS

No one plans to get sick while traveling, but it happens, so **consider signing up with a medical-assistance company.** Members get doctor referrals, emergency evacuation or repatriation, 24-hour telephone hot lines for medical consultation, cash for emergencies, and other personal and legal assistance. Coverage varies by plan, so **review the benefits carefully.**

➤ MEDICAL-ASSISTANCE COMPANIES: **International SOS Assistance** (⊠ Box 11568, Philadelphia, PA 19116, ☎ 215/244–1500 or 800/523–8930; ⊠ 1255 University St., Suite 420, Montréal, Québec H3B 3B6, ☎ 514/874–7674 or 800/363–0263; ⊠ 7 Old Lodge Pl., St. Margarets, Twickenham TW1 1RQ, England, ☎ 0181/744–0033). **MEDEX Assistance Corporation** (⊠ Box 5375, Timonium, MD 21094-5375, ☎ 410/453–6300 or 800/537–2029). **Traveler's Emergency Network** (⊠ 3100 Tower Blvd., Suite 1000B, Durham, NC 27707, ☎ 919/490–6055 or 800/275–4836, FAX 919/493–8262). **TravMed** (⊠ Box 5375, Timonium, MD 21094, ☎ 410/453–6380 or 800/732–5309). **Worldwide Assistance Services** (⊠ 1133 15th St. NW, Suite 400, Washington, DC 20005, ☎ 202/331–1609 or 800/821–2828, FAX 202/828–5896).

HOLIDAYS

NATIONAL HOLIDAYS

National holidays for 1998 are: New Year's Day, Good Friday (April 10), Easter Monday (April 13), Victoria Day (May 18), Canada Day (July 1), Labor Day (September 7), Thanksgiving (October 12), Remembrance Day (November 11), Christmas, and Boxing Day (December 26).

I

INSURANCE

Travel insurance is the best way to **protect yourself against financial loss.** The most useful policies are trip-cancellation-and-interruption, default, medical, and comprehensive insurance.

Without insurance you will lose all or most of your money if you cancel your trip, regardless of the reason. It's essential that you **buy trip-cancellation-and-interruption insurance,** particularly if your airline ticket,

THE GOLD GUIDE / SMART TRAVEL TIPS

cruise, or package tour is nonrefundable and cannot be changed. When considering how much coverage you need, look for a policy that will cover the cost of your trip plus the nondiscounted price of a one-way airline ticket, should you need to return home early. Also **consider default or bankruptcy insurance,** which protects you against a supplier's failure to deliver.

Medicare generally does not cover health-care costs outside the United States, nor do many privately issued policies. If your own policy does not cover you outside the United States, **consider buying supplemental medical coverage.** Remember that travel health insurance is different from a medical-assistance plan (☞ Health, *above*).

Citizens of the United Kingdom can buy an annual travel-insurance policy valid for most vacations during the year in which it's purchased. If you are pregnant or have a preexisting medical condition, make sure you're covered.

If you have purchased an expensive vacation, particularly one that involves travel abroad, comprehensive insurance is a must. **Look for comprehensive policies that include trip-delay insurance,** which will protect you in the event that weather problems cause you to miss your flight, tour, or cruise. A few insurers sell waivers for preexisting medical conditions. Companies that offer both features include Access America, Carefree Travel, Travel Insured International, and Travel Guard (☞ *below*).

Always **buy travel insurance directly from the insurance company**; if you buy it from a travel agency or tour operator that goes out of business you probably will not be covered for the agency or operator's default, a major risk. Before you make any purchase, **review your existing health and home-owner's policies** to find out whether they cover expenses incurred while traveling.

➤ TRAVEL INSURERS: In the U.S., **Access America** (⊠ 6600 W. Broad St., Richmond, VA 23230, ☎ 804/285–3300 or 800/284–8300), **Carefree Travel Insurance** (⊠ Box 9366, 100 Garden City Plaza, Garden City,

NY 11530, ☎ 516/294–0220 or 800/323–3149), **Near Travel Services** (⊠ Box 1339, Calumet City, IL 60409, ☎ 708/868–6700 or 800/654–6700), **Travel Guard International** (⊠ 1145 Clark St., Stevens Point, WI 54481, ☎ 715/345–0505 or 800/826–1300), **Travel Insured International** (⊠ Box 280568, East Hartford, CT 06128–0568, ☎ 860/528–7663 or 800/243–3174), **Travelex Insurance Services** (⊠ 11717 Burt St., Suite 202, Omaha, NE 68154-1500, ☎ 402/445–8637 or 800/228–9792, ℻ 800/867–9531), **Wallach & Company** (⊠ 107 W. Federal St., Box 480, Middleburg, VA 20118, ☎ 540/687–3166 or 800/237–6615). In Canada, **Mutual of Omaha** (⊠ Travel Division, 500 University Ave., Toronto, Ontario M5G 1V8, ☎ 416/598–4083, 800/268–8825 in Canada). In the U.K., **Association of British Insurers** (⊠ 51 Gresham St., London EC2V 7HQ, ☎ 0171/600–3333).

L

LANGUAGE

Canada's two official languages are English and French. Though English is widely spoken, it may be useful to **learn a few French phrases** if you plan to travel to the province of Québec or to the French Canadian communities in the Maritimes (Nova Scotia, New Brunswick, and Prince Edward Island), northern Manitoba, and Ontario. Canadian French, known as Québecois or *joual,* is a colorful language often quite different from that spoken in France.

LODGING

Aside from the quaint hotels of Québec, Canada's range of accommodations more closely resembles that of the United States than of Europe. In the cities you'll have a choice of luxury hotels, moderately priced modern properties, and smaller older hotels with perhaps fewer conveniences but more charm. Options in smaller towns and in the country include large, full-service resorts; small, privately owned hotels; roadside motels; and bed-and-breakfasts. Even here you'll need to make reservations at least on the day on which you're planning to pull into town.

Expect accommodations to cost more in summer than in the off-season. When making reservations, **ask about special deals** and packages when reserving. City hotels that cater to business travelers often offer weekend packages, and many city hotels offer rooms at up to 50% off in winter. If you're planning to visit a major city or resort area in high season, **book well in advance.** Also be aware of any special events or festivals that may coincide with your visit and fill every room for miles around.

APARTMENT & VILLA RENTALS

If you want a home base that's roomy enough for a family and comes with cooking facilities, **consider a furnished rental.** These can save you money, however some rentals are luxury properties, economical only when your party is large. Home-exchange directories list rentals (often second homes owned by prospective house swappers), and some services search for a house or apartment for you (even a castle if that's your fancy) and handle the paperwork. Some send an illustrated catalog; others send photographs only of specific properties, sometimes at a charge. Up-front registration fees may apply.

➤ RENTAL AGENTS: **Property Rentals International** (✉ 1008 Mansfield Crossing Rd., Richmond, VA 23236, ☎ 804/378–6054 or 800/220–3332, ℻ 804/379–2073).

B&BS

Bed-and-breakfasts can be found in both the country and the cities. Every provincial tourist board either has a listing of B&Bs or can refer you to an association that will help you secure reservations. Rates range from $20 to upwards of $70 a night and include a Continental or a full breakfast. Some B&B hosts lock up early; be sure to ask. Room quality varies from house to house as well, so don't be bashful about asking to see a room before making a choice.

HOME EXCHANGES

If you would like to exchange your home for someone else's, **join a home-exchange organization,** which will send you its updated listings of available exchanges for a year and will include your own listing in at least one of them. Making the arrangements is up to you.

➤ EXCHANGE CLUBS: **HomeLink International** (✉ Box 650, Key West, FL 33041, ☎ 305/294–7766 or 800/638–3841, ℻ 305/294–1148) charges $83 per year.

M
MAIL

You can buy stamps at the post office or from automatic vending machines in most hotel lobbies, railway stations, airports, bus terminals, many retail outlets, and some newsstands. Within Canada, postcards and letters up to 30 grams cost 45¢; between 31 grams and 50 grams, the cost is 71¢; and between 51 grams and a kilogram the cost is 90¢. Letters and postcards to the United States cost 52¢ for up to 30 grams, 77¢ for between 31 and 50 grams, and $1.17 for up to a kilogram. Prices include GST.

International mail and postcards run 90¢ for up to 30 grams, and $2.10 for up to 100 grams.

Telepost is a fast "next day or sooner" service that combines the CN/CP Telecommunications network with letter-carrier delivery service. Messages may be telephoned to the nearest CN/CP Public Message Centre for delivery anywhere in Canada or the United States. Telepost service is available 24 hours a day, seven days a week, and billing arrangements may be made at the time the message is called in. Intelpost allows you to send documents or photographs via satellite to many Canadian, American, and European destinations. This service is available at main postal facilities in Canada and is paid for in cash.

RECEIVING MAIL

Visitors may have mail sent to them c/o General Delivery in the town they are visiting, for pickup in person

THE GOLD GUIDE / SMART TRAVEL TIPS

within 15 days, after which it will be returned to the sender.

MONEY

American money is accepted in much of Canada (especially in communities near the border). However, visitors are encouraged to exchange at least some of their money into Canadian funds at a bank or other financial institution in order to get the most favorable exchange rate. Traveler's checks (some are available in Canadian dollars) and major U.S. credit cards are accepted in most areas.

The units of currency in Canada are the Canadian dollar (C$) and the cent, in almost the same denominations as U.S. currency ($5, $10, $20, 1¢, 5¢, 10¢, 25¢, etc.). The $1 and $2 bill are no longer used; they have been replaced by $1 and $2 coins. At press time the exchange rate was C$1.29 to US$1 and C$2.18 to £1.

ATMS

Before leaving home, **make sure that your credit cards have been programmed for ATM use.**

➤ ATM LOCATIONS: Cirrus (☎ 800/424–7787). Plus (☎ 800/843–7587).

TRAVELER'S CHECKS

Whether or not to buy traveler's checks depends on where you are headed. **Take cash if your trip includes rural areas** and small towns, traveler's checks to cities. If your checks are lost or stolen, they can usually be replaced within 24 hours. To ensure a speedy refund, buy your checks yourself (don't ask someone else to make the purchase). When making a claim for stolen or lost checks, the person who bought the checks should make the call.

P

PACKING

Layering is the best defense against Canada's cold winters; a hat, scarf, and gloves are essential. For summer travel, loose-fitting natural-fiber clothes are best; bring a wool sweater and light jacket.

Bring an extra pair of eyeglasses or contact lenses in your carry-on luggage, and if you have a health problem, **pack enough medication** to last the entire trip or have your doctor write you a prescription using the drug's generic name, because brand names vary from country to country. It's important that you **don't put prescription drugs or valuables in luggage to be checked**: it might go astray. To avoid problems with customs officials, carry medications in the original packaging. Also, don't forget the addresses of offices that handle refunds of lost traveler's checks.

LUGGAGE

In general, you are entitled to check two bags on flights within the United States and on international flights leaving the United States. A third piece may be brought on board, but it must fit easily under the seat in front of you or in the overhead compartment.

If you are flying between two foreign destinations, note that baggage allowances may be determined not by piece but by weight—generally 88 pounds (40 kilograms) in first class, 66 pounds (30 kilograms) in business class, and 44 pounds (20 kilograms) in economy. If your flight between two cities abroad *connects* with your transatlantic or transpacific flight, the piece method still applies.

Airline liability for baggage is limited to $1,250 per person on flights within the United States. On international flights it amounts to $9.07 per pound or $20 per kilogram for checked baggage (roughly $640 per 70-pound bag) and $400 per passenger for unchecked baggage. Insurance for losses exceeding these amounts can be bought from the airline at check-in for about $10 per $1,000 of coverage; note that this coverage excludes a rather extensive list of items, which is shown on your airline ticket.

Before departure, **itemize your bags' contents** and their worth, and label the bags with your name, address, and phone number. (If you use your home address, cover it so that potential thieves can't see it readily.) Inside each bag, **pack a copy of your itinerary.** At check-in, **make sure that each bag is correctly tagged** with the destination airport's three-letter code. If your bags arrive damaged or fail to arrive at all, file a written report with the airline before leaving the airport.

PASSPORTS & VISAS

Once your plans are confirmed, **get a passport even if you don't need one to enter Canada**—it's always the best form of I.D. **Make photocopies of the data page**; leave one copy with someone at home and keep another with you, separated from your passport. If you lose your passport, promptly call the nearest embassy or consulate and the local police; having a copy of the data page can speed replacement.

U.S. CITIZENS

Citizens and legal residents of the United States do not need a passport or a visa to enter Canada, but proof of citizenship (a birth certificate or valid passport) and photo identification may be requested. Naturalized U.S. residents should carry their naturalization certificate or "green card." U.S. residents entering Canada from a third country must have a valid passport, naturalization certificate, or "green card."

U.K. CITIZENS

Citizens of the United Kingdom need only a valid passport to enter Canada for stays of up to six months.

➤ INFORMATION: **London Passport Office** (☎ 0990/21010) for fees and documentation requirements and to request an emergency passport.

S

SENIOR-CITIZEN TRAVEL

To qualify for age-related discounts, **mention your senior-citizen status up front** when booking hotel reservations and before you're seated in restaurants. Note that discounts may be limited to certain menus, days, or hours. When renting a car, **ask about promotional car-rental discounts.**

➤ EDUCATIONAL TRAVEL PROGRAMS: **Elderhostel** (✉ 75 Federal St., 3rd floor, Boston, MA 02110, ☎ 617/426–8056).

STUDENTS

Persons under 18 years of age who are not accompanied by their parents should bring a letter from a parent or guardian giving them permission to travel to Canada.

To save money, **look into deals available through student-oriented travel agencies.** To qualify you'll need a bona fide student ID card. Members of international student groups are also eligible.

➤ STUDENT IDs AND SERVICES: **Council on International Educational Exchange** (✉ CIEE, 205 E. 42nd St., 14th floor, New York, NY 10017, ☎ 212/822–2600 or 888/268–6245, FAX 212/822–2699), for mail orders only, in the United States. **Travel Cuts** (✉ 187 College St., Toronto, Ontario M5T 1P7, ☎ 416/979–2406 or 800/667–2887) in Canada.

➤ HOSTELING: **Hostelling International—American Youth Hostels** (✉ 733 15th St. NW, Suite 840, Washington, DC 20005, ☎ 202/783–6161, FAX 202/783–6171). **Hostelling International—Canada** (✉ 400-205 Catherine St., Ottawa, Ontario K2P 1C3, ☎ 613/237–7884, FAX 613/237–7868). **Youth Hostel Association of England and Wales** (✉ Trevelyan House, 8 St. Stephen's Hill, St. Albans, Hertfordshire AL1 2DY, ☎ 01727/855215 or 01727/845047, FAX 01727/844126). Membership in the U.S., $25; in Canada, C$26.75; in the U.K., £9.30).

T

TAXES

A goods and services tax of 7% (GST) applies on virtually every transaction in Canada except for the purchase of basic groceries.

SALES

In addition to the GST, Prince Edward Island has a 10% sales tax on most items purchased in shops, on restaurant meals, and sometimes on hotel rooms. In New Brunswick, Newfoundland, and Nova Scotia, a single 15% HST (Harmonized sales tax) is in effect. Most provinces do not tax goods shipped directly by the vendor to the visitor's home address.

➤ GST REFUNDS: You **can get a GST refund** on purchases taken out of the country and on short-term accommodations (but not on food, drink, tobacco, car or motorhome rentals, or transportation); rebate forms, which must be submitted within 60 days of leaving Canada, may be obtained from certain retailers, duty-free shops, and customs officials or from **Revenue Canada** (✉ Visitor Rebate Program, Summerside Tax Centre, Summerside, PE C1N 6C6, ☎ 800/668-4748 in Canada or 902/432-5608 from outside of Canada). Instant cash rebates up to a maximum of $500 are provided by some duty-free shops when leaving Canada, and most provinces do not tax goods that are shipped directly by the vendor to the purchaser's home. You'll need your original receipts from stores and hotels. Be sure the name and address of the establishment is shown on the receipt. Original receipts are not returned. The total amount of GST on each receipt must be at least $3.50, and visitors have to claim at least $14 in tax per rebate application form.

TELEPHONES

CALLING HOME

AT&T, MCI, and Sprint long-distance services make calling home relatively convenient and let you avoid hotel surcharges. Typically you dial an 800 number.

➤ TO OBTAIN ACCESS CODES: **AT&T USADirect** (☎ 800/874-4000). **MCI Call USA** (☎ 800/444-4444). **Sprint Express** (☎ 800/793-1153).

TIPPING

Tips and service charges are not usually added to a bill in Canada. In general, tip 15% of the total bill. This goes for waiters, waitresses, barbers and hairdressers, taxi drivers, etc. Porters and doormen should get about $1 a bag (or more in a luxury hotel). For maid service, $1 a day is sufficient ($2 in luxury hotels).

TOUR OPERATORS

Buying a prepackaged tour or independent vacation can make your trip to Nova Scotia less expensive and more hassle-free. Because everything is prearranged you'll spend less time planning.

Operators that handle several hundred thousand travelers per year can use their purchasing power to give you a good price. Their high volume may also indicate financial stability. But some small companies provide more personalized service; because they tend to specialize, they may also be more knowledgeable about a given area.

A GOOD DEAL?

The more your package or tour includes, the better you can predict the ultimate cost of your vacation. Make sure you know exactly what is covered, and **beware of hidden costs.** Are taxes, tips, and service charges included? Transfers and baggage handling? Entertainment and excursions? These can add up.

If the package or tour you are considering is priced lower than in your wildest dreams, **be skeptical.** Also, **make sure your travel agent knows the accommodations** and other services. Ask about the hotel's location, room size, beds, and whether it has a pool, room service, or programs for children, if you care about these. Has your agent been there in person or sent others you can contact?

BUYER BEWARE

Each year consumers are stranded or lose their money when tour operators—even very large ones with excellent reputations—go out of business. So **check out the operator.** Find out how long the company has been in business, and ask several agents about its reputation. **Don't book unless the firm has a consumer-protection program.**

Members of the National Tour Association and United States Tour Operators Association are required to set aside funds to cover your payments and travel arrangements in case the company defaults. Nonmembers may carry insurance instead. Look for the details, and for the name of an underwriter with a solid reputation, in the operator's brochure. Note: When it comes to tour operators, **don't trust escrow accounts.** Although the Department of Transportation watches over charter-flight operators, no regulatory body prevents tour operators from raiding the till. You may want to protect yourself by buying travel insurance that includes a tour-operator default provision. For more information, *see* Consumer Protection, *above.*

It's also a good idea to choose a company that participates in the American Society of Travel Agents Tour Operator Program (TOP). This gives you a forum if there are any disputes between you and your tour operator; ASTA will act as mediator.

➤ TOUR-OPERATOR RECOMMENDA-TIONS: **National Tour Association** (✉ NTA, 546 E. Main St., Lexington, KY 40508, ☎ 606/226–4444 or 800/755–8687). **United States Tour Operators Association** (✉ USTOA, 342 Madison Ave., Suite 1522, New York, NY 10173, ☎ 212/599–6599, FAX 212/599–6744). **American Society of Travel Agents** (☞ *below*).

USING AN AGENT

Travel agents are excellent resources. In fact, large operators accept bookings made only through travel agents. But it's a good idea to **collect brochures from several agencies,** because some agents' suggestions may be influenced by relationships with tour and package firms that reward them for volume sales. If you have a special interest, **find an agent with expertise in that area;** ASTA (☞ Travel Agencies, *below*) has a database of specialists worldwide. Do some homework on your own, too: Local tourism boards can provide information about lesser-known and small-niche operators, some of which may sell only direct.

SINGLE TRAVELERS

Prices for packages and tours are usually quoted per person, based on two sharing a room. If traveling solo, you may be required to pay the full double-occupancy rate. Some operators eliminate this surcharge if you agree to be matched with a roommate of the same sex, even if one is not found by departure time.

GROUP TOURS

Among companies that sell tours to Nova Scotia, the following are nationally known, have a proven reputation, and offer plenty of options. The classifications used below represent different price categories, and you'll probably encounter these terms when talking to a travel agent or tour operator. The key difference is usually in accommodations, which run from budget to better, and better-yet to best.

➤ DELUXE: **Globus** (✉ 5301 S. Federal Circle, Littleton, CO 80123-2980, ☎ 303/797–2800 or 800/221–0090, FAX 303/347–2080). **Maupintour** (✉ 1515 St. Andrews Dr., Lawrence, KS 66047, ☎ 913/843–1211 or 800/255–4266, FAX 913/843–8351). **Tauck Tours** (✉ Box 5027, 276 Post Rd. W, Westport, CT 06881-5027, ☎ 203/226–6911 or 800/468–2825, FAX 203/221–6828).

➤ FIRST-CLASS: **Brendan Tours** (✉ 15137 Califa St., Van Nuys, CA 91411, ☎ 818/785–9696 or 800/421–8446, FAX 818/902–9876). **Collette Tours** (✉ 162 Middle St., Pawtucket, RI 02860, ☎ 401/728–3805 or 800/832–4656, FAX 401/728–1380). **Gadabout Tours** (✉ 700 E. Tahquitz Canyon Way, Palm Springs, CA 92262–6767, ☎ 619/325–5556 or 800/952–5068). **Mayflower Tours** (✉ Box 490, 1225 Warren Ave., Downers Grove, IL 60515, ☎ 708/960–3430 or 800/323–7064).

➤ BUDGET: **Cosmos** (☞ Globus, *above*).

PACKAGES

Like group tours, independent vacation packages are available from major tour operators and airlines. The companies listed below offer vacation packages in a broad price range.

➤ AIR/HOTEL: **Air Canada Vacations** (☎ 514/876–4141).

➤ AIR/HOTEL/CAR: **Air Canada Vacations** (☎ 514/876–4141).

➤ FROM THE U.K.: **Key to America** (✉ 1-3 Station Rd., Ashford, Middlesex TW15 2UW, ☎ 01784/248777) and **Kuoni Travel** (✉ Kuoni House, Dorking, Surrey RH5 4AZ, ☎ 01306/742–222). **Vacation Canada** (✉ Cambridge House, 8 Cambridge St., Glasgow G2 3DZ, ☎ 0345/090–905). **British Airways Holidays** (✉ Astral Towers, Betts Way, London Rd., Crawley, West Sussex RH10 2XA, ☎ 01293/723–730).

TRAVEL AGENCIES

A good travel agent puts your needs first. Look for an agency that has been in business at least five years, emphasizes customer service, and has someone on staff who specializes in your destination. In addition, **make sure the agency belongs to the American Society of Travel Agents** (ASTA). If your travel agency is also acting as your tour operator, *see* Payments *and* Tour Operators, *above.*

THE GOLD GUIDE / SMART TRAVEL TIPS

➤ LOCAL AGENT REFERRALS: **American Society of Travel Agents** (ASTA, ☎ 800/965–2782 24-hr hot line, FAX 703/684–8319). **Alliance of Canadian Travel Associations** (✉ Suite 201, 1729 Bank St., Ottawa, Ontario K1V 7Z5, ☎ 613/521–0474, FAX 613/521–0805). **Association of British Travel Agents** (✉ 55–57 Newman St., London W1P 4AH, ☎ 0171/637–2444, FAX 0171/637–0713).

TRAVEL GEAR

Travel catalogs specialize in useful items, such as compact alarm clocks and travel irons, that can **save space when packing.**

➤ MAIL-ORDER CATALOGS: **Magellan's** (☎ 800/962–4943, FAX 805/568–5406). **Orvis Travel** (☎ 800/541–3541, FAX 540/343–7053). **TravelSmith** (☎ 800/950–1600, FAX 800/950–1656).

U

U.S. GOVERNMENT

The U.S. government can be an excellent source of inexpensive travel information. When planning your trip, **find out what government materials are available.**

➤ ADVISORIES: **U.S. Department of State** (✉ Overseas Citizens Services Office, Room 4811 N.S., Washington, DC 20520); enclose a self-addressed, stamped envelope. Interactive hot line (☎ 202/647–5225, FAX 202/647–3000). Computer bulletin board (☎ 301/946–4400).

➤ PAMPHLETS: **Consumer Information Center** (✉ Consumer Information Catalogue, Pueblo, CO 81009, ☎ 719/948–3334) for a free catalog that includes travel titles.

V

VISITOR INFORMATION

For general information before you go, contact the information office of the province or provinces you are visiting. When you arrive, you can visit visitor information centers throughout eacn province; *see* the A to Z section that concludes each chapter for information.

➤ PROVINCIAL: In New Brunswick, **Tourism New Brunswick** (✉ Box 12345, Woodstock, E0J 2B0, ☎ 800/561–0123); in Newfoundland and Labrador, **Newfoundland and Labrador Department of Tourism, Recreation and Culture** (✉ Box 8730, St. John's, A1B 4K2, ☎ 800/563–6353); in Nova Scotia, **Nova Scotia Tourism** (✉ Box 130, Halifax, B3J 2M7, ☎ 800/565–0000); in Prince Edward Island, **Prince Edward Island Department of Tourism, Parks and Recreation** (✉ Box 940, Charlottetown, C1A 7M5, ☎ 800/463–4734).

➤ IN THE U.K.: **Visit Canada Center** (✉ 62–65 Trafalgar Sq., London, WC2N 5DY, ☎ 0891/715–000, FAX 0171/389–1149). Calls cost 50¢ per minute.

W

WHEN TO GO

In the maritime provinces of Nova Scotia, New Brunswick, and Prince Edward Island, the weather is relatively mild, though snow can remain on the ground well into spring and fog is common year-round. In Newfoundland and Labrador temperatures vary widely; winter days can be about 32°F (0°C) in St. John's—and as low as –50°F (–45°C) in Labrador and on the west coast.

Climate

HALIFAX

Jan.	33F	1C	May	58F	14C	Sept.	67F	19C
	20	– 7		41	5		53	12
Feb.	33F	1C	June	67F	19C	Oct.	58F	14C
	19	– 7		50	10		44	7
Mar.	39F	4C	July	73F	23C	Nov.	48F	9C
	26	– 3		57	14		36	2
Apr.	48F	9C	Aug.	73F	24C	Dec.	37F	3C
	33	1		58	13		25	4

➤ FORECASTS: **Weather Channel Connection** (☎ 900/932–8437), *95¢* per minute from a Touch-Tone phone.

1 Destination: Nova Scotia, New Brunswick, Prince Edward Island

SMALL, FRIENDLY, RELAXED

IT HAS BEEN ON TRIPS outside the city, to the more far-flung sectors of this most resolutely regional of nations, that I have found Canada at its more extreme, independent, quirky—even romantic, as un-Canadian a word as that is supposed to be. One snow-swept morning in Pouch Cove, a fishing-village-turned-suburb north of St. John's, Newfoundland, I visited William Noseworthy in his white clapboard house high on Noseworthy's Hill. Blue-eyed and ruddy-cheeked, Noseworthy sat in the kitchen by a wood stove, distractedly smoking a cigarette. He was 66 and had just retired the year before after four decades of fishing, but he still stared out the window at the North Atlantic. "There's something that draws you to it," he said in the rich accent of "the Rock."

His son, 31-year-old Barry, sipping a Labatt's beer, recalled that once, when he was 13, his father caught him whistling in a boat. "He was going to throw me overboard," said Barry. "It's just bad luck." William explained: "you don't whistle on the water. You wouldn't dare. You wouldn't launch your boat on Friday either. They're just superstitions, maybe. But several years ago, someone launched a big fishing trawler on a Friday, and she was lost on a Friday, and all the crew members, too." A minute later, William pulled out a shiny red accordion and played a jig, tapping his foot, but his eyes never left the water.

Newfoundland is also a place to sample Canadian regionalism at its most craggy and entrenched. The province's inshore fishermen claim that their very way of life is endangered by declining cod catches, which they blame on offshore trawling, often by foreigners. They blame Ottawa for not looking out for their interests—even 40 years after joining the Confederation, the old refrain still comes quickly to some residents' lips: " Newfoundlander first, a Canadian second." But in a Pouch Cove twine store, where four diehard fishermen repaired their cod traps while country music drawled from a tape player, Frank Noseworthy, a slim, mustachioed

cousin of Barry, said that he rejected the Newfoundlanders first sentiment—and would far rather be Canadian than American. "In the States," he said, "them that's got it, gets more; them that don't, gets less. The Canadian government's more generous toward people that don't have."

In general, Canadians strike me as more outward-looking than Americans. They did not, after all, grow up being told that they already live in the greatest country on earth. "Americans are like TV evangelists," maintained Roger Bill, an Indiana native who is now the Newfoundland-based Atlantic field producer for CBS Radio's *Sunday Morning* show. "They really believe theirs is the best way and everyone else should follow. Canadians aren't nearly so arrogant." They do, however, take a palpable pride in place, with a decided prejudice toward the small, friendly, and relaxed. "I wouldn't live in the States, or in Toronto or Montréal," said Richard Harvey, a high-school principal from Upper Gullies, Newfoundland. "You couldn't pay me enough."

—Bob Levin

Originally from Philadelphia, *Maclean's* foreign editor Bob Levin moved to Toronto in October 1985. He traveled from coast to coast for this article on an American's impressions of Canada.

NEW AND NOTEWORTHY

NEW BRUNSWICK➤ The **Kingsbrae Gardens,** a horticultural garden complete with mazes, is scheduled to open in spring 1998 on a historic estate in St. Andrews.

NEWFOUNDLAND AND LABRADOR➤ A new Marine Interpretation Centre in **Terra Nova National Park** in the Bonavista Bay area of eastern Newfoundland includes touch tanks, displays, and tours. It signals a change in the park's focus from land to sea. The **Ryan Premises National Historic Site** in Cape Bonavista depicts the almost

500-year history of the commercial cod fishery in a fish merchant's restored properties.

PRINCE EDWARD ISLAND➤ Travelers coming to the province via New Brunswick will see the completion of the Island's newest attraction: **Confederation Bridge,** which links the Island with the mainland.

WHAT'S WHERE

New Brunswick

New Brunswick is where the great Canadian forest, sliced by sweeping river valleys and modern highways, meets the Atlantic. To the north and east, the gentle, warm Gulf Stream washes quiet beaches. Besides the seacoast, there are pure inland streams, pretty towns, and historic cities. The province's dual heritage (35% of its population is Acadian French) provides added spice.

Newfoundland and Labrador

Canada's easternmost province, Newfoundland, was a center of the world's cod fishing industry for 400 years until the supply ran out in 1992. In summer, Newfoundland's stark cliffs, bogs, and meadows become a riot of wildflowers and greenery, and the sea is dotted with boats and buoys. St. John's, the capital, is a classic harbor city.

Nova Scotia

This little province on the Atlantic coast, compact and distinctive, has a capital city, Halifax, the same size as Christopher Marlowe's London. The days when Nova Scotians were prosperous shipwrights and merchants trading with the world left Victorian mansions in all the salty little ports that dot the coastline and created a uniquely Nova Scotian outlook: worldly, approachable, and sturdily independent.

Prince Edward Island

In the Gulf of St. Lawrence north of Nova Scotia and New Brunswick, Prince Edward Island seems too good to be true, with its crisply painted farmhouses, manicured green fields rolling down to sandy beaches, the warmest ocean water north of Florida,

lobster boats in trim little harbors, and a vest-pocket capital city, Charlottetown, packed with architectural heritage.

PLEASURES AND PASTIMES

Dining

Though there are few really distinct national dishes here, the strong ethnic presence in Canada makes it difficult not to have a good meal. This is especially true in the larger cities, where Greek, Italian, Chinese, Indian, and other immigrants operate restaurants. In addition, each province is well known for various specialties. **Seafood** usually heads the menu at restaurants in Nova Scotia, New Brunswick, Prince Edward Island, and Newfoundland. In addition, **fiddleheads,** curled young fern fronds picked in the spring, often accompany dishes in these maritime provinces.

The Great Outdoors

Most Canadians live in towns and cities within 200 miles of the American border, but the country does have a splendid backyard to play in. A network of 34 national parks, from Kluane in Yukon to Cape Breton Highlands in Nova Scotia, is backed by dozens of provincial and regional parks. All this wilderness provides abundant opportunities for bicycling, camping, canoeing, hiking, boating, horseback riding, mountain climbing, skiing, white-water sports, and fishing. The Gulf of St. Lawrence and the Atlantic provinces are ideal for whale-watching. The chapters in this book and provincial tourism authorities have information on all these activities.

BIKING➤ Eastern Canada offers some of the best bicycling in the country, from the flats of Prince Edward Island to the varied terrain in New Brunswick and Nova Scotia. Write to the provincial tourist boards for their road maps (which are more detailed than the maps available at gas stations) and information on local cycling associations.

BOATING➤ With the Atlantic coastline, major rivers, and smaller lakes, boating is extremely popular throughout Eastern

Canada. Boat rentals are widely available, and provincial tourism departments can provide lists of sources.

CAMPING➤ Canada's 2,000-plus campgrounds range from simple roadside turnoffs with sweeping mountain vistas to fully equipped facilities with groomed sites, trailer hookups, recreational facilities, and vacation-village atmosphere. Many of the best sites are in Canada's national and provincial parks, with nominal overnight fees. Commercial campgrounds offer more amenities, such as electrical and water hookups, showers, and even game rooms and grocery stores. They cost more and are—some think—antithetical to the point of camping: getting a little closer to nature. Contact tourist offices for listings.

CANOEING AND KAYAKING➤ Your degree of expertise and experience will dictate where you canoe. Beginners can try waterways in more settled areas; pros head north to the streams and rivers that flow into the Arctic Ocean. Provincial tourist offices can be of assistance, especially in locating an outfitter to suit your needs.

FISHING➤ Anglers can find their catch in virtually any region of the country, though restrictions, seasons, license requirements, and catch limits vary from province to province. In addition, a special fishing permit is required to fish in all national parks; it can be obtained at any national park site, for a nominal fee. **Nova Scotia** has some of the most stringent freshwater restrictions in Canada, but the availability of Atlantic salmon, speckled trout, and striped bass makes the effort worthwhile. Salmon, trout, and black bass are abundant in the waters of **New Brunswick,** and although many salmon pools in the streams and rivers are leased to private freeholders, either individuals or clubs, fly fishing is still readily available for visitors. The waters surrounding **Prince Edward Island** have some of the best deep-sea tuna fishing. **Newfoundland** offers cod, mackerel, salmon, and sea trout in the Atlantic and speckled trout and rainbow trout in its fresh waters.

HIKING➤ Miles and miles of trails weave through all of Canada's national and provincial parks. Write to the individual provincial tourist offices.

NATIONAL PARKS➤ The country's first national park was established in 1885, and since then the national park system has grown to encompass 34 national parks and 112 national historic sites. Because of Canada's eagerness to preserve its environment, new lands are continually being added to this network. Almost every park offers camping—either primitive camping or campsites with various facilities that can accommodate recreational vehicles. Hiking trails weave their way through each of the parks. One of the most popular preserves is **Fundy National Park** in New Brunswick.

SCUBA DIVING➤ More than 3,000 shipwrecks lie off the coast of **Nova Scotia,** making it particularly attractive to divers. The provincial Department of Tourism can provide details on the location of wrecks and where to buy or rent equipment.

WHALE-WATCHING➤ The Atlantic waters around Newfoundland offer excellent whale-watching, and giant humpback, right whales, finback, and minke whales can be seen in the Bay of Fundy. Boat trips are available from New Brunswick and Nova Scotia.

WINTER SPORTS➤ If asked, most Canadians would probably claim they hate winter. Whining about the cold is a national pastime. But the fact is, the country revels in winter. Every town and village has at least a few skating rinks, and everyone has a favorite toboggan hill. In January and February, fishermen erect villages of huts on frozen rivers and lakes, and dog teams yap through the forest as soon as the snow is deep enough. There are thousands of miles of cross-country ski trails. One of the fastest-growing sports is snowmobiling. A network of 112,255 km (69,600 mi) of trails with its own restaurants, road signs, and maps crisscrosses much of the country.

Shopping

ARTS AND CRAFTS➤ Sweaters, silver objects, pottery, and Acadian crafts can be found in abundance in New Brunswick. For pewter, head for Fredericton. For woven items, visit the village of St. Andrews.

MAPLE SYRUP➤ Eastern Canada is famous for its sugar maples. The trees are tapped in early spring, and the sap is collected in buckets to be boiled down into maple syrup. This natural confection is sold all year. Avoid the tourist shops and department stores; for the best prices and information, stop at farm stands and markets in New Brunswick. A small can of syrup costs about $6 to $9.

FODOR'S CHOICE

No two people will agree on what makes a perfect vacation, but it's fun and helpful to know what others think. We hope you'll have a chance to experience some of Fodor's Choices yourself in Nova Scotia, New Brunswick and Prince Edward Island. For detailed information about each entry, refer to the appropriate chapter.

Historic Site

★ **Kings Landing Historical Settlement, outside Fredericton, New Brunswick.** This reconstructed village—including homes, an inn, a forge, a store, a church, a school, working farms, and a sawmill—illustrates life in the central Saint John River valley between 1790 and 1900.

Parks

★ **Cape Breton Highlands National Park, Nova Scotia.** A wilderness of wooded valleys, plateau barrens, and steep cliffs, it stretches across the northern peninsula of Nova Scotia's Cape Breton Island.

★ **Prince Edward Island National Park, Prince Edward Island.** Along the north shore of the island on the Gulf of St. Lawrence, sky and sea meet red sandstone cliffs, rolling dunes, and long stretches of sand.

Views to Remember

★ **Peggy's Cove, Nova Scotia.** At the mouth of a bay facing the open Atlantic, the cove, with its houses huddled around the narrow slit in the boulders, has the only Canadian post office in a lighthouse.

★ **Signal Hill National Historic Site, St. John's, Newfoundland.** Overlooking the snug, punch-bowl harbor of St. John's and the sea, this hilltop was taken and retaken by opposing forces in the 17th and 18th centuries.

Hotel

★ **West Point Lighthouse, West Point, Prince Edward Island.** A functioning lighthouse in a provincial park, this small inn sits next to the beach. *$$*

FESTIVALS AND SEASONAL EVENTS

Contact local or provincial tourist boards for more information about these and other festivals.

WINTER

DECEMBER➤ Newfoundland and Labrador: In St. John's, **New Year's** revelers pour out of downtown pubs to gather on the waterfront to ring in the new year.

Prince Edward Island: The Prince Edward Island Crafts Council **Annual Christmas Craft Fair** brings juried producers to Charlottetown for the largest event of its kind on the Island.

SPRING

MAY➤ Nova Scotia: In the Annapolis Valley, the **Apple Blossom Festival** includes dancing, parades, and entertainment.

SUMMER

JUNE➤ New Brunswick: St. John's Day commemorates the city's birthday and includes a parade, street dance, concerts, and sporting and cultural events.

Nova Scotia: The **International Blues Festival** draws music lovers to Halifax.

Prince Edward Island: Charlottetown Festival Theatre offers concerts and musicals (through September). In Summerside the annual **Summerside Highland Gathering** kicks off a summer of concerts and "Come to the Ceilidh" evenings.

JULY➤ New Brunswick: Loyalist City Festival, in St. John, celebrates the town's founding with parades, dancing, and sidewalk festivities. The **Shediac Lobster Festival** takes place in the town that calls itself the Lobster Capital of the World. There's an **Irish Festival** in Miramichi. The **New Brunswick Highland Games & Scottish Festival** is in Fredericton. In Edmunston the **Foire Brayonne** has music, cultural events, and sports; it's the biggest Francophone festival outside Québec's Winter Carnival.

Newfoundland and Labrador: The **Hangashore Folk Festival** is in Corner Brook, the **Exploits Valley Salmon Festival** in the Grand Falls area, the **Fish, Fun and Folk Festival** in Twillingate, and the **Conception Bay Folk Festival** in Carbonear. **Musicfest** in Stephenville celebrates music, from rock and roll to traditional Newfoundland. **Signal Hill Tattoo** in St. John's (through August) reenacts the final 1762 battle of the Seven Years' War between the British and the French. The **Burin Peninsula**

Festival of Folk Song and Dance features traditional Newfoundland entertainment.

Nova Scotia: Antigonish Highland Games, staged annually since 1861, has Scottish music, dance, and such ancient sporting events as the caber toss. Halifax hosts the **Nova Scotia International Tattoo.** The **Atlantic Jazz Festival** is a Halifax highlight.

Prince Edward Island: The **Annual Outdoor Scottish Fiddle and Dance Festival** skirls through Richmond. Rollo Bay hosts a **Fiddle Festival.** Summerside's **Lobster Carnival** is a weeklong feast of lobster. **Canada Day** festivities abound in even the smallest community on the first of the month.

AUGUST➤ New Brunswick: The **Miramichi Folk Song Festival** features traditional and contemporary folk songs steeped in Maritime lore. **Acadian Festival,** at Caraquet, celebrates the region's Acadian heritage with folk singing and food. The **Chocolate Festival** in St. Stephen includes suppers, displays, and children's events.

Newfoundland and Labrador: Gander's **Festival of Flight** celebrates this town as the aviation "Crossroads of the World," with dances, parades, and a folk festival. *Une Longue Veillée* folk festival, celebrating western Newfoundland's French heritage, brings traditional musicians, singers, and dancers to Cape St. George.

Nova Scotia: There's Lunenburg's **Nova Scotia Fisheries Exhibition and Fishermen's Reunion.** The **Nova Scotia Gaelic Mod** in St. Ann's celebrates Scottish culture on the grounds of the only Gaelic college in North America. The **Halifax International Buskerfest** has daily outdoor shows by street performers, a food festival, and stage entertainment.

Prince Edward Island: Eldon's **Highland Games** gathers Scotsmen and women. The **Annual Community Harvest Festival** animates Kensington. **Old Home Week** fills Charlottetown with nostalgia. An **International Hydroplane Regatta** brings speed to the Summerside waterfront.

AUTUMN

SEPTEMBER➤ **Newfoundland and Labrador:** Deer Lake hosts the **Humber Valley Agricultural Home and Handicraft Exhibition.**

Prince Edward Island: Festival Acadien de la Region Evangeline is an agricultural fair with Acadian music, a parade, and lobster suppers, at Wellington Station.

OCTOBER➤ **Nova Scotia:** There's the **Shearwater International Air Show.**

2 Nova Scotia

Compact and distinctive, this little province on the Atlantic Coast is a mélange of cultures: Gaelic street signs in Pugwash and Mabou, French masses in Chéticamp and Point de l'Eglise, black gospel choirs in Halifax, Mi'Kmaq handicrafts in Eskasoni, onion-dome churches in Sydney, sauerkraut in Lunenburg, and Yankee Puritanism in Clark's Harbour. Though quiet coastal villages may set the tone, urban centers like Halifax and Sydney exist with a pleasant mix of big-city life and small-town charm.

INFINITE RICHES IN A LITTLE ROOM," wrote Elizabethan playwright Christopher Marlowe. He might have been referring to Nova Scotia, Canada's second-smallest province, which packs an impossible variety of cultures and landscapes into an area half the size of Ohio.

Updated by
Julie V. Watson

Nova Scotia's landscapes echo every region of Canada. Mountain clefts in Cape Breton Island could pass for crannies in British Columbia. Stretches of the Tantramar Marshes are as board-flat as the prairies. The glaciated interior, spruce-swathed and peppered with lakes, closely resembles the Canadian Shield in northern Manitoba. The apple blossoms in the Annapolis Valley are as glorious as those in Niagara, and parts of Halifax could masquerade as downtown Toronto. A massive Catholic church in a tiny French village recalls Québec. The warm saltwater and long sandy beaches of Prince Edward Island are also found on the mainland side of Northumberland Strait, and the brick-red mud flats of the Bay of Fundy echo their counterparts in New Brunswick. Neil's Harbour looks just like a Newfoundland outport—and sounds like one, too.

The people are as varied as the landscape. The Mi'Kmaq Indians have been here for 10,000 years. The French came to the Annapolis Basin in 1605. In the 1750s, cockneys and Irish settled in Halifax and "Foreign Protestants"—chiefly Germans—in Lunenburg. By then Yankees from New England were putting down roots in Liverpool, Cape Sable Island, and the Annapolis Valley. In the 1780s they were joined by thousands of "Loyalists," many of them black, displaced by the American Revolution. Soon after, the Scots poured into northern Nova Scotia and Cape Breton, evicted from the Highlands by their landlords' preference for sheep. The last wave of immigrants, in the 1890s, became steelworkers and coal miners in Cape Breton; they came from Wales, the West Indies, Poland, Ukraine, and the Middle East. They're all Nova Scotians, and they're all still here, eating their own foods and worshiping in their own churches.

This is a little buried nation, with a capital city the same size as Marlowe's London. Before Canada was formed in 1867, Nova Scotians were prosperous shipwrights and merchants, trading with the world. Who created Cunard Lines? A Haligonian, Samuel Cunard. Those days brought democracy to the British colonies, left Victorian mansions in the salty little ports that dot the coastline, and created a uniquely Nova Scotian outlook: worldly, approachable, and sturdily independent.

Pleasures and Pastimes

Dining

Skilled chefs find their abilities enhanced by the availability of ingredients such as succulent blueberries, crisp apples, wild mushrooms, home-raised poultry, quality beef, fresh-from-the-sea lobster, cultivated mussels, Digby scallops, and the famous Atlantic salmon. The quality of ingredients comes from the closeness of the harvest. Agriculture, fisheries (both wild harvest and aquaculture) are never far from the doorstep of the food and hospitality industry.

Helping travelers discover for themselves the best tastes of this beautiful province, the Nova Scotian culinary industry has formed an organization called the Taste of Nova Scotia. It pulls together the producers and the preparers, setting quality standards to ensure that patrons at member restaurants receive authentic Nova Scotian food. Look for their symbol: a golden oval porthole framing food and a ship.

CATEGORY	COST*
$$$$	over $50
$$$	$35–$50
$$	$15–$35
$	under $15

per person, excluding drinks, service, and 15% harmonized sales tax (HST).

Lodging

Nova Scotia's strength lies within a sprinkling of first-class resorts that have retained the traditional feel, top country inns where a dedication to fine dining with an emphasis on local products and high-level accommodation rule, and a smattering of exceptional corporate hotels. Bed-and-breakfasts, particularly those in smaller towns, are often exceptional. Most of the resorts and many B&Bs are seasonal.

In addition to the reliable chains, Halifax and Dartmouth have a number of excellent hotels; reservations are necessary year-round and can be made by calling Check In (☞ Contacts and Resources *in* Nova Scotia A to Z, *below*). Expect to pay considerably more in the capital district than elsewhere.

CATEGORY	COST*
$$$$	over $80
$$$	$65–$80
$$	$45–$65
$	under $45

All prices are for a standard double room, excluding 15% harmonized sales tax (HST).

Music

Talented musicians abound in Nova Scotia, ranging from traditional fiddlers to folk singers and rock bands. Names to watch for include the Rankin Family, the Barra MacNeills, the Minglewood Band, Sam Moon, Rita MacNeil, David MacIsaac, Scott Macmillan, and such traditional fiddlers as Buddy MacMaster, Ashley MacIsaac, Sandy MacIntyre, Lee Cremo, and Jerry Holland.

Outdoor Activities and Sports

BEACHES

The province is one big seashore. The warmest beaches are found on the Northumberland Strait shore. The west coast of Cape Breton and the Bras d'Or Lake also offer fine beaches and warm saltwater.

BIRD-WATCHING

One of the highest concentrations of bald eagles in North America is found in Cape Breton, along the Bras d'Or Lake and in Cape Breton Highlands National Park. July and August are the best eagle-watching months. The Bird Islands, off the coast of Cape Breton, are home to a variety of seabirds, including the rare Atlantic puffin and the endangered Piping Plover.

FISHING

Nova Scotia has more than 9,000 lakes and 100 brooks; practically all lakes and streams are open to anglers. The catch includes Atlantic salmon (June–September), brook and sea trout, bass, rainbow trout, and shad. You can get a nonresident fishing license from any Department of Natural Resources office in the province and at most sporting-goods stores. Before casting a line in national park waters, it is necessary to obtain a transferrable National Parks Fishing License, available at park offices. Licenses are not required for saltwater fishing. South of Shelburne, from Barrington to Digby, is the most prosperous fishing region in the province.

The shoreline along the Bay of Fundy contains some of the oldest rocks and fossils in the world. Fossilized trees, insects, plants, and ferns can be seen at the famous fossil cliffs of Joggins on Chignecto Bay. The Minas Basin near Parrsboro has dinosaur fossils as well as semiprecious stones such as agate and amethyst. Rock hounds are welcome to gather what they find along the beaches, but a permit from the Nova Scotia Museum is required to dig along the cliffs. Organized rock hounding tours are available in Joggins and Parrsboro.

Wineries

Nova Scotian wineries are becoming exceedingly popular. While local wines are featured in many restaurants, they can be sampled for free and bought by the bottle for as little as $6 (U.S.) at the vineyards they come from. Wineries to visit include Jost Vineyards in Malagash and Sainte Famille Winery in Falmouth.

Exploring Nova Scotia

On the eastern edge of North America, Nova Scotia is astonishing in its variety. Along the coast, the North Atlantic breaks on rocky shores and beaches of fine, white sand. To the west the world's largest tides ebb and flow along the Bay of Fundy. Inland, dense forests and country roads weave among hundreds of lakes and rivers. The rugged terrain continues in central Nova Scotia and Cape Breton, where there are spectacular cliffs.

When arriving in Nova Scotia from New Brunswick via the Trans-Canada Highway (Hwy. 104), you are presented with three ways to proceed into the province. Amherst is the first community you will enter upon crossing the border. From Amherst, Highway 104 will take you toward Halifax, only a two-hour drive away. Touring alternatives lie to the north and south. Route 6, to the north, leaves Amherst to follow the shore of the Northumberland Strait; farther east is Cape Breton. Route 2, to the south, is a less travelled road and a favorite with children because of nearby fossil studded shores. Connect to branch roads to reach the Annapolis Valley and other points south. Please be aware that driving on rural roads warrants careful attention; while well surfaced, these roads are often without shoulders and unposted blind crests and sharp curves pop up unexpectedly in keeping with the rugged landscape.

Numbers in the text correspond to numbers in the margin and on the Nova Scotia and Halifax maps.

Great Itineraries

The province naturally divides itself into regions that can be explored in three to seven days. Some visitors do a whirlwind drive around, taking in only a few sights. But Nova Scotia's varied cultural landscape deserves careful exploration. If you have the time, try linking up to two or more tours.

IF YOU HAVE 3 DAYS

Start in **Halifax** ①–⑫, where remnants of a maritime past provide the setting for a surprisingly urban present. Explore the South Shore and Annapolis Valley, taking in the Lighthouse Route and Evangeline Trail. The two trails form a loop that begins and ends in Halifax (via Route 3, 103, or 333, the scenic road around the shore), covering a distance of approximately 850 km (527 mi) with no side trips. Leaving Halifax, head for **Peggy's Cove,** a picturesque fishing village surrounded by bare granite and coastal barrens. Explore **Mahone Bay** and travel on to **Lunenburg** ⑮, where the culture of Atlantic Coast fisheries is ex-

PRINCE EDW

Borden

Cape Tormentine

NEW BRUNSWICK

Northumberland

Amherst

Oxford

Pugwash

Malaga

6
28

Tatam

Trans-Canada

Joggins

30

29 **Springhill**

Balmora

Mills

Masstown

Great
Village

Debert

Bib

Chignecto Game
Sanctuary

2

Five Islands

104

Advocate
Harbour

209

Parrsboro

31

2

Cobequid Bay

Trur

Cap d'Or
Scots Bay

Cape
Split

Cape
Blomidon

Minas
Basin

Maitland

Stewi

St. John

358

2

Bay of Fundy

Minas Channel

Wolfville

Kentville

Hantsport

Windsor

22

Shubena

Mount
Uniacke

Evangeline Trail

Berwick

23

Three
Mile Plains

101

Annapolis
Royal

Kingston

Middleton

Upper Sackville
Middle Sackville

102

Lower
Sackville

21

Port Royal

101

Bridgetown

12

Hubbards

Bedford

13 **Dartmout**

Digby Neck

Clements Port

103

St.
Margarets
Bay

Eastern

Digby

Bear
River

8

New Ross

Mahone
Bay

Chester

Peggy's
Cove

333

Herring
Cove

Halifa

Long
Island

1

Tiverton

St. Bernard

KEJIMKUJIK
NATIONAL PARK

Bridgewater

15

1

12

20

Westport

Evangeline Trail

TOBEATIC
WILDLIFE
MANAGEMENT AREA

Lake
Rossignol

3

Lunenburg

14 **Big and Little**
Tancook Islands

Brier
Island

19 **Point de**
l'Eglise

101

210

La Have
Greenfield

103

Milton

Brooklyn

ATLANT

TO
BAR HARBOR
[MAINE]

1

16 **Liverpool**

18 **Yarmouth**

3

TO
PORTLAND
[MAINE]

Pubnico

Shelburne

17

103

Lockeport

Woods
Harbour

Barrington

330

Cape
Sable
Island

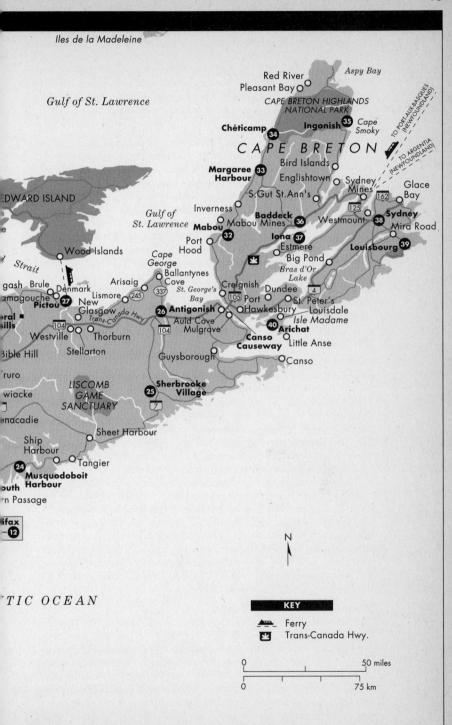

Iles de la Madeleine

Gulf of St. Lawrence

Aspy Bay

Red River
Pleasant Bay

CAPE BRETON HIGHLANDS
NATIONAL PARK

Chéticamp · **34** · Ingonish · **35** · Cape
Smoky

C A P E   B R E T O N

TO PORT AUX BASQUES
(NEWFOUNDLAND)

TO ARGENTIA
(NEWFOUNDLAND)

Margaree
Harbour · **33** · Bird Islands
Englishtown · Sydney
Mines

S.Gut St.Ann's

Glace
Bay

EDWARD ISLAND

Gulf of
St. Lawrence

Inverness

162

125

Sydney

Baddeck · **36** · Westmount · **38**

Mira Road

Mabou · **32** · Mabou Mines

Port
Hood

Iona · **37**
Estmere

Big Pond

Louisbourg · **39**

Wood Islands

Cape
George

Bras d'Or
Lake

Strait

Ballantynes
Cove

Creignish

Dundee

4

St. Peter's

Arisaig

337

St. George's
Bay

105

Port
Hawkesbury

Louisdale

Denmark

245

gash Brule

Lismore

amagouche

New
Glasgow

Pictou · **27**

Antigonish · **26**

Auld Cove
Mulgrave

Isle Madame

Arichat · **40**

Little Anse

ral
ills

Trans-Canada Hwy.

104

Westville Thorburn

Canso
Causeway

Canso

Bible Hill

Stellarton

Guysborough

ruro

wiacke

LISCOMB
GAME
SANCTUARY

Sherbrooke
Village · **25**

7

nacadie

Sheet Harbour

Ship
Harbour

Tangier

24

Musquodoboit
Harbour

outh

n Passage

ifax · **12**

TIC OCEAN

N

KEY

Ferry

Trans-Canada Hwy.

0 ——————————————— 50 miles

0 ——————————————— 75 km

plored in the Fisheries Museum. Overnight in Lunenburg before continuing on Route 3 or 103 to **Shelburne** ⑰. Begin day two with a visit to **Yarmouth** ⑱ and travel on to **Digby** for a lunch of scallops. **Annapolis Royal** ㉑, with its gardens, historic sites, and harbor-front boardwalk, is a lovely spot to spend an afternoon. Travel on to ⊡ **Wolfville** ㉒ for an overnight stay. The next day check tide times and plan a drive to the shore of Minas Basin, where the tides are the highest in the world. A leisurely drive will put you back in Halifax by late noon.

IF YOU HAVE 5 DAYS

The Eastern Shore, the Atlantic Coast east of Halifax, is perhaps the most scenic and unspoiled stretch of coastline in mainland Nova Scotia. Route 7 winds along a deeply indented, glaciated coastline of rocky waters interspersed with pocket beaches, long, narrow fjords, and fishing villages. **Musquodoboit Harbour** ㉔ is a haven for fishing enthusiasts. Nearby is **Martinique Beach,** one of Nova Scotia's best beaches. Continue north to **Sherbrooke Village** ㉕, full of refurbished late 19th century structures. Route 7 turns inland and follows the St. Mary's River towards **Antigonish** ㉖ on the Sunrise Trail. Historians will appreciate a visit to **Hector Heritage Quay** in ⊡ **Pictou** ㉗, where the Scots landed in 1773. From Pictou, Route 6 runs beside an apparently endless string of beaches with many summer homes plunked in the adjoining fields. Turn right to Malagash, where **Jost Vineyards** invites wine tasting and tours. Be sure to visit **Seagull Pewter** in **Pugwash** ㉘. A half-hour drive will take you to ⊡ **Amherst.** Continue on to **Joggins** ㉚ and search for souvenirs in its sandstone cliffs.

IF YOU HAVE 7 DAYS

Cape Breton Island, with its lush natural areas, wonderful small towns, and spectacular National Park, is perfect for a leisurely seven-day tour. Follow the coastal route (described in the following pages), which takes you on a west-to-east loop from the Canso Strait Causeway. Overnight in ⊡ **Margaree Harbour** ㉝ so that you can enjoy the Cabot Trail and **Cape Breton Highlands National Park** for at least a full day. Spend a night or more in Margaree Harbour, a good base from which to seek out orchids, photograph spectacular scenery, walk the trails to hidden waterfalls, or go whale-watching (whale-watching opportunities abound on the northeastern side of the peninsula). Allow time for a visit to the **Alexander Graham Bell National Historic Site** in **Baddeck** ㊱, and spend the night in ⊡ **Iona** ㊲. ⊡ **Sydney** ㊳, with its casino for evening entertainment, will position you for a daylong visit to **Fortress of Louisbourg National Historic Park,** the largest historic restoration in Canada, and the town of **Louisbourg** ㊴, which has an interesting shipwreck museum. Take Route 4 back to Canso Causeway through **Big Pond,** home of singer Rita McNeil.

When to Tour Nova Scotia

The best time of year to visit Nova Scotia is mid-June to mid-September; in fact, many resorts, hotels, and attractions are only open during July and August. Nova Scotia, particularly the Cape Breton area, is a very popular destination in the fall due to the spectacular changing of the leaves. Lobster lovers will find the region's most popular seafood plentiful in May and June. Whale-watching, wildlife cruises, and sea kayaking outfitters generally operate from July to mid-September. Most golf courses stay open from June until late September, and some into October. Skiing (both downhill and cross-country) is popular at a variety of locations including Kejimkujik and Cape Breton Highlands from mid-December to early April.

HALIFAX AND DARTMOUTH

The Halifax and Dartmouth metro area, now known, along with the whole former County of Halifax, as the Halifax Regional Municipality, surrounds the second-largest natural harbor in the world, Halifax Harbour. It bustles with activity day and night and flavors the rest of the city with its presence. Pubs, shops, museums, parks, and public gardens buzz with activity. Jazz, buskers, outdoor festivals, and cultural and sporting events abound. Galleries, concerts, theater, and fine dining combine to make the twin cities a destination for any season, with a mix of big-city life and small-town charm.

Halifax

1,137 km (705 mi) northeast of Boston; 275 km (171 mi) southeast of Moncton, New Brunswick.

Salty and urbane, learned and plain-spoken, Halifax is large enough to have the trappings of a capital city, yet small enough to retain the warmth and convenience of a small town.

A Good Walk

Begin on Upper Water Street at **Purdy's Wharf** ①, for unobstructed views of Halifax Harbour and the architectural wonder it inspired. Continue south to the restored warehouses of **Historic Properties** ②, a cluster of boutiques and restaurants linked by cobblestoned footpaths. Stroll along the piers to the **Maritime Museum of the Atlantic** ③: The wharves outside frequently welcome visiting transatlantic yachts and sail-training ships. Walk to the end of the block and cross the street to **Brewery Market** ④, restored waterfront property abundant with eateries. Take the elevator at the office-end of the Brewery Market and emerge on Hollis Street. Turn left, past several elegant Victorian town houses—notably Keith Hall—once the executive offices of the brewery.

Turn right onto Bishop Street and right again onto Barrington Street, Halifax's main downtown thoroughfare. The stone mansion on your right is **Government House** ⑤, the official residence of Nova Scotia's lieutenant governor. Take a detour from Barrington Street onto Spring Garden Road, and head for the **Halifax Public Gardens** ⑥, where you can rest your legs on shaded benches amidst flower beds and rare trees. Only one block away on Summer Street is the **Nova Scotia Museum of Natural History** ⑦.

On your way back to Barrington Street, you'll notice the **Halifax Citadel National Historic Site** ⑧, dominated by the fortress that once commanded the city. On a lot defined by Barrington, Argyle, and Prince streets lies **St. Paul's Church** ⑨; one wall within its historic confines contains a fragment of the great Halifax Explosion of 1917. A block farther and facing City Hall is the Grand Parade, where musicians perform at noon on summer days. From here, the waterfront side of Citadel Hill, look uphill: The tall, stylish brick building is the World Trade and Convention Centre and is attached to the 10,000-seat Halifax Metro Centre—the site of hockey games, rock concerts, and political conventions. Farther to the right are the office towers above Scotia Square, the leading downtown shopping mall. Look also for **Province House** ⑩, Canada's oldest legislative building, and, across from Province House at Cheapside, the **Art Gallery of Nova Scotia** ⑪, which showcases a large collection of folk art. If time permits, end your tour at **Anna Leonowens Gallery** ⑫ on Granville Street and peruse the work of local artists.

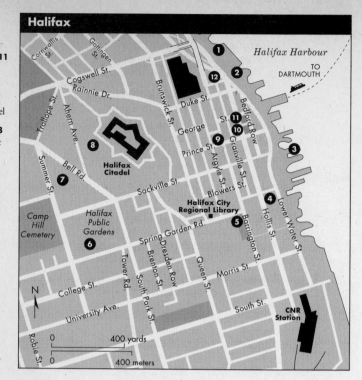

TIMING

The city of Halifax is fairly compact: Depending on your tendency to stop and study or sit back and savor the moment, the above tour can take from a half to a full day. You can drive from sight to sight, but parking is a problem, and you will miss out on much of the flavor of the city.

Sights to See

12 **Anna Leonowens Gallery.** Though the gallery is named for the Victorian woman whose memoirs served as fodder for Rodgers' and Hammerstein's *The King and I*, it has nothing to do with the Broadway production—founding the Nova Scotia College of Art and Design is just another of her life's chapters. Three exhibition spaces serve as a public showcase for the college, faculty and students alike, as well as visiting artists. The displays, which change frequently, focus on contemporary studio and media art. ⊠ *1891 Granville St.,* ☎ *902/494–8223.* ▦ *Free.* ☉ *Tues.–Fri. 11–5, Sat. noon–4.*

11 **Art Gallery of Nova Scotia.** Sheltered within this historic building is an extensive permanent collection of over 4,000 works, including an internationally recognized collection of maritime and folk art. ⊠ *1741 Hollis St., at Cheapside,* ☎ *902/424–7542,* FAX *902/424–0750.* ▦ *$2.50.* ☉ *June–Aug., Tues., Wed., and Fri. 10–5, Thurs. 10–9, weekends noon–5; Sept.–May, Tues.–Fri. 10–5, weekends noon–5.*

4 **Brewery Market.** This sprawling ironstone complex was once Keith's Brewery (named for Alexander Keith, a 19th-century brewer); now it houses offices, restaurants, and shops. It's a favored haunt of Haligonians on Saturday mornings year-round and on Fridays in summer when a farmer's market invites the opportunity to sample local produce, meats, and cheeses. ⊠ *Between Hollis and Lower Water Sts.*

❺ Government House. Built between 1799 and 1805 for Sir John Wentworth, the Loyalist governor of New Hampshire, and his racy wife, Fannie (Thomas Raddall's novel *The Governor's Lady* tells their story), this house has since been gubernatorial quarters. The house is not open to the public.

★ **❽ Halifax Citadel National Historic Site.** The Citadel, erected between 1826 and 1856, was the heart of the city's fortifications, and was linked to smaller forts and gun emplacements on the harbor islands and on the bluffs above the harbor entrance. Kilted soldiers drill in front of the **Army Museum,** once the barracks, and a cannon is fired every day at noon. Audiovisual programs and special events are offered several times throughout the year. Before leaving, take in the view from the Citadel: the spiky downtown crowded between the hilltop and the harbor; the wooded islands at the harbor's mouth; and the naval dockyard under the Angus L. MacDonald Bridge, the nearer of the two bridges connecting Halifax with its sister city of Dartmouth. The handsome four-sided **Town Clock** on Citadel Hill was given to Halifax by Prince Edward, Duke of Kent, military commander from 1794 to 1800. ⊠ *Citadel Hill,* ☎ *902/426–5080.* 🎦 *June 15–Aug. $5.75; May 15–June 14 and Sept.–Oct. 15 $3.50; rest of year free.* ☉ *June 15–Aug., daily 9–6; May 15–June 14, Sept.–Oct. 15, and rest of year, daily 9–5.*

NEED A BREAK?

Bud the Spud, a chip-wagon parked at the curb in front of the Halifax City Regional Library, supplies summer crowds with snacks perfect for listening to the buskers who make stages of the library's lawn. ⊠ *5381 Spring Garden Rd.*

❻ Halifax Public Gardens. One of the oldest formal Victorian gardens in North America, this city oasis had its start in 1753 as a private garden. Its layout was completed in 1875 by Richard Power, former gardener to the Duke of Devonshire in Ireland. Gravel paths wind among ponds, trees, and flower beds, revealing an astonishing variety of plants from all over the world. The centerpiece is a filigreed gazebo erected in 1887 for Queen Victoria's Golden Jubilee; today it stages Sunday afternoon concerts in summer. ⊠ *Bounded by Sackville, Summer, and S. Park Sts. and Spring Garden Rd.*

❷ Historic Properties. Dating from the early 19th century when trade and war made Halifax prosperous, these waterfront warehouses are Canada's oldest. They were built by such raffish characters as Enos Collins, a privateer, smuggler, and shipper whose vessels defied Napoléon's blockade to bring American supplies to the Duke of Wellington. Collins was also a prime mover in the Halifax Banking Company, which evolved into the Royal Bank of Canada, the country's largest bank. The buildings have since been taken over by quality shops and restaurants, boisterous pubs, and chic offices.

❸ The Maritime Museum of the Atlantic. The exhibits in this restored chandlery and warehouse on the waterfront include small boats once used around the coast, as well as displays describing Nova Scotia's proud sailing heritage, from the days when the province, on its own, was one of the world's foremost shipbuilding and trading nations. Other exhibits explore the Halifax Explosion of 1917, shipwrecks, and lifesaving. Permanently moored outside, after a long life of charting the coasts of Labrador and the Arctic, is the hydrographic steamer *Acadia.* At the next wharf, in summer, is Canada's naval memorial, **HMCS** *Sackville,* the sole survivor of a fleet that escorted convoys of ships from Halifax to England during World War II. ⊠ *1675 Lower Water St.,* ☎ *902/424–7490 or 902/424–7491,* 𝔽𝔸𝕏 *902/424–0612.* ☉ *June–mid-*

Oct., Mon. and Wed.–Sat. 9:30–5:30, Tues. 9:30–8, Sun. 1–5:30; mid-Oct.–May, Wed.–Sat. 9:30–5, Tues. 9:30–8, Sun. 1–5.

❼ Nova Scotia Museum of Natural History. Nova Scotia's natural wonders are preserved in several galleries that focus on both land and sea. Stand next to a Sei whale skeleton and admire Mi'Kmaq quillwork. The museum is most easily recognized by the huge fiberglass model of the tiny northern spring peeper (a frog), which "clings" to the side of the building May through October. ✉ *1747 Summer St.,* ☎ *902/424-7353,* ℻ *902/424–0560.* 🎫 *$3.* ☉ *Mid-May–Oct., Mon., Tues., and Thurs.–Sun. 9:30–5:30, Wed. 9:30–8; Nov.–mid-May, Tues. and Thurs.–Sun. 9:30–5, Wed. 9:30–8.*

Point Pleasant Park. Most of the city's secondary fortifications have been turned into public parks. This one encompasses 186 wooded acres, veined with walking trails and seafront paths. The park was leased from the British Crown by the city for 999 years, at a shilling a year. Its major military installation is a massive round martello tower dating from the late 18th century. Point Pleasant is about 12 blocks down South Park Street from Spring Garden Road.

❿ Province House. Charles Dickens proclaimed this structure "a gem of Georgian architecture." It's now a national historic site. Erected in 1819 to house Britain's first overseas self-government, the sandstone building still serves as the meeting place for the provincial legislature. ✉ *1726 Hollis St.,* ☎ *902/424–4661.* 🎫 *Free.* ☉ *July and Aug., weekdays 9–5, weekends 10–4; Sept.–June, weekdays 8:30–4:30.*

❶ Purdy's Wharf. Named after a famous shipping family from the 19th century, this wharf is composed of a pier and twin office towers that stand right in the harbor. An architectural first, the buildings use ocean water to generate air-conditioning. ✉ *Upper Water St.*

❾ St. Paul's Church. St. Paul's, opened in 1750, is Canada's oldest Protestant church, Britain's first overseas cathedral, and the burial site of many colonial notables. Inside, on the north end, a piece of metal is embedded in the wall. It is a fragment of the *Mont Blanc,* one of the two ships whose collision caused the Halifax Explosion of December 6, 1917, the greatest human-caused explosion prior to Hiroshima. ✉ *1749 Argyle St.,* ☎ *902/429–2240.* ☉ *Sept.–May, weekdays 9–4:30; June–Aug., Mon.–Sat. 9–4:30; services Sun. at 8:30, 10:30, and 7:30.*

Dining and Lodging

$$$ ✕ **MacAskill's Restaurant.** Experience a continuing tradition of Nova Scotian hospitality in this romantic dining room overlooking beautiful Halifax Harbour. Award-winning chefs will delight you with a unique selection of seafood dishes prepared with only the finest, freshest fish available. Specialties include pepper steak, flambéed tableside. ✉ *88 Alderney Dr., Dartmouth Ferry Terminal Bldg.,* ☎ *902/466–3100. AE, DC, MC, V.*

$$–$$$ ✕ **Salty's on the Waterfront.** This restaurant, overlooking Privateer's
★ Wharf and the entire harbor, gets the prize for the best location in the city. Request a table with a window view, and save room for their famous dessert, called "Cadix" (chocolate mousse over praline crust). The **Salty Dog Bar & Grill** on the ground level is less expensive and serves lunches outside on the wharf in summer. ✉ *1869 Upper Water St.,* ☎ *902/423–6818. Reservations essential. AE, DC, MC, V.*

$–$$ ✕ **Privateer's Warehouse.** History surrounds you in this 200-year-old building, where three restaurants share early 18th-century stone walls and hewn beams. **Upper Deck Waterfront Fishery & Grill** (☎ 902/422–1289), done in a nautical theme, affords great views of the harbor, and assures lobsters straight from their holding tank. **Middle Deck Pasta**

Works & Beverage Co. (☎ 902/426–1500) has a bistro-style atmosphere and serves innovative pastas as well as traditional cuisine; there's also a children's menu. **Lower Deck Good Time Pub** (☎ 902/426–1501) is a boisterous bar with long trestle tables and a patio; fish-and-chips and other pub food is served. ⊠ *Historic Properties, Lower Water St. AE, DC, MC, V.*

$ ✕ **Satisfaction Feast.** This small, vegetarian restaurant is informal, friendly, and usually packed at lunchtime. The food is simple and wholesome; try the fresh whole-wheat bread and one of the daily curries. ⊠ *1581 Grafton St.,* ☎ *902/422–3540. AE, MC, V.*

$$$$ ✕⊞ **Hotel Halifax.** This first-class Canadian Pacific hotel has spacious, attractive rooms, the majority with a panoramic view of the harbor. An aboveground pedway network provides easy access to the Scotia Square shopping mall and Historic Properties. The **Crown Bistro** has a unique blend of elegant dishes and lighter fare. **Sam Slicks**, a cozy piano bar, has nightly entertainment and serves great food. ⊠ *1990 Barrington St., B3J 1P2,* ☎ *902/425–6700 or 800/441–1414,* FAX *902/425–6214. 279 rooms, 21 suites. Restaurant, piano bar, indoor pool, hot tub, sauna, exercise room. AE, DC, MC, V.*

$$$$ ✕⊞ **Prince George Hotel.** Contemporary mahogany furnishings in
★ this luxurious and understated business-oriented hotel include writing desks. **Georgio's Restaurant** serves Californian cuisine in a casual setting. The hotel is conveniently connected by underground tunnel to the World Trade and Convention Centre; pedway access to shops, offices, and entertainment is also provided. ⊠ *1725 Market St., B3J 3N9,* ☎ *902/425–1986, 800/565–1567 in Canada. 207 rooms, 9 suites. Restaurant, bar, pool, hot tub, exercise room, concierge. AE, DC, MC, V.*

$$$$ ⊞ **Cambridge Suites.** This hotel, in a convenient location, takes pride in its motto, "A suite for the price of a room." Choose from among three suite sizes; all have sitting rooms and kitchenettes. ⊠ *1583 Brunswick St., B3J 3P5,* ☎ *902/420–0555 or 800/565–1263,* FAX *902/ 420–9379. 200 suites. Restaurant, bar, kitchenettes, hot tub, sauna, exercise room. CP. AE, D, MC, V.*

$$$$ ⊞ **Haliburton House Inn.** Halifax's only four-star registered Heritage property, this hotel is an elegant renovation of three 19th-century town houses. Comfortable rooms are furnished with period antiques, lending a homey ambience. Wild game and Atlantic seafood are served in an elegant dining room. ⊠ *5184 Morris St., B3J 1B3,* ☎ *902/420–0658,* FAX *902/423–2324. 25 rooms, 2 suites. Dining room, library. CP. AE, DC, MC, V.*

$$$$ ⊞ **Sheraton Halifax.** This waterfront hotel, built low to match neighboring historic ironstone buildings, strays in appearance from others of its chain. Its convenient location in Historic Properties contributes to its elegance. Other assets include an indoor pool with a summer sundeck. Halifax's only casino is in the lobby. ⊠ *1919 Upper Water St., B3J 3J5,* ☎ *902/421–1700 or 800/325–3535,* FAX *902/422–5805. 335 rooms, 19 suites. Restaurant, bar, room service, health club, dock, casino, concierge, meeting rooms. AE, DC, MC, V.*

$$$ ⊞ **Inn on the Lake.** A great value in a quiet, relaxing location, this small country club–style hotel is on 5 acres of parkland on the edge of Fall River Lake, 10 minutes from Halifax and the airport. ⊠ *Box 29, Waverly, B0N 2S0,* ☎ *902/861–3480,* FAX *902/861–4883. 34 rooms, 12 suites. Restaurant, lounge, beach, airport shuttle, free parking. AE, MC, V.*

Nightlife and the Arts

THE ARTS

Halifax has a dynamic film industry, the product of which is presented at the **Atlantic Film Festival** (☎ 902/422–3456), held in Halifax the third week in September. The festival also showcases feature films, TV movies, and documentaries made elsewhere in the Atlantic Provinces.

Wormwood's Dog and Monkey Cinema (✉ 2112 Gottingen St., ☎ 902/422–3700) shows Canadian, foreign-language, and experimental films.

Scotia Festival of Music (☎ 902/429–9469) presents internationally recognized classical musicians via concert and master classes each May and June. The **du Maurier Atlantic Jazz Festival** (☎ 902/492–2225) takes place in mid-July.

The **Neptune Theatre** (✉ 1593 Argyle St., B3J 2B2 ☎ 902/429–7300, 902/429–7070 box office), Canada's oldest professional repertory playhouse, stages year-round performances ranging from classics to contemporary Canadian drama. During the first week of September, the **Atlantic Fringe Festival** presents 40 shows in eight venues. The **Historic Feast Company** (☎ 902/420–1840) presents shows set in the 19th-century at Historic Properties on Thursday, Friday, and Saturday evenings. **Grafton Street Dinner Theatre** (✉ 1741 Grafton St., ☎ 902/425–1961) holds performances Wednesday through Saturday.

NIGHTLIFE

The multilevel entertainment center in Historic Properties, **Privateer's Warehouse** (✉ Lower Water St., ☎ 902/422–1289), is a popular nighttime hangout. At the ground-level **Lower Deck** tavern you can quaff a beer to Celtic music. **Cheers** (✉ 1743 Grafton St., ☎ 902/421–1655), with bands and entertainment nightly, is a popular spot. **O'Carroll's** (✉ 1860 Upper Water St., ☎ 902/423–4405) has a restaurant, oyster bar, and lounge where you can hear live Irish music nightly.

Shopping

The **Spring Garden Road** area has two stylish shopping malls, with shops selling everything from designer clothing to fresh pasta. **Jennifer of Nova Scotia** (✉ 5635 Spring Garden Rd., ☎ 902/425–3119) sells locally made jewelry, pottery, wool sweaters, and soaps. You can find fine crafts in **Historic Properties** (☞ *above*) and the **Barrington Inn Complex** (✉ 1875 Barrington St.). **Pewter House** (✉ 1875 Granville St., ☎ 902/423–8843), across the street from the Barrington Inn Complex, sells locally made and imported pewter goods from knickknacks and tableware to clocks and jewelry. The **Plaid Place** (✉ 1903 Barrington Pl., ☎ 902/429–6872 or 800/563–1749) has an array of tartans and Highland accessories. The **Wool Sweater Outlet** (✉ 1870 Hollis St., ☎ 902/422–9209) sells wool and cotton sweaters at reasonable prices.

Dartmouth

⓭ *North of Halifax via the A. Murray Mackay and Angus L. Macdonald bridges.*

You can either drive or take the ferry from Halifax to Dartmouth. If you walk along the water behind the modern Law Courts in Halifax, near Historic Properties, you'll soon reach the Dartmouth ferry terminal, jammed with commuters during the rush hour. The terminal is home to the oldest operational saltwater ferry service in North America, which began operation in 1732. Suburban in demeanor, Dartmouth was first settled by Quaker whalers from Nantucket. The 23 lakes within Dartmouth's boundaries provided the Mi'Kmaqs with a canoe route to the province's interior and to the Bay of Fundy. A 19th-century canal system connected the lakes for a brief time, but today there are only ruins, which have been partially restored as heritage sites.

The **Black Cultural Centre for Nova Scotia,** in Westphal (a neighborhood of Dartmouth), is in the heart of the oldest black community in the area. The museum, library, and educational complex are dedicated to the preservation of the history and culture of blacks in Nova Scotia, who first arrived here in the 1600s. ⊠ *Rte. 7 and Cherrybrooke Rd.,* ☎ *902/434–6223.* ☞ *$2.* ☉ *Weekdays 9–5; June–Sept. also Sat. 10–4.*

Lodging

$$$$ ☒ **Ramada Renaissance.** In Dartmouth's Burnside Industrial Park, this luxury hotel is aimed at the business traveler as well as families. There is a 108-foot indoor water slide. ⊠ *240 Brownlow Ave., B3B 1X6,* ☎ *902/468–8888, 800/561–3733 in Canada,* FAX *902/468–8765. 178 rooms, 30 suites. Restaurant, bar, room service, pool, hot tub, sauna, exercise room, meeting rooms. AE, DC, MC, V.*

THE SOUTH SHORE AND ANNAPOLIS VALLEY

Mainland Nova Scotia is a long, narrow peninsula; no point in the province is more than 56 km (35 mi) from saltwater. The South Shore is on the Atlantic side, the Annapolis Valley on the Fundy side, and though they are less than an hour apart by car, the two destinations seem like different worlds. The South Shore is rocky coast, island-dotted bays, fishing villages, and shipyards; the Annapolis Valley is lumber yards, farms, vineyards, and orchards. The South Shore is German, French, and Yankee; the Valley is stoutly British. The sea is everywhere on the South Shore; in the Valley the sea is blocked from view by a ridge of mountains.

Route 103, Route 3, and various secondary roads form the province's designated Lighthouse Route, which leads from Halifax down the South Shore. It touches the heads of several big bays and small harbors, revealing an ever-changing panorama of shoreline, inlet, and island. Charming little towns and fishing villages are spaced out every 50 km (31 mi). The Lighthouse Route ends in Yarmouth and the Evangeline Trail begins, winding along the shore of St. Mary's Bay, through a succession of Acadian villages collectively known as the French Shore. Here, you'll notice the Acadian flag, tricolored with a gold star representing *stella maris,* the star of the sea. The star guides the Acadians during troubled times, which have been frequent. In 1755, after residing for a century and a half in Nova Scotia, chiefly in the Annapolis Valley, the Acadians were expelled by the British—an event that inspired Longfellow's famous *Evangeline.* Some eluded capture and others slowly crept back, but many settled in New Brunswick and along this shore of Nova Scotia. The villages blend seamlessly into one another for about 32 km (nearly 20 mi), each one, it seems, with its own wharf, fish plant, and enormous Catholic church. This tour mostly focuses on the towns along Route 1, but you should follow the side roads whenever the inclination strikes; the South Shore rewards slow, relaxed exploration.

The Annapolis Valley runs northeast like a huge trench, flat on the bottom, sheltered on both sides by the long ridges of the North and South mountains. Occasional roads over the South Mountain lead to the South Shore; short roads over the North Mountain lead to the Fundy shore. Like the South Shore, the Valley is punctuated with pleasant small towns, each with a generous supply of extravagant Victorian homes and churches. For most visitors, the Valley towns, each with its own distinction, go by like charming milestones. The rich soil of the valley bottom supports dairy herds, hay, grain, root vegetables, tobacco, and fruit. Apple blossom season (late May and early June) and the fall harvest are the loveliest times to visit.

Peggy's Cove

48 km (30 mi) southwest of Halifax.

Peggy's Cove, on Route 333, stands at the mouth of St. Margaret's Bay. The cove, with its houses huddled around the narrow slit in the boulders, is probably the most photographed village in Canada. It also has the only Canadian post office located in a lighthouse (open April–November). Be careful exploring the bald, rocky shore. Incautious visitors have been swept to their deaths by the towering surf that sometimes breaks here.

Dining and Lodging

$$$ ✕🏨 **Dauphinee Inn.** On the shore of Hubbards Cove, about 12 miles before Chester, this charming country inn has first-class accommodations and an excellent restaurant. Try the Hot Rocks, a social dining concept where guests are invited to cook fresh vegetables, seafood, beef, or chicken on a hot slab of South Shore granite. Opportunities abound for bicycling, bird-watching, and deep-sea fishing nearby, and walking trails lead to the shore. ✉ *167 Shore Club Rd., Hubbard B0J 1T0 (Exit 6 off Rte. 103)*, ☎ *902/857–1790 or 800/567–1790,* FAX *902/857–9555. 6 rooms, 2 suites. Restaurant, lounge, boating, fishing. AE, D, DC, MC. Closed Nov.–Apr.*

Chester

79 km (49 mi) west of Peggy's Cove.

Chester, on Lunenburg County's Mahone Bay, has a population of just over 1,100 people. In summer, however, this seaside retreat swells with a well-established population of U.S. visitors and Haligonians, and with the sailing and yachting community. Mid-August brings **Chester Race Week,** the largest regatta in Atlantic Canada.

The **Ross Farm Museum** is a restored 19th-century living museum that illustrates the evolution of agriculture from 1600 to 1925 and has the types of animals found on a farm of the 1800s—draft horses, oxen, and older breeds or types of animals—not the genetically developed, purebred animals of today. At the Pedlar's Shop, on the premises, you can purchase items made in the community. ✉ *Rte. 12, New Ross (20-min drive inland from Chester)*, ☎ *902/689–2210.* ✉ *$3.* ☉ *June–mid-Oct., daily 9:30–5:30; winter programs Jan.–mid-Mar. (call to confirm).*

⑭ A passengers-only ferry runs from the dock in Chester to the scenic **Big and Little Tancook Islands,** 8 km (5 mi) out in Mahone Bay. Reflecting its part-German heritage, Big Tancook claims to make the best sauerkraut in Nova Scotia. Exploration of the island is made easy by walking trails. The boat runs four times daily Monday through Thursday; six times daily Friday; and twice daily on weekends. The 45-minute trip costs $1.

Dining

$ ✕ **The Galley.** Decked out in nautical bric-a-brac and providing a spectacular view of the ocean, this restaurant has a pleasant, relaxed atmosphere. Try the seafood chowder, live lobster from their in-house pond, and homemade desserts. ✉ *Rte. 3, 115 Marina Rd., Marriots Cove (Exit 8 off Rte. 103, 3 km, or 2 mi, west of Chester)*, ☎ *902/275–4700. Reservations essential. AE, D, MC, V. Closed mid-Dec.–mid-Mar.*

En Route   The town of **Mahone Bay** presents a dramatic face to visitors: Three tall wooden churches—of different denominations—stand side by side, their images reflected in the harbor. Once a shipbuilding community, Mahone Bay is now a crafts center.

Lunenburg

★ **⑮**   *9½ km (6 mi) south of the town of Mahone Bay.*

A feast of Victorian-era architecture, wooden boats, steel draggers (a fishing boat that operates a trawl), historic inns, and good restaurants, Lunenburg is, among other things, visually delightful. The center of town, known as **old town,** is a UNESCO world heritage site, and the fantastic old school on the hilltop is the region's finest remaining example of Second Empire architecture, an ornate style that began in France.

Lunenburg is home port to *Bluenose II*, a replica of the great racing schooner depicted on the back of the Canadian dime. Built in 1921, the original *Bluenose,* which sank years ago, was the undefeated champion of the North Atlantic fishing fleet and winner of four international schooner races. Its twin, built in 1963, is open to visitors through the Fisheries Museum (☞ *below*) when in port.

The **Fisheries Museum of the Atlantic** sets off on a nautical journey that explores a day in the life of Canada's Atlantic coast fishermen. Among the attractions are the last of the Grand Bank schooners, the *Theresa E. Connor,* a steel stern trawler, *Cape Sable,* and an aquarium. ⊠ *68 Bluenose Dr.,* ☎ *902/634–4794.* ⊡ *$6. June–mid-Oct., daily 9:30–5:30; off-season, weekdays by appointment only.*

The **Houston North Gallery** represents both trained and self-taught Nova Scotian artists as well as Inuit (Eskimo) soapstone carvers and printmakers. ⊠ *110 Montague St.,* ☎ *902/634–8869.* ☉ *Feb.–Dec., Mon.–Sat. 10–6, Sun. 1–6.*

Lodging

$$–$$$ ⊞ **Boscawen Inn and MacLachlan House.** Period antiques adorn and fireplaces warm this elegant 1888 mansion and its 1905 annex, located in the middle of Lunenburg's historic old town. Guests can take afternoon tea in one of the drawing rooms or on the balcony. All rooms and suites have either water or park views. ⊠ *Box 1343, 150 Cumberland St., B0J 2C0,* ☎ *902/634–3325,* ℻ *902/634–9293. 20 rooms. Restaurant. AE, D, DC, MC, V. Closed Jan.–Easter.*

$$–$$$ ⊞ **Pelham House Bed & Breakfast.** Close to downtown, this sea captain's home, circa 1906 and decorated to period throughout, has a large collection of books and periodicals about the sea, sailing, and wooden boats. Sit back and relax on the veranda overlooking the harbor. Full breakfast and afternoon tea are included in the room rate. ⊠ *Box 358, 224 Pelham St., B0J 2C0,* ☎ *902/634–7113,* ℻ *902/634–7114. 3 rooms. Business services. MC, V.*

Bridgewater

18 km (11 mi) west of Lunenburg.

This is the main market town of the South Shore. The town's main attraction, the **DesBrisay Museum,** explores the nature and people of Lunenburg County and presents exhibits on art, science, technology, and history from museums around the world. The gift shop carries books by local authors and art and crafts by local artisans. ⊠ *130 Jubilee Rd.,* ☎ *902/543–4033.* ⊡ *$2.50.* ☉ *Mid-May–Sept., Mon.–Sat. 9–5, Sun. 1–5; Oct.–mid-May, Tues.–Sun. 1–5, Wed. 1–9.*

Liverpool

 46 km (29 mi) south of Bridgewater.

Nestled on the estuary of the Mersey River, Liverpool was settled around 1760 by New Englanders and is now a fishing and paper-milling town. During the American Revolution and the War of 1812, Liverpool was a privateering center; later, it became an important shipping and trading port.

In the center of town is the **Simeon Perkins House,** built in 1766, which was the home of a prominent early settler who kept an extensive and revealing diary. The Perkins diary was used extensively by Thomas Raddall, whose internationally successful novels and stories are sometimes set in and around Liverpool. ⊠ *109 Main St.,* ☎ *902/354–4058.* ☒ *Free.* ⊗ *June–mid-Oct., Mon.–Sat. 9:30–5:30, Sun. 1–5:30.*

Fishing

The **Mersey** is the oldest documented canoe route on the continent. It drains Lake Rossignol, Nova Scotia's largest freshwater lake, and provides good trout and salmon fishing. For canoe and fishing outfitters, go to the town of Greenfield, on Route 210, off Route 8.

Kejimkujik National Park

67 km (42 mi) west of Liverpool.

This is a 381-square-km (147-square-mi) inland wilderness about 45 minutes from Liverpool in the interior of the western part of the province. Kejimkujik has many lakes with well-marked canoe routes that have primitive campsites. Nature trails are marked for hikers, boat rentals are available, and there's freshwater swimming. Look for white-tail deer, porcupine, loons, owls and beaver. Kejimkujik also operates the Seaside Adjunct near Port Joli on the Atlantic shore that protects one of the last undeveloped tracts of coastline on the Eastern Seaboard. There are two mile-long beaches, both reached by hiking trails (no visitor services; day use only). Sections of beaches are closed from late April to late July so that nesting birds, such as the endangered piping plover, remain undisturbed. ⊠ *Rte. 8 from Liverpool or Annapolis Royal, Maitland Bridge,* ☎ *902/682–2772.* ☒ *$3 per day, 4-day pass $9, annual pass $15, camping $9–$13.50 per day.*

Shelburne

❶❼ *69 km (43 mi) south of Liverpool.*

The high noon of Shelburne occurred right after the Revolution, when 16,000 Loyalists briefly made it one of the largest communities in North America. Today it is a fishing and shipbuilding town situated at the mouth of the Roseway River.

Many of Shelburne's homes date back to the late 1700s, including the **Ross-Thomson House,** which is now a provincial museum. Inside, the only surviving 18th-century store in Nova Scotia contains all the necessities of the period in which it originated. ⊠ *9 Charlotte La.,* ☎ *902/875–3141.* ☒ *Free.* ⊗ *June–mid-Oct., daily 9:30–5:30; call for winter hours.*

Barrington

40 km (25 mi) south of Shelburne.

Barrington harbors a cluster of museums that explore various aspects of life in the 18th and 19th centuries. The **Barrington Woolen Mill Museum** (☎ 902/637–2185), built in 1882, displays machinery and has exhibits that explain how wool is woven into bolts of twills and flannels, blankets, and suitings. Early New England settlers converged at the **Old Meeting House Museum** (☎ 902/637–2185) for town meetings, elections, and religious services. A five-story climb to the top of the **Seal Island Light Museum** affords beautiful views of Barrington Bay. The **Western Counties Military Museum** (☎ 902/768–2161) houses an array of old military artifacts.

Cape Sable Island

8 km (5 mi) south of Barrington over the Causeway.

Connected to the mainland via a bridge, Cape Sable Island has a 13-mile loop that includes Nova Scotia's southernmost extremity. Like Barrington, Cape Sable Island is a Yankee community, as common family names attest; everyone seems to be named "Smith" or "Nickerson." Interestingly, there is a bewildering variety of small evangelical churches, which presumably reflects the Puritan enthusiasm for irreconcilable disagreements over fine points of doctrine. The largest community on Cape Sable is **Clark's Harbour,** where the first Cape Islander fishing boat was developed—with its pilothouse forward and its high, flaring bow and low stern, the Cape Islander is Nova Scotia's standard inshore fishing boat.

Pubnico

48 km (30 mi) west of Barrington.

Upon reaching Pubnico you enter the Acadian milieu; from here to Digby the communities are mostly French-speaking. Favorite local fare includes *fricot,* a stew made mostly of vegetables, sometimes mixed with rabbit meat, and rappie pie, made of meat or poultry with potatoes from which much of the starch has been removed.

You'll no doubt notice that there are no fewer than seven towns bearing the name Pubnico: Lower West Pubnico, Middle West Pubnico, and West Pubnico, all on the west shore of Pubnico Harbour; three East Pubnicos on the eastern shore; and just plain Pubnico, at the top of none other than Pubnico Harbour. These towns were founded by Phillipe Muis D'Entremont, and they once constituted the only barony in French Acadia. D'Entremont was a prodigious progenitor: To this day, many of the people in the Pubnicos are D'Entremonts, and most of the rest are D'Eons or Amiraults.

Yarmouth

⑱   *82 km (51 mi) north of Barrington.*

The largest town (with some 8,500 inhabitants) in southern Nova Scotia and the biggest port west of Halifax, Yarmouth is the point of entry for travelers arriving by ferry from Maine. The ferries are a major reason for Yarmouth's prosperity as they pull in much revenue by providing quick, inexpensive access for merchants and consumers going to the Boston market for fish, pulpwood, boxes and barrels, knitwear, Irish moss, Christmas trees, and berries.

In the 19th century Yarmouth was an even bigger shipbuilding center than it is now, and its location put the port on all the early steamship routes. The **Yarmouth County Museum,** in a late-19th-century church, unravels the region's history with displays of period furniture, costumes, tools, and toys, as well as a significant collection of ship models and paintings. Also in the building is a research library and archives, where local history and genealogy are documented. ✉ *22 Collins St.,* ☎ *902/742–*

5539, FAX *902/749–1120.* ☞ *$2.50, archive $5 per half day.* ☉ *June–mid-Oct., Mon.–Sat. 9–5, Sun. 2–5; mid-Oct.–May, Tues.–Sun. 2–5.*

The **Firefighters Museum of Nova Scotia,** one block from the waterfront, presents the evolution of fire fighting through its displays of equipment from the leather bucket to the chemical spray. ⊠ *451 Main St.,* ☎ *902/742–5525.* ☞ *$2.* ☉ *June, Mon.–Sat. 9–5; July and Aug., Mon.–Sat. 9–9, Sun. 10–5; Sept., Mon.–Sat. 9–5; Oct.–May, weekdays 10–noon and 2–4.*

<table>
<tr><td>

NEED A
BREAK?

</td><td>

Harris's Quick 'n' Tasty is the place for good, old-fashioned food such as rappie pie and lobster cooked up in more ways than you can imagine. ⊠ *Rte. 1, Dayton,* ☎ *902/742–3467.*

</td></tr>
</table>

Dining and Lodging

$$ ✕▥ **Manor Inn.** This country inn in a colonial mansion beside Doctors Lake on Rte. 1 offers a choice of four grades of rooms, settings, and price ranges to choose from: coach-house units, lakeside or rose-garden lodges, or the main estate. Prime rib and lobster are the specialties in the dining room; reservations are required. ⊠ *Box 56, Rte. 1, Hebron, B0W 1X0 (Rte. 1., 5 mi northeast of Yarmouth),* ☎ *902/ 742–2487, 888/626–6746,* FAX *902/742–8094. 53 rooms. 2 dining rooms, 2 bars, outdoor café, pool, tennis court. AE, DC, MC, V.*

Point de l'Eglise (Church Point)

⑲ *70 km (43 mi) north of Yarmouth.*

Point de l'Eglise is the site of **Université Ste-Anne,** the only French-language institution among Nova Scotia's 17 degree-granting colleges and universities. Founded in 1891, this small university off Route 1 is a focus of Acadian studies and culture in the province.

St. Mary's Church, on the side of the main road that runs through Point de l'Eglise, was finished in 1905. It's the tallest and largest wooden church in North America, at 190 feet long and 185 feet high. The steeple requires 40 tons of rock ballast to keep it steady in the ocean winds and can be seen for miles on the approach. Inside the church is a small museum. Tours are given by appointment. ⊠ *Main road,* ☎ *902/769– 2832.* ☞ *$1.* ☉ *July–mid-Oct., daily 9:30–5:30.*

En Route   **St. Bernard,** a few miles north of Point de l'Eglise, marks the end of the French Shore. It's known for an impressive granite Gothic church that seats 1,000 people.

Digby

35 km (22 mi) north of Point de l'Eglise.

Digby is the terminus of the ferry service from St. John, New Brunswick, and an important fishing port with several good restaurants and a major resort, The Pines (☞ *below*). The town is on the otherwise-landlocked Annapolis Basin, into which the Annapolis River flows after its long course through the valley. The town is particularly famous for its scallops and for smoked herring known as "Digby Chicks." For a real treat go down to the wharf and visit seafood retailers: They'll cook up the delicious scallops and lobster that you buy.

<table>
<tr><td>

OFF THE
BEATEN PATH

</td><td>

BEAR RIVER – This jewel of a village, 15 km (9 mi) inland from Digby, is called the "Switzerland of Nova Scotia." It has a large arts-and-crafts community and an Ethnographic Museum (⊠ *18 Chute Rd.,* ☎ *902/ 467–3762*) devoted to folk costumes and artifacts from exotic lands.

</td></tr>
</table>

Dining and Lodging

$$$$ ✕▦ **Pines Resort Hotel.** Complete with fireplaces, sitting rooms, and a view of the Annapolis Basin, this casually elegant property, composed of a Norman Chateaux–style hotel, 30 cottages, and lavish gardens, offers myriad amenities. Local seafood with a French touch is served daily in the restaurant, and the lounge is perfect for quiet relaxation. ✉ *Box 70, Shore Rd., B0V 1A0,* ☎ *902/245–2511 or 800/667–4637,* ℻ *902/245–6133. 144 rooms. Restaurant, bar, pool, sauna, 18-hole golf course, 2 tennis courts, health club, walking trails. AE, D, DC, MC. Closed mid-Oct.–May.*

Long Island and Brier Island

㉓ *10-minute ferry ride between East Ferry and Tiverton.*

Digby Neck is extended seaward by two narrow islands, Long Island and Brier Island. Because the surrounding waters are rich in plankton they attract a variety of whales, including fins, humpbacks, minkes, and right whales, as well as harbor porpoises. This is also an excellent spot for bird-watching.

Ferries going between the islands have to crab sideways against the ferocious Fundy tidal streams that course back and forth through the narrow gaps. They operate hourly, 24 hours a day, with a fare of $1 each way. One of the boats is called *Joshua Slocum* and the other is *Spray*; the former is named after Westport's most famous native, and the latter for the 36-foot oyster sloop that he rebuilt and in which from 1894 to 1896 he became the first man to circumnavigate the world singlehandedly. At the southern tip of Brier Island is a **cairn,** commemorating the voyage.

Whale-Watching

Pirate's Cove Whale Cruises (✉ Rte. 217, Tiverton, Long Island, ☎ 902/839–2242) operates whale-watching cruises from June through October. The fare is $33.

Annapolis Royal

★ **㉑** *29 km (18 mi) north of Digby.*

This town is well supplied with imposing mansions, particularly along the upper end of St. George Street, the oldest town street in Canada. Local businesses (or the tourist information center in the Annapolis Royal Tidal Power Building) can provide *Footprints with Footnotes,* a self-guided walking tour of the town; guided tours leave from the lighthouse on St. George Street, daily at 10 and 2:30.

Fort Anne National Historic Site was fortified in 1643; the present structures are the remnants of the fourth fort erected here and garrisoned by the British as late as 1854. The officers' quarters are now a museum with exhibits on the site's history. ✉ *St. George St., Box 9, B0S 1A0,* ☎ *902/532–2397 or 902/532–2321,* ℻ *902/532–2232.* ▦ *Grounds free, museum $3.* ☉ *Mid-May–mid-Oct., daily 9–6; mid-Oct.–mid-May, by appointment.*

The **Annapolis Royal Historic Gardens** are 10 acres of magnificent theme gardens connected to a wildlife sanctuary. ✉ *441 St. George St.,* ☎ *902/532–7018.* ▦ *$3.50.* ☉ *Mid-May–mid-Oct., daily 8–dusk.*

The **Annapolis Royal Tidal Power Project,** ¼ mile from Annapolis Royal, was designed to test the feasibility of generating electricity from tidal energy. This pilot project is the only tidal generating station in North America and one of only three operational sites in the world. The interpretive center explains the process with guided tours. ⊠ *Annapolis River Causeway,* ☎ *902/532–5454.* ☜ *Free.* ⊙ *Mid-May–mid-June, daily 9–5:30; mid-June–Aug., daily 9–8; Sept.–mid-Oct., daily 9–5:30.*

Lodging

$$$ ⚲ **Auberge Wandlyn Royal Anne Motel.** This modern, no-frills motel has a pleasant, quiet setting on 20 acres of land. ⊠ *Box 628, Rte. 1, B0S 1A0,* ☎ *902/532–2323,* 🖷 *902/532–7277. 30 rooms. Restaurant, hot tubs, sauna, meeting rooms. AE, DC, MC, V.*

$$ ⚲ **Moorings Bed & Breakfast.** Built in 1881, this tall, beautiful home overlooking Annapolis Basin has a fireplace, tin ceilings, antiques, and contemporary art. ⊠ *Box 118, Granville Ferry B0S 1K0,* ☎ 🖷 *902/532–2146. 1 room with ½ bath, 2 rooms share bath. V.*

Port Royal

8 km (5 mi) downriver from Annapolis Royal on the opposite bank.

One of the oldest settlements in Canada, Port Royal was Nova Scotia's first capital (for both the French and English) until 1749, and the province's first military base. A national historic site commemorates the period.

The **Port Royal National Historic Site,** a reconstructed French fur-trading post, dates back to 1605 when Sieur deMonts and Samuel de Champlain built it. Here, amid the hardships of the New World, North America's first social club—the Order of Good Cheer—was founded, and Canada's first theatrical presentation was written and produced by Marc Lescarbot. ⊠ *Rte. 1 to Granville Ferry, left 12 km (7 mi),* ☎ *902/532–2898, 902/532–5589.* ☜ *$3.* ⊙ *Mid-May–mid-Oct., daily 9–6.*

OFF THE
BEATEN PATH

CAPE BLOMIDON – At Greenwich, take Route 358 to Cape Blomidon via Port Williams and Canning for a spectacular view of the Valley and the Bay of Fundy from the Lookoff.

HALL'S HARBOUR – This is one of the best natural harbors on the upper Bay of Fundy and can be reached via Route 359. Go for a walk on a gravel beach bordered by cliffs; try sea kayaking or wilderness camping, or seek out the intaglio printmaking studio.

Wolfville

㉒   *20 km (12 mi) east of Kentville.*

Settled in the 1760's by New England Planters, Wolfville is a charming college town with stately trees and ornate Victorian homes. Chimney swifts, aerobatic birds that fly in spectacular formation at the brink of dusk, are so abundant there's an interpretive display devoted to them at the **Robie Tufts Nature Centre** on Front Street. At the end of Front, by the harbor, are dikes built by the Acadians in the 1600s.

OFF THE
BEATEN PATH

GRAND PRÉ NATIONAL HISTORIC SITE – Follow Route 101 through Wolfville about 5 km (3 mi) to the site that was once an Acadian village. A small stone church commemorates Longfellow's hero in *Evangeline* and houses an exhibit on the 1755 deportation of the Acadians from the Valley. ☎ *902/542-3631.* ⊙ *Mid-May–mid-Oct., daily 9–6.*

Dining and Lodging

$$$–$$$$ ✕⚲ **Blomidon Inn.** This 19th-century sea captain's mansion with 4 acres of lawns and gardens was restored in 1981. Guest rooms are uniquely furnished, most with four-poster beds, and all with hand-made quilts. Relax over lunch or dinner in one of the dining rooms or on the terrace, enjoying fresh fare from the valley and sea. Lobster bisque and fresh Atlantic salmon are among the menu favorites, and their home-made bread baked with oats and molasses will leave you begging for the recipe. Afternoon tea is served daily, and there's a weekend brunch (reservations advised). ✉ *127 Main St., Box 839, B0P 1X0,* ☎ *902/542–2291 or 800/565–2291,* ℻ *902/542–7461. 26 rooms. 2 dining rooms, tennis court, horseshoes, shuffleboard, meeting room. MC, V.*

Hiking

A popular hiking trail, 25 km (16 mi) north of Wolfville, leads from the end of Route 358 to the dramatic cliffs of Cape Split, a 13-km (8-mi) round-trip.

Windsor

㉓ *25 km (16 mi) southeast of Wolfville.*

Windsor, the last of the Valley towns, sits midway between the equa-tor and the North Pole and was settled in 1703 as an Acadian com-munity. Here, tide's average rise and fall is over 40 feet; you can see the tidal bore (the leading edge of the incoming tide) rushing up the Meander River and sometimes reaching a height of 3 feet.

Sainte Famille Winery in Falmouth, 5 km (3 mi) west of Windsor, is a family-owned vineyard where tours are offered that combine the re-gion's ecological history with the intricacies of growing grapes and aging wine. Wine tasting is done in the gift shop, where bottles are sold at a steal. ✉ *Dyke Rd. and Dudley Park La.,* ☎ *902/798–8311 or 800/565–0993,* ℻ *902/798–9418.* ⊙ *June–Sept., Mon.–Sat. 9–6, Sun. noon–5; call for off-season hours and tour schedule.*

Fort Edward, one of the assembly points for the expulsion of the Aca-dians, still stands as the only remaining colonial blockhouse in Nova Scotia. ✉ *Exit 6 off Rte. 1, 1st left at King St., left up street facing fire station,* ☎ *902/542–3631.* ⊙ *Mid-June–Labor Day, daily 10–6.*

The **Haliburton House Museum,** a provincial museum on a manicured 25-acre estate, was the home of Judge Thomas Chandler Halibur-ton—lawyer, politician, historian, and humorist. His best-known work, *The Clockmaker,* pillories Nova Scotian follies from the viewpoint of a Yankee clock peddler, Sam Slick, whose witty sayings are still com-monly used. ✉ *414 Clifton Ave.,* ☎ *902/798–2915.* ⊙ *June–Oct. 15, Mon.–Sat. 9:30–5:30, Sun. 1–5:30.*

OFF THE
BEATEN PATH

UNIACKE ESTATE MUSEUM PARK – Off of Route 1, 25 km (16 mi) east of Windsor, lies a summerhouse built about 1815 for Richard John Uni-acke, attorney general and the advocate general to the Admiralty court during the War of 1812. The house, a superb example of colonial archi-tecture on spacious grounds near a lake, is now a provincial museum. It's preserved in its original condition with many authentic furnishings. Several walking trails surround the estate. ✉ *758 Main Rd., 30 km (19 mi) east of Windsor,* ☎ *902/866-2560.* ✇ *Free.* ⊙ *June–Oct. 15, Mon.–Sat. 9:30-5:30, Sun. 1-5:30.*

NORTHERN NOVA SCOTIA

The area that lies between Halifax and Cape Breton Island includes the rugged coastline on the Atlantic, the gentler Bay of Fundy and Northumberland Strait. Fishing villages, sandy beaches, and remote cranberry barrens range along the eastern shore. The salt marshes, Scottish clans, and feasts of lobster along Northumberland Strait give way to mills, rolling hills, hiking trails, and farms as you move inland. A land of high tides, million-year-old fossils, and semiprecious stones borders the Bay of Fundy. Walk on the bottom of the sea when the mighty Fundy tide recedes, or ride the tidal bore as it comes rushing back.

This region takes in parts of three of the official Scenic Trails, including Marine Drive (315 km, or 195 mi), the Sunrise Trail (316 km, or 196 mi), and the Glooscap Trail (365 km, or 226 mi). Any one leg of the routes could be done comfortably as an overnight trip from Halifax; for the whole tour, allow at least three or four days.

Musquodoboit Harbour

㉔ *45 km (28 mi) east of Dartmouth.*

Musquodoboit Harbour, with about 930 residents, is a substantial village at the mouth of the Musquodoboit River. The river itself offers good trout and salmon fishing, and the village touches on two slender and lovely harbors.

Lodging

$$–$$$ ⊞ **Salmon River House.** About 35 minutes east of Dartmouth, where Route 7 crosses the Salmon River, is this unpretentious white-frame inn on 30 acres that provides glorious views. The home has a sun room and one room with a waterbed and whirlpool bath. ⊠ *9931 #7 Hwy., Salmon River Bridge, B0J 1P0,* ☎ *902/889–3353 or 800/565–3353,* FAX *902/889–3653. 6 rooms with bath or shower. Dining room, boating, fishing. MC, V.*

Beach

One of the Eastern Shore's best beaches, **Martinique Beach,** is about 12 km (7 mi) south of Musquodoboit Harbour. Other fine beaches are at Clam Bay and Clam Harbour, several kilometers east of Martinique.

OFF THE
BEATEN PATH

MOOSE RIVER GOLD MINES – This small local museum, about 30 km (19 mi) north of Tangier on Route 224, commemorates the small gold rush that occurred during the first part of this century, complete with a 1936 mine disaster. During the turmoil, the first live, on-the-spot radio newscasts were made throughout Canada and the world. It's open July through August.

En Route   As you travel through **Ship Harbour** take note of the strings of white buoys, marking one of North America's largest cultivated mussel farms.

Sherbrooke Village

★ **㉕** *83 km (51 mi) north of Sheet Harbour.*

This living history village, though it has fewer than 400 residents, is this shore's leading tourist center. The St. Mary's River, which flows through the hamlet, is one of Nova Scotia's best salmon rivers. Twenty-five buildings have been restored on their original sites by the Nova Scotia Museum to their late 19th-century character, including a blacksmith shop, water-powered sawmill, horse-drawn wagons, tearooms, and stores. ⊠ *Rte. 7,* ☎ *902/522–2400.* 🖾 *$4.* ☉ *June–mid-Oct., daily 9:30–5:30.*

Antigonish

26 *62 km (38 mi) north of Sherbrooke Village on Hwy. 104.*

Antigonish is the home of **St. Francis Xavier University,** a center for Gaelic studies and the first coeducational Catholic institution to graduate women.

Dining

$$ ✕ **Lobster Treat Restaurant.** This cozily decorated brick, pine, and stained-glass restaurant was once a two-room schoolhouse. The varied menu includes fresh seafood, chicken, pastas, and bread and pies baked on the premises. Because of its relaxed atmosphere and children's menu, families enjoy coming here. ✉ *241 Post Rd. (Trans-Canada Hwy.),* ☎ *902/863–5465. AE, DC, MC, V. Closed Nov.–mid-Apr.*

En Route Follow Route 337, the Sunrise Trail, for a glorious drive along St. George's Bay with its many good swimming beaches, before the road abruptly climbs 1,000 feet up and over to Cape George. There's a little take-out shop on the wharf at **Ballantyne's Cove,** a tiny artificial harbor near the tip of Cape George, that has some of the best fish-and-chips in Nova Scotia. Grab an order and enjoy the views. After following the Cape, high above the sea, the road runs along Northumberland Strait through lonely farmlands and tiny villages, such as **Arisaig,** where on the Arisaig shore, you can search for fossils. **Lismore,** just a few kilometers west of Arisaig, affirms the Scottish origin of its people with a stone cairn commemorating Bonnie Prince Charlie's Highland rebels, slaughtered by the English at Culloden in 1746. Lobster is landed and processed in shoreside factories here—a great place to buy some of the freshest lobster possible.

Pictou

★ **27** *74 km (46 mi) west of Antigonish.*

First occupied by the Mi'kmaqs, this well-developed town on Pictou Harbour became a Scottish settlement in 1773, when a land grant to the Philadelphia Company gave access to nearly 200 Highland Scots. Now one of the largest communities on the Northumberland Strait, it's considered the "birthplace of New Scotland."

Free factory tours at **Grohmann Knives** introduce the art of knife making. ✉ *116 Water St.,* ☎ *902/485–4224.* ☉ *Weekdays 9–3.*

At the **Hector Heritage Quay,** a replica of the *Hector* is under construction. In 1773 the *Hector*—the nearest thing to a Canadian *Mayflower*—came to Pictou Harbour, inaugurating the torrent of Scottish immigration that permanently altered the character of the province and the nation. An interpretive center with audio and visual displays that tell the story of Pictou's Scottish settlement are on the grounds, as well as working blacksmith and carpentry shops. ✉ *73 Harbour Dr.,* ☎ *902/485–6057.* ▭ *$4.* ☉ *May–Oct., daily 9–8.*

Under the inspired leadership of such men as the pioneering educator Thomas McCulloch, Pictou quickly became a center of commerce, education, theological disputation, and radical politics. **McCulloch House,** a restored 1806 building with displays of McCulloch's scientific collection and such personal items as furniture, is preserved as part of the Nova Scotia Museum. ✉ *Old Haliburton Rd.,* ☎ *902/485–4563.* ▭ *Free.* ☉ *June–mid-Oct., Mon.–Sat. 9:30–5:30, Sun. 11:30–5:30.*

Dining and Lodging

$$–$$$ ✕⊡ **Braeside Inn.** Built in 1938, this inn, on a 5-acre hillside in the center of historic Pictou, has well-appointed accommodations and fine food. Beaches are nearby, and a shuttle services Pictou's two marinas. The dining room specializes in fresh seafood dishes. ⊠ *Box 1810, 126 Front St., B0K 1H0,* ☎ *902/485–5046 or 800/613–7701,* FAX *902/485–1701. 20 rooms. 2 dining rooms, meeting room. AE, MC, V.*

$$ ⊡ **Walker Inn.** A hospitable and energetic couple run this downtown inn in their brick Georgian-style town house, built in 1865. Every room is different. ⊠ *Box 629, 34 Coleraine St., B0K 1H0,* ☎ *902/485–1433 or 800/370–5553. 10 no-smoking rooms. Dining room (guests only), library, meeting room. AE, MC, V.*

Beach

About 23 km (14 mi) east of Pictou, follow the shore road from Highway 104 to **Melmerby Beach,** one of the warmest beaches on the province.

- -

OFF THE   **BALMORAL GRIST MILL MUSEUM –** A water-powered gristmill serves as
BEATEN PATH   the centerpiece for this museum, 25 km (16 mi) southeast of Pictou. Built in 1860, it's the oldest operating mill in Nova Scotia. Observe the milling demonstrations, then have a picnic in the park on the grounds. ⊠ *660 Matheson Brook Rd., Balmoral Mills,* ☎ *902/657–3016.* ⊠ *Free.* ☉ *June–mid-Oct., Mon.–Sat. 9:30–5:30, Sun. 1–5:30; demonstrations daily 10–noon and 2–4.*

- -

Malagash

65 km (40 mi) west of Pictou.

Malagash is best known for a winery that flourishes in the warm climate influenced by the Northumberland Strait. **Jost Vineyards** produces a surprisingly wide range of international award-winning wines, including an ice wine that's making a name for the vineyard. Tours run at 3 PM daily, from mid-June through September. Allow time to enjoy the deli-bar, patio deck, children's playground, and picnic area. ⊠ *Off Hwy. 104, on Rte. 6,* ☎ *902/257–2636, 800/565–4567 in Atlantic Canada.*

Pugwash

28 *26 km (16 mi) west of Malagash.*

Pugwash was the home of Cleveland industrialist Cyrus Eaton, at whose estate numerous Thinkers' Conferences brought together leading intellectual figures from the West and the Soviet Union during the 1950s and 1960s. Pugwash is still Scottish terrain, as the Gaelic street signs attest.

Seagull Pewter (⊠ Durham St., ☎ 902/243–2516), a husband-and-wife crafts operation that has grown into a $25 million business of exporting pewter vessels, picture frames, and other artifacts worldwide, has a showroom that fronts on the main highway.

Amherst

44 km (27 mi) west of Pugwash.

Amherst stands on one of the glacial ridges that borders the Tantramar Marsh, said to be the largest marsh in the world. It was once a thriving manufacturing center for many products, including pianos and furnaces. In 1917, en route from New York to Russia, the Communist leader Leon Trotsky was confined here for a month in a prisoner-of-war camp.

Lodging

$$$ 🛏 **Amherst Shore Country Inn.** This seaside country inn, with a beau-
★   tiful view of Northumberland Strait, has comfortable rooms, suites, and cottages fronting 600 feet of private beach. Incredibly well-prepared four-course dinners incorporating home-grown produce are served at one daily seating (7:30, by reservation only). ⊠ *Lorneville (32 km, or 20 mi, from Amherst on Rte. 366), R.R. 2, Amherst, B4H 3X9,* ☎ *902/661–4800. 4 rooms, 4 suites, 1 cottage. Dining room. AE, DC, MC, V. Closed late Oct.–Apr.*

Springhill

㉙ *42 km (26 mi) southeast of Amherst.*

Route 2 leads through the coal-mining town of Springhill, the site of the famous mine disaster immortalized in the folk song "The Ballad of Springhill" by Peggy Seeger and Ewen McColl.

Tour a real coal mine at the **Spring Hill Miners Museum.** ⊠ *Black River Rd., off Rte. 2,* ☎ *902/597–3449.* 🎫 *$5.* ☉ *Mid-May–mid-Oct.*

Springhill is the hometown of internationally acclaimed singer Anne Murray, whose career is celebrated in the **Anne Murray Centre.** ⊠ *Main St.,* ☎ *902/597–8614.* 🎫 *$5.* ☉ *May–Oct., daily 9–5.*

Joggins

㉚ *40 km (25 mi) west of Springhill.*

Joggins's main draw is the coal-age fossils embedded in its 150-foot sandstone cliffs. Visit the **Joggins Fossil Centre,** where you can learn about the region's geological and archaeological history. Guided tours of the fossil cliffs are available, but departure times depend on the tides. Maps are issued for independent fossil hunters. ⊠ *30 Main St.,* ☎ *902/251–2727.* 🎫 *Centre $3.50, tour $10.* ☉ *June–Sept., daily 9–6:30.*

En Route   **Advocate Harbour,** 66 km (41 mi) south of Joggins, was named by Champlain for his friend Marc Lescarbot, who was a lawyer, or "avocat." Built on flat shore land with a tall ridge backdrop and a broad harbor before it, Advocate is eerily beautiful.

Cap d'Or

5 km (3 mi) east of Advocate Harbour.

Cape d'Or, land jutting out and dividing the waters of the main Bay of Fundy from the narrow enclosure of the Minas Basin, has a spectacular vista and lighthouse. As the tides change, fierce riptides create stunning waves. The view from the ridge down to the lighthouse is superb—keep your eyes peeled for peregrine falcons. The view from the lighthouse itself is almost equally magnificent, but the road down is rather primitive and should be attempted only in four-wheel-drive vehicles. Those who can handle the steep return climb can park at the top of the hill and walk down.

En Route   **Spencer's Island** (not really an island) is a 19th-century shipbuilding community on Route 209. A cairn commemorates the construction of the famous *Mary Celeste,* which was found in 1872 sailing in the mid-Atlantic without a crew; she had been abandoned at sea with the table still set for dinner.

Parrsboro

㉛ *45 km (28 mi) east of Spencer's Island.*

Parrsboro, a center for rock hounds and fossil hunters, is the main town on this shore, and hosts the **Rockhound Roundup** every August. Among the exhibits and festivities are geological displays, concerts, and other special events.

Parrsboro is an appropriate setting for the **Fundy Geological Museum** since it's not far from the Minas Basin area, the site where some of the oldest dinosaur fossils in Canada were found. Two-hundred-million-year-old dinosaur fossils are displayed here alongside exhibits of amethysts, agates, zeolites, and other mineral, plant, and animal relics that have washed out of nearby cliffs. ⊠ *6 Two Island Rd.,* ☎ *902/254–3814.* ⊡ *$3.* ☉ *June–Oct. 15, daily 9:30–5:30.*

The "world's smallest dinosaur footprints" are on display at the **Parrsboro Rock and Mineral Shop and Museum** (⊠ 39 Whitehall Rd., ☎ 902/254–2981), run by Eldon George.

Although fossils have become Parrsboro's claim to fame, this harbor town was also a major shipping and shipbuilding port, and its history is described at the **Ottawa House Museum-by-the-Sea,** 3 km (2 mi) east of Parrsboro. Ottawa House, which overlooks the Bay of Fundy, was the summer home of Sir Charles Tupper, a former premier of Nova Scotia who was briefly prime minister of Canada. ⊠ *Whitehall Rd.,* ☎ *902/254–2376.* ⊡ *$1.* ☉ *July–early Sept., daily 10–8.*

The Arts

Parrsboro's professional **Ship's Company Theatre** (☎ 902/254–3425) has a summer season of plays based on historical events of the region, performed aboard the MV *Kipawo,* a former Minas Basin ferry.

Hiking

Ward's Falls is a beautiful 6 km (4 mi) interpreted hiking trail about 5 km (3 mi) east of Parrsboro.

En Route   The 125-foot-high **Hidden Falls,** near Route 2, are about 5 km (3 mi) east of Parrsboro. Although the falls are located on private property, the path leading from the gift shop is open to the public and parking is available.

Five Islands

24 km (15 mi) east of Parrsboro.

Among the most beautiful scenic areas along Route 2 is Five Islands, which, according to Mi'Kmaq legend, was created when the god Glooscap threw handfuls of sod at beaver. **Five Islands Provincial Park** (⊠ Rte. 2, ☎ 902/254–2980), on the shore of Minas Basin, has a campground, a beach, hiking trails, and some interpretation of the region's unusual geology.

Lodging

$$–$$$ 🏠 **Shady Maple B&B.** Here's a unique property: a working farm where you can breakfast on fresh eggs and the farm's own maple syrup, jams, and jellies. Enjoy the smoke-free rooms and sun-dried bed linen, and take a dip in the pool. One of the three rooms is a deluxe suite with a waterbed. Full breakfast included. ⊠ *R.R. 1, Masstown B0M 1G0,* ☎ *902/662–3565,* ℻ *902/662–3565. 3 rooms. Pool. MC, V.*

CAPE BRETON ISLAND

The highways and byways of the Island of Cape Breton make up one of the most spectacular drives in North America. Wind through the rugged coastal headlands of Cape Breton Highlands National Park where you can climb mountains and plunge back down to the sea in a matter of minutes. The Margaree River is a cultural dividing line: South of the river the settlements are Scottish, up the river they are largely Irish, and north of the river they are Acadian French. Visit villages where ancient dialects can still be heard, and explore a fortress where period players bring history to life. This is a place where heritage is alive, where the atmosphere is maritime, and where inventors Marconi and Bell share the spotlight with coal miners and singers like Rita MacNeil.

Bras d'Or Lake, a vast, warm, almost-landlocked inlet of the sea, occupies the entire center of Cape Breton. The coastline of the lake is more than 967 km (600 mi) long, and people sail yachts from all over the world to cruise its serene, unspoiled coves and islands. Bald eagles have become so plentiful around the lake that they are now exported to the United States to restock natural habitats. Four of the largest communities along the shore are Mi'Kmaq Indian reserves.

If Halifax is the heart of Nova Scotia, Cape Breton is its soul, complete with soul music: flying fiddles, boisterous rock, velvet ballads. Cape Breton musicians—weaned on Scottish jigs and reels—are among Canada's finest, and you can hear them all over the island all summer long at dozens of local festivals and concerts.

Allow three or four days for this meandering tour of approximately 710 km (about 440 mi) that begins by entering the island via the Canso Causeway on Highway 104. Turn left at the rotary and take Route 19, the Ceilidh Trail (129 km, or 80 mi), which winds along the mountainside through green wooden glens and hidden farms, with fine views across St. George's Bay to Cape George. This western shoreline of Cape Breton faces the Gulf of St. Lawrence and is famous for its sandy beaches and warm saltwater.

Mabou

32 *13 km (8 mi) northeast of Port Hood on Rte. 19.*

Mabou has been called "the prettiest village in Canada," and it is also perhaps the most Scottish, with its Gaelic signs and a deep tradition of Scottish music and dancing. This is the hometown of national recording and performing artists such as John Allan Cameron and the Rankin Family; stop at a local gift shop and pick up some tapes to play as you drive down the long fjord of Mabou Harbour.

Lodging

$$$ **Glenora Inn & Distillery.** This friendly inn is home to North America's only single malt whisky distillery. Sample a "wee dram" of their own whiskey—billed as Canada's first legal moonshine. Stop in for a distillery tour, fine cuisine, and traditional Cape Breton music even if you don't plan to stay overnight. From November through April, rooms are available by reservation only. ⊠ *Glenville (Rte. 19 between Mabou and Inverness), B0E 1X0,* ☎ *902/258–2662. 9 inn rooms, 6 chalets. Restaurant, pub, gift shop, convention facilities. AE, MC, V.*

Mabou Mines

> *10 km (6 mi) northwest of Mabou.*

This town, known as "the mines," is a place so hauntingly exquisite that you expect to meet the *sidhe*, the Scottish fairies, capering on the hillsides. Within the hills of Mabou Mines is some of the finest hiking in the province, and above the land fly bald eagles, plentiful in this region. Inquire locally or at the tourist office on Margaree Forks for information about trails.

En Route   Take Route 19 to Route 219 and follow the coast to **Chimney Corner.** A nearby beach has "sonorous sands": When you step on the sand or drag a foot through it, it squeaks and moans.

Margaree Harbour

> ③③ *28 km (17 mi) north of Inverness.*

The Ceilidh Trail joins the Cabot Trail at Margaree Harbour at the mouth of the Margaree River, a famous salmon-fishing stream and a favorite canoe route.

Dining and Lodging

$$$ ✕▦ **Normaway Inn.** This secluded 1920s inn, nestled on 250 acres in the hills of the Margaree Valley at the beginning of the Cabot Trail, has distinctive rooms and cabins, most with wood stoves and screened porches; some have hot tubs. Take advantage of the traditional entertainment or films featured nightly, and the weekly square dances in the "Barn." The inn is known for its country cuisine, particularly the vegetable chowders and fresh seafood ragoût. ⌧ *Box 326, Egypt Rd., 2 mi off Cabot Trail, B0E 2C0,* ☎ *902/248–2987 or 800/565–9463,* ℻ *902/248–2600. 9 rooms, 19 cabins. Restaurant, tennis court, hiking and walking trails, bicycles, travel services. MC, V. Closed mid-Oct.–mid-June.*

$–$$ ▦ **Heart of Hart's Inn.** This 100-year-old rural farmhouse is within walking distance of the village of North East Margaree. The theme is "very country," with wood stove, antiques, colonial colored glass, and an array of flowers in the gardens. A full breakfast is included in the room rate, and four-course country dinners of local and regional foods are served nightly by reservation, at $30 per person. ⌧ *Cabot Trail, Box 21, B0E 2H0,* ☎ *902/248–2765,* ℻ *902/248–2606. 5 rooms. Travel services. MC, V.*

Chéticamp

> ③④ *26 km (16 mi) north of Margaree Harbour.*

Chéticamp, an Acadian community, has the best harbor and the largest settlement on this shore. With its tall silver steeple towering over the village, it stands exposed on a wide lip of flat land below a range of bald green hills, behind which lies the high plateau of the Cape Breton Highlands. Chéticamp is famous for its hooked rugs, available at many local gift shops.

The **Dr. Elizabeth LeFort Gallery and Museum** displays artifacts and fine hooked embroidery work, rugs, and tapestries. ⌧ *Les Trois Pignons.* ▦ *$3. May–Oct., weekdays 9–5; July and Aug., daily 9–6.*

Whale-Watching

Chéticamp is known for its whale-watching cruises, which depart in June, twice daily, and in July and August, three times daily, from the government wharf. **Whale Cruisers Ltd.** (☎ 902/224–3376 or 800/813–3376) is a reliable charter company. Cruises cost $25 for adults.

Cape Breton Highlands National Park

★ *At the outskirts of Chéticamp.*

This 950-square-km (361-square-mi) wil... plateau barrens, and steep cliffs stretches ... of Cape Breton from the Gulf Shore t... through the park is magnificent as it rises t... tains and descends through tight switchbacks to the ... has been compared to a 106-km (66-mi) roller coaster ride, stretching from Chéticamp to Ingonish. Good brakes and an attentive driver are advised. Pull-offs provide photo opportunities. For wildlife watchers there's much to see, including moose, eagle, deer, bear, fox, and bobcat. Your chances of seeing wildlife are better if you venture off the main road at dusk or dawn. High altitude marshlands are home to delightful wild orchids and other unique flora and fauna. If you plan to hike, fish or camp in the park, or want to maximize your appreciation for the nature and history associated within the park, stop at the Chéticamp Information Centre for advice and necessary permits. A guide to the park's 27 hiking trails, *Walking in the Highlands,* can be purchased. Trails range from easy 20-minute strolls to tough overnight treks. ☎ *902/285–2535, 902/285–2270 in winter. ✉ May–Oct. $3.50 per person per day, 4-day pass $10.50, seasonal pass $17.50; Nov.–Apr. free (including use of Cabot Trail lookouts within park, roadside exhibits, walking trails, picnic areas); camping $13–$19.*

OFF THE BEATEN PATH **GAMPO ABBEY –** The most northerly tip of the island is not part of the National Park; a spur road creeps along the cliffs to Red River, beyond which, on a broad flat bench of land high above the sea, is this Tibetan Buddhist monastery. It's the only one in America.

Ingonish

③⑤ *113 km (70 mi) northeast of Chéticamp.*

Ingonish, one of the leading holiday destinations on the island, is actually several villages on two bays, divided by a long narrow peninsula called Middle Head. Each bay has a sandy beach.

Dining and Lodging

$$$$ ✕🖼 **Keltic Lodge.** Spread across cliffs overlooking the ocean, the provincially owned Keltic Lodge sits on the Cabot Trail in Cape Breton Highlands National Park (☞ *above*). Guests can choose among the Main Lodge, White Birch Inn, and two- or four-bedroom cottages. A wide variety of activities is offered, including golfing on the world-class Highlands Links. Seafood stars on the menu in the Purple Thistle Dining Room. ✉ *Middlehead Peninsula, Ingonish Beach, B0C 1L0,* ☎ *902/285–2880 or 800/565–0444. 98 rooms. 2 Restaurants, pool, golf, hiking, beaches. Closed Apr., May, Nov., and Dec.*

OFF THE BEATEN PATH **BIRD ISLANDS –** From Big Bras d'Or, 100 km (62 mi) south of Ingonish, notice the small islands on the far side of the mouth of St. Ann's Bay: These are the Bird Islands, breeding grounds for Atlantic puffins, black guillemots, razor-billed auks, and cormorants. Boat tours are available from **Bird Islands Boat Tour** (☎ 902/674–2384). Landing on the islands is forbidden, however.

65 km (40 mi) south of Ingonish on Rte. 312.

Take the short (about 2 minutes) ferry ride from Jersey Cove across St. Ann's Bay to Englishtown, home of the celebrated Cape Breton Giant, Angus MacAskill. Ferries run 24 hours a day, and the fare is 50¢. The **Giant MacAskill Museum** holds artifacts and the remains of the 7'9" man who traveled with P.T. Barnum's troupe in the 1800s. ⊠ *Rte. 312,* ☎ *902/929–2875.* 🎟 *$1.* ☉ *May–Oct., daily 9–6.*

South Gut St. Ann's

12 km (7 mi) south of Jersey Cove.

Settled by the Highland Scots, South Gut St. Ann's is home to North America's only **Gaelic College** (☎ 902/295–3441). Its Great Hall of the Clans depicts Scottish history and has an account of the Great Migration. The college offers courses in Gaelic language and literature, Scottish music and dancing, weaving, and other Scottish arts. There's also a Scottish gift shop.

Baddeck

36 *20 km (12 mi) south of South Gut St. Ann's.*

Baddeck, the most highly developed tourist center in Cape Breton, has more than 1,000 motel beds, a golf course, many fine gift shops, and numerous restaurants. It was also the summer home of Alexander Graham Bell until he died here at the age of 75. In summer the town celebrates **Centre Bras d'Or Festival of the Arts,** which offers live music and drama every evening during summer. The annual **regatta** of the Bras d'Or Yacht Club is held in the first week of August. Sailing tours and charters are available locally, as are bus tours along the Cabot Trail.

Discover how Alexander Graham Bell bridged the world between sound and silence at the **Alexander Graham Bell National Historic Site.** Participate in experiments, kite making, and other hands-on activities designed especially for children, and take in a presentation in Mr. Bell Theatre, where you can view films, artifacts, and photographs to learn how ideas led Bell to create man-carrying kites, airplanes, and a marine record-setting hydrofoil boat. ⊠ *Chebucto St.,* ☎ *902/295–2069,* FAX *902/295–3496.* 🎟 *$3.75.* ☉ *July and Aug., daily 9–8; June and Sept., daily 9–7; Oct.–May (reduced service), daily 9–5.*

Dining and Lodging

$$$$ ✕⊞ **Inverary Inn Resort.** On the shores of the magnificent Bras d'Or Lake, this resort has stunning views and a lot of activities for the money. Choose from cozy pine-paneled cottages, modern hotel units, or the elegant 100-year-old main lodge. There's boating and swimming in close proximity to the village, but the resort remains tranquil. Families will appreciate the on-site children's playground and the choice of dining in the Lakeside Cafe or the elegant main dining room. ⊠ *Box 190, Rte. 205 and Shore Rd., B0E 1B0,* ☎ *902/295–3500 or 800/565–5600,* FAX *902/295–3527. 137 rooms. Restaurant, café, indoor pool, sauna, 3 tennis courts, boat rental. AE, D, MC, V.*

Beach

A free ferry (passengers only) shuttles between the government wharf and the sandy beach by the lighthouse at Kidston Island.

Iona

㊲ *56 km (35 mi) south of Baddeck.*

From Baddeck, take Trans-Canada Highway 105 to Exit 6, which leads
to Little Narrows where you can take a short ferry ride to the Washabuck
Peninsula. From here, take Route 223 to Iona, the site of the **Nova Scotia Highland Village,** set high on a mountainside, with a spectacular
view of Bras d'Or Lake and the narrow Barra Strait. The village's 10
historic buildings were assembled from all over Cape Breton to depict
Highland Scots' way of life from their origins in the Hebrides to the
present day. Among the participants at this living-history museum are
a smith in the blacksmith shop and a clerk in the store. Ferries run 24
hours a day, and the fare is 25¢. ✉ *Rte. 233,* ☎ *902/725–2227.* ✇
$4. ☉ *Reception desk and museum June–Sept., Mon.–Sat. 9–5, Sun.
10–6; Welcome Center Oct.–May, weekdays 9–5.*

Dining and Lodging

$$ ✕▦ **Highland Heights Inn.** The rural surroundings, the Scottish home-
style cooking served near the dining room's huge stone fireplace, and
the view of the lake substitute nicely for the Scottish Highlands. The
inn is on a hillside beside the Nova Scotia Highland Village, overlooking
the village of Iona, where some residents still speak the Gaelic language
of their ancestors. Enjoy the salmon (or any fish in season), fresh-baked
oat cakes, and homemade desserts. ✉ *Box 19, Rte. 223,* ☎ *902/725–
2360,* ℻ *902/725–2800. 26 rooms. Dining room. D, MC, V. Closed
mid-Oct.–mid-May.*

En Route   The Barra Strait Bridge joins Iona to Grand Narrows. A few kilome-
ters from the bridge, bear right toward East Bay. (If you miss this turn,
don't worry; you'll have just as scenic a drive along St. Andrews Chan-
nel.) The East Bay route runs through the Mi'Kmaq village of **Eska-
soni,** the largest native community in the province. This is one of the
friendliest villages, with a fascinating cultural heritage.

Sydney

㊳ *60 km (37 mi) northeast of Iona.*

The heart of Nova Scotia's second-largest urban cluster, Sydney is
known as "Industrial Cape Breton." It encompasses villages, unorga-
nized districts, and a half-dozen towns—most of which sprang up
around the coal mines, which fed the steel plant at Sydney. These are
warmhearted, interesting communities with a diverse ethnic popula-
tion, including Ukrainians, Welsh, Poles, Lebanese, West Indians, Ital-
ians; most residents descended from the miners and steelworkers who
arrived a century ago when the area was booming. Sydney is also the
only significantly industrialized district in Atlantic Canada, and it has
suffered serious environmental damage.

Sydney has the island's only real airport, its only university, and a lively
entertainment scene that specializes in Cape Breton music. The town
is also a departure point: Fast ferries leave from North Sydney for New-
foundland, and scheduled air service to Newfoundland and the French
islands of St. Pierre and Miquelon departs from Sydney Airport.

Dining and Lodging

$$$ ✕▦ **Delta Sydney.** This hotel is on the harbor, beside the yacht club,
and close to the center of town. The attractively decorated guest rooms
each have a view of the harbor. The intimate dining room specializes
in seafood and Continental cuisine. ✉ *300 Esplanade, B1P 6J4,* ☎
902/562–7500 or 800/887–1133, 800/268–1133 in Canada, ℻

902/562–3023. 152 rooms. Restaurant, lounge, indoor pool, sauna, exercise room. AE, DC, MC, V.

Nightlife and the Arts

The **Cape Breton Summertime Revue,** based in Sydney, performs an annual original revue of music and comedy that tours Nova Scotia during June and August. Many leading fiddlers appear at the **Big Pond Concert** in mid-July. At the **Sheraton Casino** (✉ 625 George St., ☎ 902/563–7777), try the slot machines, roulette, or gaming tables, or enjoy live entertainment in the lounge. Glace Bay's opulent old opera house, the **Savoy Theatre** (✉ Union St., ☎ 902/842–1577) is the home of the summer-long Festival on the Bay. The **University College of Cape Breton** (✉ 1250 Grand Lake Rd., ☎ 902/539–5300) has many facilities for the public, such as the **Boardmore Playhouse** and the island's only public **art gallery.**

Louisbourg

㊴ *33 km (20 mi) southeast of Sydney.*

Though best known as the home of the largest National Historic Site in Canada, Louisbourg is also an important fishing community with ★ a lovely harborfront. **Fortress of Louisbourg National Historic Park,** the most remarkable site in Cape Breton, is about 30 minutes from Sydney. After the French were forced out of mainland Nova Scotia in 1713, they established their headquarters here in a walled and fortified town on a low point of land at the mouth of Louisbourg Harbour. The fortress was twice captured, once by New Englanders and once by the British; after the second siege, in 1758, it was razed. Its capture essentially ended the French Empire in America. A quarter of the original town has been rebuilt on its foundation, just as it was in 1744, before the first siege. Costumed actors re-create the lives and activities of the original inhabitants; you can watch a military drill, see nails and lace being made, and eat food prepared from 18th-century recipes in the town's two inns. Plan on spending at least a half day. Louisbourg tends to be chilly, so pack a warm sweater or windbreaker. ✉ *Rte. 22,* ☎ *902/733–2280 or 800/565–9464.* 🎟 *$7.50.* ☉ *June and Sept., daily 9:30–5; July and Aug., daily 9–6.*

At the **Sydney and Louisburg Historical Society,** a restored 1895 railway station exhibits the history of the S&L Railway, railway technology, and marine shipping. The rolling stock includes a baggage car, coach, and caboose. ✉ *7336 Main St.,* ☎ *902/733–2720.* 🎟 *Free.* ☉ *June and Sept., weekdays 9–5; July and Aug., daily 9–7.*

Atlantic Statiquarium is a marine museum devoted largely to underwater treasure. ✉ *7523 Main St.,* ☎ *902/733–2721.* 🎟 *$2.50.* ☉ *June–Sept., daily 10–8.*

Big Pond

40 km (25 mi) west of Sydney.

Take Route 22 to Route 125. From here, turn onto Route 4 and follow it to this little town comprised of just a few houses. One of them is the home of singer/songwriter Rita MacNeil, who operates a tearoom in a tranquil setting with seating indoors and out. Stop in for Rita's special blend of tea and home-baked goodies such as oatcakes. A display room contains Rita's awards and memorabilia.

En Route   Route 4 rolls along the lake, sometimes close to the shore and sometimes high in the hills. At **St. Peter's** the Atlantic Ocean is connected with the Bras d'Or Lake by the century-old St. Peter's Canal, still heavily used by pleasure craft and fishing vessels. From St. Peter's to Port Hawkesbury the population is largely Acadian French.

Arichat

 43 km (27 mi) south of Dundee.

Take Route 247 to Route 320 and head for Isle Madame, a 27-square-km (10-square-mi) island named for Madame de Maintenon, second wife of Louis XIV. Route 320 leads through the villages of Poulamon and D'Escousse, and overlooks the protected waterway of Lennox Passage, with its spangle of islands. Route 206 meanders through the low hills to a maze of land and water at West Arichat. Together, the two routes encircle the island, meeting at Arichat, the principal town of Isle Madame.

Arichat was once the seat of the local Catholic diocese. Notre Dame de l'Assumption church, built in 1837, still retains the grandeur of its former cathedral status. Its bishop's palace, the only one in Cape Breton, is now a law office. The two cannons overlooking the harbor were installed after the town was sacked by John Paul Jones, founder of the U.S. Navy, during the American Revolution.

The town was an important shipbuilding and trading center during the 19th century, and some fine old houses from that period still remain, along with the 18th-century **LeNoir Forge,** a restored French 18th-century stone blacksmith shop. ⊠ *Rte. 320 off Rte. 4,* ☎ *902/226–9364.* ⊙ *May–Sept., weekdays 9–5, Sat. 10–3.*

OFF THE   **LITTLE ANSE –** With its rocky red bluffs, cobble shores, tiny harbor, and
BEATEN PATH   brightly painted houses, Little Anse is particularly attractive to artists and photographers.

NOVA SCOTIA A TO Z

Arriving and Departing

By Bus

Greyhound Lines (☎ 800/231–2222) from New York, and **Voyageur Inc.** (☎ 613/238–5900) from Montréal, connect with **Scotia Motor Tours** or **SMT** (☎ 506/458–6000) through New Brunswick, which links (rather inconveniently) with **Acadian Lines Limited** (☎ 902/454–8279), which provides inter-urban services within Nova Scotia.

By Car

Throughout Nova Scotia, the highways numbered from 100 to 199 are all-weather, limited-access roads, with 100-km-per-hour (62-mi-per-hour) speed limits. The last two digits usually match the number of an older trunk highway along the same route, numbered from 1 to 99. Thus, Route 102, between Halifax and Truro, matches the older Route 2, between the same towns. Roads numbered from 200 to 399 are secondary roads that usually link villages. Unless otherwise posted, the speed limit on these and any roads other than the 100-series highways is 80 km per hour (50 mi per hour).

Most highways in the province lead to Halifax and Dartmouth. Routes 3/103, 7, 2/102, and 1/101 terminate in the twin cities.

By Ferry

Three car ferries connect Nova Scotia with Maine and New Brunswick. **Marine Atlantic** (☎ 902/794–5700 or 800/341–7981) sails from Bar Harbor, Maine, and **Prince of Fundy Cruises** (☎ 800/341–7540) from

Portland; both arrive in Yarmouth. From Saint John, New Brunswick, to Digby, Nova Scotia, ferry service is provided by **Marine Atlantic** (☎ 800/341–7981; in Canada, 800/565–9470).

Marine Atlantic also operates ferries between New Brunswick and Prince Edward Island, and between Cape Breton and Newfoundland (☎ 902/794–5700, 709/772–7701, or 800/341–7981). Between May and December, **Northumberland Ferries** (☎ 902/566–3838; in Nova Scotia and Prince Edward Island, 800/565–0201) operate between Caribou, Nova Scotia, and Wood Islands, Prince Edward Island.

By Plane
The **Halifax International Airport** is 40 km (25 mi) northeast of downtown Halifax. **Sydney Airport** is 13 km (8 mi) east of Sydney.

Air Canada (☎ 902/429–7111 or 800/776–3000) provides regular, daily service to Halifax and Sydney, Nova Scotia, from New York, Boston, Toronto, Montréal, and St. John's, Newfoundland, as well as Frankfurt, Germany, twice weekly. **Canadian Airlines International** (☎ 800/527–8499) has service to Halifax via Toronto and Montréal. **Air Nova** (☎ 902/429–7111 or 800/776–3000) and **Air Atlantic** (☎ 800/426–7000; in Canada, 800/665–1177) provide regional service to both airports with flights to Toronto, Montréal, and Boston. **Canada 3000** (☎ 902/873–3555) offers service with Toronto, Calgary, Edmonton, Vancouver, London, Amsterdam, and Hamburg. **Northwest Air** (☎ 800/225–2525) provides summer service between Halifax and Detroit. **Icelandair** (☎ 902 873–2029) offers flights from Halifax to Reykjavik.

Visiting pilots will find aviation-related information for the flying tourist from the **Aviation Council of Nova Scotia** (⊠ Box 100, Debert, Nova Scotia B0M 1G0, ☎ 902/895–1143). A publication, *Air Tourist Information: Canada,* is available on request from the **Aeronautical Information and Publications Office** (⊠ Ministry of Transport, Place de Ville, Tower C, Ottawa, Ontario K1A 0N5).

BETWEEN THE AIRPORT AND CITY CENTER
Limousine and taxi service, as well as car rentals, are available at Halifax, Sydney, and Yarmouth airports. Airport bus service to most Halifax and Dartmouth hotels costs $20 round-trip, $12 one-way. Regular taxi fare is $35 each way, but if you book in advance with **Aero Cab** (☎ 902/445–3393) the fare is $26 if you pay cash, slightly more with a credit card (MC, V). The trip takes 30–40 minutes.

By Train
VIA Rail (☎ 800/561–3949) provides service from Montréal to Halifax via Moncton, in New Brunswick, and Amherst and Truro, in Nova Scotia. **Amtrak** (☎ 800/872–7245) from New York City makes connections in Montréal.

Getting Around

Halifax
BY BUS
Metro Transit (☎ 902/421–6600) provides bus service throughout the cities of Halifax and Dartmouth, the town of Bedford, and (to a limited extent) the county of Halifax. The base fare is $1.35; exact change only.

BY FERRY
Metro Transit (☞ *above*) runs three passenger ferries from the Halifax Ferry Terminal on the hour and half hour from 6:30 AM to 11:57 PM. During the weekday commuter rush, ferries cross continuously to the

Woodside Terminal from 6:52 AM to 10:04 AM and 3:37 PM to 6:19 PM only. Ferries also operate on Sunday during the summer (June–September). Free transfers are available from the ferry to the bus system (and vice versa). The fare for a single crossing is $1.10 and is well worth it considering you get an up-close view of both waterfronts.

BY TAXI

Rates begin at about $2.50 and increase based on mileage and time. A crosstown trip should cost $5–$6, depending on traffic. Hailing a taxi can be difficult, but there are taxi stands at major hotels and shopping malls. Most Haligonians simply phone for a taxi service; try **Aero Cab** (☞ By Plane, *above*).

Elsewhere in Nova Scotia

BY BUS

There are a number of small, regional bus services; however, connections are not always convenient. Outside of Halifax there are no inner-city bus services. For information, call **Nova Scotia Visitors Services** (☎ 800/565–0000).

BY CAR

The recommended mode of travel within the province is by car. As you explore Nova Scotia, be on the lookout for the 10 designated "Scenic Travelways" that appear throughout the province and are easily identified by roadside signs with icons that correspond with trail names. These routes, as well as tourist literature (maps and the provincial *Travel Guide*) published in accordance with this scheme, have been developed by the Nova Scotia Economic Renewal Agency. **Nova Scotia Tourism** (☞ Visitor Information, *below*) provides information and reservation services.

Many of the roads in rural Nova Scotia require attentive driving as they are not well signed, are narrow, and do not always have a paved shoulder. They are generally well surfaced.

BY PLANE

Internal air travel is very limited. **Air Nova** (☎ 902/429–7111 or 800/776–3000) and **Air Atlantic** (☎ 800/426–7000; in Canada, 800/665–1177) provide regional service to other provinces and to Sydney.

Contacts and Resources

Car Rentals

Halifax is the most convenient place from which to begin your driving tour of the province. It is recommended that you book a car through your own travel agent. The following list details city and airport venues of rental-car agencies. **Avis** (✉ 5600 Sackville St., ☎ 902/423–6303; airport, ☎ 902/873–3523). **Budget** (✉ 1558 Hollis St., ☎ 902/421–1242; airport, ☎ 902/873–3509). **Hertz** (✉ Halifax Sheraton, ☎ 902/421–1763; airport, ☎ 902/873–3700). **Thrifty** (✉ 6930 Lady Hammond, ☎ 902/422–4455; airport, ☎ 902/873–3527). **Tilden** (✉ 1130 Hollis St., ☎ 902/422–4433; airport, ☎ 902/873–3505).

Emergencies

Dial **"0"** for operator in emergencies; check the front of the local phone book for specific medical services.

Guided Tours

There are more than 20 tour operators specializing in specific areas, modes of transportation, tour topics, and types of groups. For information, and to connect with the tour company most suited to your needs, contact **Nova Scotia Tourism** (☎ 800/565–0000).

Boat tours have become very popular in all regions of the province. For details contact **Nova Scotia Tourism** (☞ *above*).

Murphy's on the Water (☎ 902/420–1015) sails various vessels: *Harbour Queen I,* a paddle wheeler; *Haligonian III,* an enclosed motor launch; *Stormy Weather I,* a 40-foot Cape Islander (fishing boat); and *Mar II,* a 75-foot sailing ketch. All operate from mid-May to late October from berths at 1751 Lower Water Street on Cable Wharf next to the Historic Properties in Halifax. Costs vary, but a basic tour of the Halifax Harbour ranges from $10 to $15.

Both **Gray Line Sightseeing** (☎ 902/454–8279) and **Cabana Tours** (☎ 902/423–6066) run coach tours through Halifax, Dartmouth, and Peggy's Cove. **Halifax Double Decker Tours** (☎ 902/420–1155) offers two-hour tours on double-decker buses that leave daily from Historic Properties in Halifax.

Outdoor Activities and Sports

Bicycle Tours in Nova Scotia ($7) is published by **Bicycle Nova Scotia** (✉ Box 3010, 5516 Spring Garden Rd., Halifax B3J 3G6, ☎ 902/425–5450). **Backroads** (✉ 1516 5th St., Suite Q333, Berkeley, CA 94710, ☎ 510/527–1555 or 800/245–3874) offers five- and six-day bike trips in the province.

Nova Scotia is located on the "Atlantic Flyway" and is an important staging point for migrating species. An excellent, beautifully illustrated book, *Birds of Nova Scotia,* by Robie Tufts, is a must on every ornithologist's reading list.

Nova Scotia is seamed with small rivers and lakes, by which the Mi'Kmaq Indians roamed both Cape Breton and the peninsula. Especially good canoe routes are within Kejimkujik National Park. The publication *Canoe Routes of Nova Scotia* and a variety of route maps are available from the **Nova Scotia Government Bookstore** (✉ Box 637, 1700 Granville St., Halifax B3J 2T3, ☎ 902/424–7580). Canoeing information is also available from **Canoe NS** (✉ Box 3010S, Halifax B3J 3G6, ☎ 902/425–5450, ext. 316; FAX 902/425–5606).

The province has a wide variety of trails along the rugged coastline and inland through forest glades, which enable you to experience otherwise inaccessible scenery, wildlife, and vegetation. *Hiking Trails of Nova Scotia* ($12.95) is available through **Gooselane Editions** (✉ 469 King St., Fredericton, New Brunswick, E3R 1E5, ☎ 506/450–4251).

Visiting snowmobilers can get information on trails, activities, clubs, and dealers through the **Snowmobile Association of Nova Scotia** (✉ Box 3010 South, Halifax B3J 3G6, ☎ 902/425–5450).

Reservation Service

Nova Scotia has a computerized system called **Check In** (☎ 902/425–5781 or 800/565–0000), which provides information and makes reservations with more than 700 hotels, motels, inns, campgrounds, and car-rental agencies. Check In also represents most properties in Prince Edward Island and some in New Brunswick.

Shopping

Changes to the collection of sales tax have combined the current provincial tax and the federal GST to a 15% harmonized sales tax (HST), which is charged on most goods and services. A decision regarding a refund of sales tax for foreign visitors is pending. Contact the **Nova Scotia Government** (☏ 902/421–8736) or the **Provincial Tax Commission** (✉ Tax Refund Unit, Box 755, Halifax B3J 2V4, ☏ 902/424–5946; in Nova Scotia, 902/424–6708) for current information on refunds.

Visitor Information

Nova Scotia Tourism (✉ Box 130, Halifax B3J 2M7, ☏ 902/424–5000 or 800/341–6096; in Canada, 800/565–0000; FAX 902/420–1286) publishes a wide range of literature, including an exhaustive annual travel guide. **Nova Scotia Tourism Information Centre** (✉ Old Red Store at Historic Properties, Halifax, ☏ 902/424–4248) and **Tourism Halifax & Nova Scotia Tourism** (✉ International Visitors Centre, 1595 Barrington St., ☏ 902/421–8736 or 902/421–2842) are open mid-June–Labor Day, daily 9–6; Labor Day–mid-June, weekdays 9–4:30.

3 Excursions from Nova Scotia to Coastal Maine

Purists hold that the Maine coast begins at Penobscot Bay. Here you'll find the rugged, "downeast" experience: classic townscapes, rocky shorelines, sandy beaches, and quaint downtown districts. Maine's principal tourist attraction, Acadia National Park, has 34,000 acres to explore. Others go to explore Freeport, north of Portland, where a bewildering assortment of outlets has sprung up around the famous outfitter L.L. Bean.

Updated
by Hilary
M. Nangle

MAINE IS A LIKELY EXCURSION from Nova Scotia thanks to two ferry systems that make commuting easy. Boats depart from Yarmouth, Nova Scotia, and arrive in either Portland or Bar Harbor, Maine. Consider taking your car across, though, so you can travel up the Maine coast, taking in history, seafood, and fine shopping in the many outlet shops.

The coast is several places in one. South of the rapidly gentrifying city of Portland, such resort towns as Ogunquit, Kennebunkport, and Old Orchard Beach (sometimes called the Québec Riviera because of its popularity with French Canadians) predominate along a reasonably smooth shoreline. Development has been considerable; north of Portland and Casco Bay, secondary roads turn south off Route 1 onto so many oddly chiseled peninsulas that it's possible to drive for days without retracing your route and to conclude that motels, discount outlets, and fried-clam stands are taking over the domain of presidents and lobstermen. Freeport is an entity unto itself, a place where a bewildering assortment of off-price, name-brand outlets has sprung up around the famous outfitter L.L. Bean.

The visitor seeking an untouched fishing village with locals gathered around a pot-bellied stove in the general store may be sadly disappointed; that innocent age has passed in all but the most remote of villages. Tourism has supplanted fishing, logging, and potato farming as Maine's number one industry, and most areas are well equipped to receive the annual onslaught of visitors. But whether you are stepping outside a motel room for an evening walk or watching a boat rock at its anchor, you can sense the infinity of the natural world. Wilderness is always nearby, growing to the edges of the most urbanized spots.

Numbers in the margin correspond to points of interest on the Southern Maine Coast, Portland, Penobscot Bay, and Mount Desert Island maps.

PORTLAND TO PEMAQUID POINT

Maine's largest city, Portland, is small enough to be seen in a day or two. It continues to undergo a cultural and economic renaissance: New inns, renewed hotels, and a performing arts center have joined the neighborhoods of historic homes. The Old Port Exchange, perhaps the finest urban renovation project on the East Coast, balances modern commercial enterprise with a salty waterfront character in an area bustling with restaurants, shops, and galleries. The piers of Commercial Street abound with opportunities for water tours of the harbor and excursions to the Calendar Islands. Downtown Portland, in a funk for years, is now a burgeoning arts district connected to the Old Port by a revitalized Congress Street, where L. L. Bean operates a factory store.

Freeport, north of Portland, is a town made famous by the L. L. Bean store, whose success led to the opening of scores of other clothing stores and outlets. Brunswick is best known for Bowdoin College. Bath has been a shipbuilding center since 1607, and the Maine Maritime Museum preserves its history. Wiscasset offers a multitude of antiques shops and galleries.

The Boothbays—the coastal areas of Boothbay Harbor, East Boothbay, Linekin Neck, Southport Island, and the inland town of Boothbay—attract hordes of vacationing families and flotillas of pleasure craft. The Pemaquid peninsula juts into the Atlantic south of Damariscotta

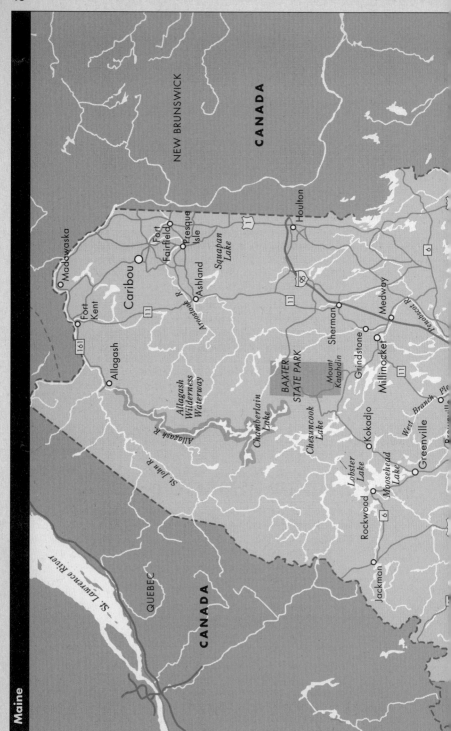

ATLANTIC OCEAN

Passamaquoddy Bay

Campobello Island

Grand Manan Island

NEW HAMPSHIRE

Portsmouth
Kittery
York
Ogunquit
Kennebunkport
Kennebunk
Biddeford
Portland
Casco Bay
Freeport
Brunswick
Bath
Phippsburg
Boothbay Harbor
Georgetown
Muscongus Bay
Damariscotta
Newcastle
Rockland
Camden
Belfast
Penobscot Bay
Castine
Islesboro
Deer Isle
Stonington
ACADIA NAT'L PARK
Mt. Desert Island
Isle au Haut
Frenchman Bay
Bar Harbor
Hancock
West Gouldsboro
Ellsworth
Bangor
Old Town
Newport
Waterville
Augusta
Lewiston
Auburn
Farmington
Bethel
Lovell
Sebago Lake
WHITE MOUNTAIN NAT'L FOREST
Rangeley
Rangeley Lake
Mooselookmeguntic Lake
Androscoggin R.
Kennebec R.
Dead R.
Pleasant R.
Brownville Junction
Passadumkeag

40 miles
60 km

and just east of the Boothbays, and near Pemaquid Beach one can view the objects unearthed at the Colonial Pemaquid Restoration.

This south mid-coast area gives visitors an overview of Maine: a little bit city, a little more coastline, and a nice dollop of history and architecture. The towns are arranged in such a manner as to drive easily to a selection of spots and return to Portland in a single day or to make an overnight along the way.

Portland

105 mi northeast of Boston, 320 mi northeast of New York City, 215 mi southwest of St. Stephen, New Brunswick.

Portland's first home was built on the peninsula now known as Munjoy Hill in 1632. When the Civil War broke out in 1861, Maine was asked to raise only a single regiment to fight, but the state raised 10 and sent the 5th Maine Regiment into the war's first battle at Bull Run. Not long after, much of Portland was destroyed on July 4 in the Great Fire of 1866 when a boy threw a celebration firecracker into a pile of wood shavings; 1,500 buildings burned to the ground. Poet Henry Wadsworth Longfellow said at the time his city reminded him of the ruins of Pompeii. The Great Fire started not far from where tourists now wander the streets of the Old Port Exchange. Portland offers many aspects of a large city without big-city problems.

Congress Street, Portland's main street, runs the length of the peninsular city from alongside the Western Promenade in the southwest to the Eastern Promenade on Munjoy Hill in the northeast, passing through the small downtown area. A few blocks southeast of downtown, the bustling Old Port Exchange sprawls along the waterfront. Just below Munjoy Hill is India Street, where the city's Great Fire of 1866 started.

8 One of the notable homes on Congress Street is the **Neal Dow Memorial,** a brick mansion built in 1829 in the late Federal style by General Neal Dow, a zealous abolitionist and prohibitionist. The library has fine ornamental ironwork, and the furnishings include the family china, silver, and portraits. Don't miss the grandfather clocks and the original deed granted by James II. ⊠ *714 Congress St.,* ☎ *207/773–7773.* ⛟ *Free.* ☉ *Tours weekdays 11–4.*

9 For well more than a century, the tower of the Morse-Libby House, better known as the **Victoria Mansion,** has been a landmark visible from Casco Bay and Portland's harbor. A National Historic Landmark, the Italianate-style villa, built between 1858 and 1860, is widely regarded as the most sumptuously ornamented dwelling of its period remaining in the country. The lavish exterior is understated compared to the interior, with its colorful frescoed walls and ceilings, ornate marble mantelpieces, gilded gas chandeliers, stained-glass windows, and a mahogany flying staircase. ⊠ *109 Danforth St.,* ☎ *207/772–4841.* ⛟ *$4.* ☉ *Columbus Day–Labor Day, Tues.–Sat. 1–5, Sun. 1–4; Labor Day–Columbus Day, weekends 1–4.*

10 Touching is okay at the **Children's Museum of Maine,** where little ones can pretend they are fishing for lobster or are shopkeepers or computer experts. Camera Obscura, on the third floor, charges a separate admission fee ($2). ⊠ *142 Free St.,* ☎ *207/828–1234.* ⛟ *$4.* ☉ *Summer and school vacations, Mon.–Sat. 10–5, Sun. noon–5; during school yr, Wed.–Sat. 10–5, Sun. noon–5.*

11 The distinguished **Portland Museum of Art** has a strong collection of seascapes and landscapes by such masters as Winslow Homer, John Marin, Andrew Wyeth, and Marsden Hartley. Homer's *Pulling the Dory*

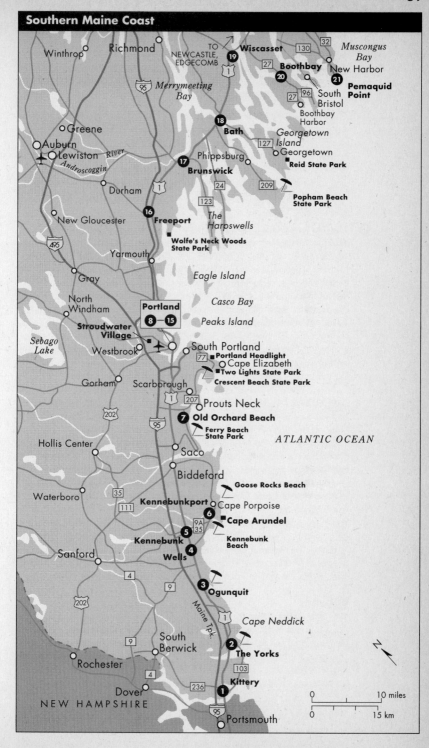

and *Weatherbeaten,* two quintessential Maine coast images, are here. The Joan Whitney Payson Collection includes works by Monet, Picasso, and Renoir. The strikingly modern Charles Shipman Payson building was designed by Harry N. Cobb, an associate of I. M. Pei, in 1983. ☒ *7 Congress Sq.,* ☎ *207/775–6148.* ☞ *$6; free Fri. evenings 5–9.* ☉ *Tues.–Wed. and Sat. 10–5, Thurs.–Fri. 10–9, Sun. noon–5; also Mon. July–Columbus Day 10–5.*

⑫ The **Wadsworth Longfellow House** of 1785, the boyhood home of the poet and the first brick house in Portland, is worth a special stop. The late Colonial–style structure sits back from the street and has a small portico over its entrance and four chimneys surmounting the hip roof. Most of the furnishings are original to the house. Christmas is celebrated with special tours of the house to highlight a particular period in the history of the poet. ☒ *485 Congress St.,* ☎ *207/879–0427.* ☞ *$4.* ☉ *June–Oct., Tues.–Sun. 10–4.*

⑬ The **Old Port Exchange,** the primary reason to visit downtown Portland, bridges the gap between yesterday and today. Allow a couple of hours to wander at leisure on Market, Exchange, Middle, and Fore streets. Like the Customs House, the brick buildings and warehouses of the Old Port Exchange were built following the Great Fire of 1866 and were intended to last for ages. When the city's economy slumped in the middle of the present century, however, the Old Port declined and seemed slated for demolition. Then artists and craftspeople began opening shops here in the late 1960s, and restaurants, chic boutiques, bookstores, and gift shops followed. You can park your car either at the city garage on Fore Street (between Exchange and Union streets) or opposite the U.S. Customs House at the corner of Fore and Pearl streets.

OFF THE
BEATEN PATH

CAPE ELIZABETH – This upscale Portland suburb juts out into the Atlantic and is home to three lighthouses and two state parks. Take Route 77 from Portland and follow signs to Two Lights State Park, home to one lighthouse, where you can wander through old World War II bunkers and picnic on the rocky coast. Stay on Two Lights Road to the end, where you'll find the other lighthouse, now privately owned, and the Lobster Shack, a seafood-in-the-rough restaurant where you can dine inside or out. Return to the center of Cape Elizabeth and turn right on Shore Road, which winds along the coast to Portland. About 2 mi from town center is Fort Williams, a town-owned park where you'll find Portland Head Light, commissioned by George Washington in 1791. The keeper's house is now a museum, **The Museum at Portland Head Light.** ☒ *1000 Shore Rd., Cape Elizabeth (7 mi south of Portland),* ☎ *207/799-2661.* ☞ *$2.* ☉ *June–Oct., daily 10–4; Nov.–mid-Dec. and Apr.–May, weekends 10–4.*

Beaches

Crescent Beach State Park (☒ Rte. 77, Cape Elizabeth, ☎ 207/767–3625), about 8 mi south from Portland, has a sand beach, picnic tables, seasonal snack bar, and bathhouse. Popular with families with young children, it charges a nominal fee for admittance. **Scarborough Beach Park** (☒ Rte. 207, Scarborough, ☎ 207/283–0067) is a long sand beach on open ocean with primitive facilities; admission is charged in season.

Dining and Lodging

$$$–$$$$
★

✕ **Back Bay Grill.** Mellow jazz, a 28-ft mural, an impressive wine list, and good food make this simple, elegant restaurant a popular spot. Appetizers such as pan-fried baby artichokes with romesco sauce or wild mushroom and garlic sandwich are followed by aged New York sirloin with cippolini onions and salsify crisp, chicken with garlic mashed potatoes or Maine brook trout, mezuna-fennel salad and smoked bacon mashed

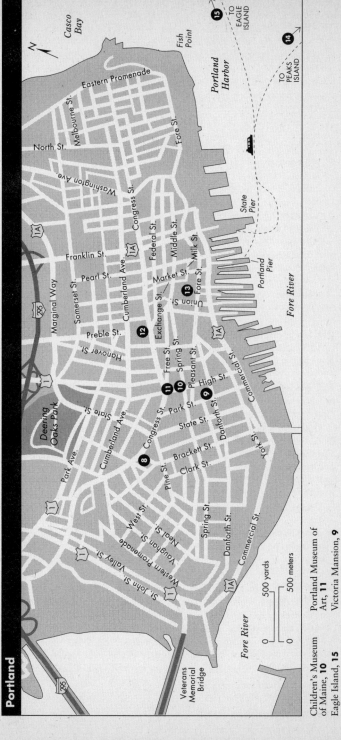

Portland

Children's Museum
of Maine, **10**
Eagle Island, **15**
Neal Dow
Memorial, **8**
Old Port
Exchange, **13**
Peaks Island, **14**

Portland Museum of
Art, **11**
Victoria Mansion, **9**
Wadsworth
Longfellow
House, **12**

potatoes. Don't miss the desserts—the crème brûlée is legendary. ⊠ *65 Portland St.,* ☎ *207/772–8833. AE, D, DC, MC, V. Closed Sun.*

$$–$$$ ✕ **Street and Co.** You enter through the kitchen, with all its wonder-
★ ful aromas, and dine amid dried herbs and shelves of staples on one of a dozen copper-topped tables (so your waiter can place a skillet of steaming seafood directly in front of you). In one dining room is a beer and wine bar. Fish and seafood are the specialties here, and you won't find any better, or any fresher. Choose from an array of superb entrées, ranging from lobster diavolo for two, scallops in Pernod and cream, or sole Française to blackened, broiled, or grilled seafood. A vegetarian entrée is the only alternative to seafood. ⊠ *33 Wharf St.,* ☎ *207/775–0887. AE, MC, V. No lunch.*

$$–$$$ ✕ **Wharf Street Café & Café Club.** Tucked away on cobblestoned Wharf Street, an alley that runs parallel to Fore Street between Moul-
ton and Union, this restaurant is really two finds in one. The small, informal restaurant has a partially exposed kitchen, brick walls, and a painted floor. The menus changes seasonally, but the house specialty, lobster and Brie ravioli with roasted grapes and caramelized onion sauce, is a mainstay. After dinner, head upstairs to the Café Club (☞ Nightlife and the Arts, *below*). ⊠ *38 Wharf St.,* ☎ *207/773–6667 for restaurant, 207/772–6976 for wine bar. AE, D, MC, V. Reservations essen-
tial. No lunch.*

$$ ✕ **Katahdin.** Somehow, the painted tables, flea-market decor, mis-
matched dinnerware, and log-pile bar work together here. The cuisine, large portions of home-cooked New England fare, is equally unpre-
tentious and fun: Try the chicken potpie, fried trout, crab cakes, or the nightly blue-plate special—and save room for the fruit cobbler. ⊠ *106 High St.,* ☎ *207/774–1740. No lunch. D, MC, V.*

$$$$ ✕🏠 **Inn by the Sea.** On greater Portland's most prime real estate, this all-suite inn is set back from the shoreline and has views of the ocean—
Crescent Beach and Kettle Cove in particular. The dining room, open to the public, serves fine seafood and other regional cuisine. The ar-
chitecture throughout is typical New England: One-bedroom suites have Chippendale furnishings; two-bedroom cottages are decorated in white pine and wicker. ⊠ *40 Bowery Beach Rd., Cape Elizabeth (7 mi south of Portland) 04107,* ☎ *207/799–3134 or 800/888–4287,* FAX *207/799–
4779. 25 suites, 18 cottage condominiums. Restaurant, pool, tennis, croquet, bicycles. AE, D, MC, V.*

$$$–$$$$ 🏠 **Portland Regency Hotel.** The only major hotel in the center of the Old Port Exchange, the Regency building was Portland's armory in the late 19th century. Rooms have four-poster beds, tall standing mirrors, floral curtains, and loveseats. ⊠ *20 Milk St., 04101,* ☎ *207/774–4200 or 800/727–3436,* FAX *207/775–2150. 95 rooms, 8 suites. Restaurant, massage, sauna, steam room, aerobics, health club, nightclub, meet-
ing rooms. AE, D, DC, MC, V.*

$$$–$$$$ 🏠 **Radisson Eastland.** This 1927 hotel has a prime location in Port-
land's up-and-coming arts district. Rooms in the tower section have floor-to-ceiling windows; higher floors have harbor views. ⊠ *157 High St., 04101,* ☎ *207/775–5411 or 800/777–6246,* FAX *207/775–
2872. 204 rooms. 2 restaurants, 2 bars, sauna, exercise room, meet-
ing rooms. AE, D, DC, MC, V.*

Nightlife and the Arts

NIGHTLIFE

The Pavillion (⊠ 115 Middle St., ☎ 207/773–6422), a dance club in a former bank, attracts a young crowd. The gay and lesbian crowd goes to the **Underground** (⊠ 3 Spring St., ☎ 207/773–3315).

Gritty McDuff's—Portland's Original Brew Pub (⌧ 396 Fore St., ☎ 207/ 772–2739) serves fine ales, brewed on the premises, along with British pub fare and local seafood dishes. **Stone Coast Brewery** (⌧ 14 York St., ☎ 207/773–2337) is a brew pub with entertainment. **Brian Boru** (⌧ 57 Center St., ☎ 207/780–1506) is an Irish pub with occasional entertainment and an outside deck in summer. **Three Dollar Dewey's** (⌧ 241 Commercial St., ☎ 207/772–3310), long a popular night spot, is an English-style ale house. **Top of the East** (⌧ Radisson East-land hotel, 157 High St., ☎ 207/775–5411) has a view of the city and live entertainment—jazz, piano, and comedy. **The Café Club** (⌧ 38 Wharf St., ☎ 207/772–6976) has a cozy atmosphere with comfortable chairs, couches, and a fireplace and offers approximately 250 wines by the bottle and a dozen nightly by the glass. It's also an espresso bar with a light menu and desserts.

THE ARTS

Portland Performing Arts Center (⌧ 25A Forest Ave., ☎ 207/774–0465) hosts music, dance, and theater performances. **Cumberland County Civic Center** (⌧ 1 Civic Center Sq., ☎ 207/775–3458) hosts concerts, sporting events, and family shows in a 9,000-seat auditorium.

Portland Symphony Orchestra (⌧ 30 Myrtle St., ☎ 207/773–8191) gives concerts October through August.

Mad Horse Theatre Company (⌧ 955 Forest Ave., ☎ 207/797–3338) performs classic, contemporary, and original works. **Portland Stage Company** (⌧ 25A Forest Ave., ☎ 207/774–0465), a producer of national reputation, mounts productions year-round at the Portland Performing Arts Center.

Outdoor Activities and Sports

BASEBALL

The stadium at Hadlock Field (⌧ 271 Park Ave.) is the site of home games for the **Portland Seadogs** (☎ 207/879–9500), a farm team of the Florida Marlins. The season begins in mid-April and goes to about Labor Day. Ticket prices range from $2 to $6.

BOAT TRIPS

For tours of the harbor, Casco Bay, and the nearby islands, try **Bay View Cruises** (⌧ Fisherman's Wharf, ☎ 207/761–0496), **The Buccaneer** (⌧ Long Wharf, ☎ 207/799–8188), **Casco Bay Lines** (⌧ Maine State Pier, ☎ 207/774–7871), **Eagle Tours** (⌧ Long Wharf, ☎ 207/774–6498), or **Old Port Mariner Fleet** (⌧ Long Wharf, ☎ 207/775–0727).

DEEP-SEA FISHING

Half- and full-day fishing charter boats are operated out of Portland by *Devils Den* (⌧ DiMillo's Marina, ☎ 207/761–4466).

HOCKEY

Portland is home to the **Portland Pirates,** the farm team of the Washington Capitals. Each season the Pirates play 40 home games at the Cumberland County Civic Center, beginning in October and running into April, depending upon whether they make the playoffs. ⌧ *85 Free St., 04101,* ☎ *207/828–4665.* ⌧ *$8–$13.*

Shopping

ART AND ANTIQUES

The **Pine Tree Shop & Bayview Gallery** (⌧ 75 Market St., ☎ 207/773–3007 or 800/244–3007) has original art and prints by prominent Maine painters. **Stein Glass Gallery** (⌧ 20 Milk St., ☎ 207/772–9072) specializes in contemporary glass, both decorative and utilitarian. **Abacus** (⌧ 44 Exchange St., ☎ 207/772–4880) has unusual gift items in glass, wood, and textiles, plus fine modern jewelry.

F. O. Bailey Antiquarians (⊠ 141 Middle St., ☎ 207/774–1479), Portland's largest retail showroom, carries antique and reproduction furniture and jewelry, paintings, rugs, and china.

BOOKS

Carlson and Turner (⊠ 241 Congress St., ☎ 207/773–4200) is an antiquarian book dealer with an estimated 50,000 titles.

MALL

Those who require mall shopping with national-brand stores should go 5 mi south of Portland to the **Maine Mall** (⊠ Maine Mall Rd., South Portland, ☎ 207/774–0303), which has 145 stores and is anchored by Sears, Filene's, JCPenney, Jordan Marsh, and Lechmere.

Casco Bay Islands

The islands of Casco Bay are also known as the Calendar Islands because an early explorer mistakenly thought there was one for every day of the year (in reality there are only 140). The brightly painted ferries of Casco Bay Lines are the islands' lifeline. There is frequent service to the most populated ones, including Peaks, Long, Little Diamond, and Great Diamond.

⓮ **Peaks Island,** nearest Portland, is the most developed, and some residents commute to work in Portland. Yet you can still commune with the wind and the sea on Peaks, explore an old fort, and ramble along the alternately rocky and sandy shore. This trip by boat is particularly enjoyable at or near sunset. Take the boat to the island and order a lobster sandwich or cold beer on the outdoor deck of **Jones' Landing** restaurant, steps from the dock. A circle trip without stops takes about 90 minutes. On the far side of the island you can stop on the rugged shoreline and have lunch. A small museum with Civil War artifacts is maintained in the **Fifth Maine Regiment** building.

⓯ The 17-acre **Eagle Island,** owned by the state and open to the public for day trips in summer, was the home of Admiral Robert E. Peary, the American explorer of the North Pole. Peary built a stone-and-wood house on the island as a summer retreat in 1904, then made it his permanent residence. The house remains as it was when Peary was here with his stuffed Arctic birds and the quartz he brought home and set into the fieldstone fireplace. The *Kristy K.,* departing from Long Wharf, makes a four-hour narrated tour; there are also tours of Portland Headlight and seal-watching cruises on the *Fish Hawk.* ⊠ *Long Wharf,* ☎ *207/774–6498.* ⊡ *Excursion tour $15, Headlight tour $8.* ⊙ *Departures mid-June–Labor Day, daily beginning 10 AM.*

Chebeague Island measures about 5 mi long and is less than 2 mi across at its widest. Service to the island is via **Casco Bay Lines** (☎ 207/774–7871) from Portland or via the **Chebeague Transportation Company** (☎ 207/846–3700) from the dock on Cousins Island, north of Portland and accessible by car. You can take along your bicycle or plan to stay overnight at the **Chebeague Island Inn** (☎ 207/846–5155), open April through October, or the **Chebeqgue Orchard Inn** (☎ 207/846–9488).

Dining and Lodging

$$$$ ✕⊡ **Diamond Cove.** At the turn of the century, nearly 700 soldiers were stationed at Fort McKinley on Great Diamond Island, which was created to protect Portland's harbor. By the mid-1900s, however, the fort was obsolete. Now it's a gem of a resort, with an art gallery, a summer theater, a general store, beaches, and walking trails. The property had a B&B planned at press time, but for now guests stay in town houses

with living rooms and kitchens. The menu in the topnotch restaurant changes regularly, but entrées may include brochette made with Maine lobster tails, jumbo shrimp, scallops, tuna, and vegetables over basmati rice. ⊠ *Great Diamond Island (Box 3572, Portland 04101),* ☎ *207/766–5804,* FAX *207/766–2973. 17 3-bedroom town homes. Restaurant, bar, pool, 5 beaches, health club, tennis courts. MC, V.*

Outdoor Activities and Sports

SEA KAYAKING

Maine Island Kayak Co. (⊠ 70 Luther St., Peak's Island, ☎ 800/796–2373) provides instruction, expeditions, and tours along the Maine coast.

Freeport

16 *17 mi northeast of Portland, 10 mi southwest of Brunswick.*

Freeport, on Route 1, northeast of Portland, has charming back streets lined with old clapboard houses and a small harbor on the Harraseeket River, but the overwhelming majority of visitors come to shop—L. L. Bean is the store that put Freeport on the map. Besides the shops that conform to strict local building guidelines, the town has many historical buildings and lovely New England architecture.

Dining and Lodging

$ ╳ **Freeport Café.** This small restaurant south of Freeport's shopping district serves creative homemade food, including soups, salads, sandwiches, and dinner entrées. Breakfast is available all day. There's a children's menu and outdoor seating on the deck in good weather. ⊠ *Rte. 1,* ☎ *207/865–3106. AE, D, MC, V.*

$ ╳ **Harraseeket Lunch & Lobster Co.** This no-frills, bare-bones, genuine lobster pound and fried-seafood place is beside the town landing in South Freeport. Seafood baskets and lobster dinners are what it's all about; you can eat outside at picnic tables in good weather. ⊠ *Main St., South Freeport,* ☎ *207/865–4888. Reservations not accepted. No credit cards.* ☽ *May–mid-Oct.*

$$$–$$$$ ╳🏨 **Harraseeket Inn.** Despite modern appointments such as elevators and whirlpools, this gracious 1850 Greek Revival home gives its visitors a country-inn experience. Afternoon tea is served in the mahogany drawing room, and guest rooms have reproductions of Federal canopy beds. The formal, no-smoking dining room, serving New England–influenced Continental cuisine, is a simply decorated, airy space with picture windows facing the inn's garden courtyard. The Broad Arrow Tavern appears to have been furnished by L. L. Bean, with fly rods, snowshoes, and moose heads; the hearty fare includes ribs, burgers, and charbroiled skewered shrimp and scallops. At press time, the inn was awaiting final approval to build an addition with an indoor pool, a health club, and more rooms. ⊠ *162 Main St., 04032,* ☎ *207/865–9377 or 800/342–6423,* FAX *207/865–1684. 52 rooms, 2 suites. Restaurant, bar, croquet. AE, D, DC, MC, V.*

Outdoor Activities and Sports

BOAT TRIPS

Atlantic Seal Cruises (⊠ South Freeport, ☎ 207/865–6112) has daily trips to Eagle Island, where you can tour Admiral Peary's museum home, and evening seal and osprey watches on the *Atlantic Seal* and *Arctic Seal.*

NATURE WALKS

Wolfe's Neck Woods State Park has 5 mi of hiking trails along Casco Bay, the Harraseeket River, and a fringe salt marsh, as well as walks led by naturalists. There are picnic tables and grills, but no camping.

⊠ *Wolfe's Neck Rd. (follow Bow St. opposite L. L. Bean off Rte. 1),* ☎ *207/865–4465.* ⊡ *$2 Memorial Day–Labor Day, $1 off-season.*

Bradbury Mountain State Park has moderate trails to the top of Bradbury Mountain, which offers views to the sea. A picnic area and shelter, ball field, playground, and 41 campsites are available. ⊠ *Pownal (5 mi from Freeport-Durham exit off I–95),* ☎ *207/688–4712.* ⊡ *$2 Memorial Day–Labor Day, $1 off-season.*

Shopping

Freeport's name is almost synonymous with shopping: L. L. Bean and the more than 100 other **factory outlets** and shops that opened during the 1980s are here. Outlet stores are in the **Fashion Outlet Mall** (⊠ 2 Depot St.) and the **Freeport Crossing** (⊠ 200 Lower Main St.), and many others crowd **Main Street** and **Bow Street.** The *Freeport Visitors Guide* (⊠ Freeport Merchants Association, Box 452, Freeport 04032, ☎ 207/865–1212 or 800/865–1994) has a complete listing.

Founded in 1912 as a small mail-order merchandiser of products for hunters, guides, and fisherfolk, **L. L. Bean** now attracts some 3.5 million shoppers a year to its giant store in the heart of Freeport's shopping district. Here you can still find the original hunting boots, along with cotton, wool, and silk sweaters; camping and ski equipment; comforters; and hundreds of other items for the home, car, boat, or campsite. Across the street from the main store, a Bean factory outlet has seconds and discontinued merchandise at discount prices. ⊠ *Rte. 1,* ☎ *800/341–4341.* ⊙ *24 hrs.*

Harrington House Museum Store (⊠ 45 Main St., ☎ 207/865–0477) is a restored 19th-century merchant's home owned by the Freeport Historical Society; all the period reproductions that furnish the rooms are for sale. In addition, you can buy books, rugs, jewelry, crafts, Shaker items, toys, and kitchen utensils.

DeLorme's Map Store (⊠ Rte. 1, ☎ 207/865–4171) carries an exceptional selection of maps and atlases of Maine, New England, and the rest of the world, also nautical charts and travel books.

Brunswick

⓱ *10 mi north of Freeport, 11 mi west of Bath.*

Brunswick is best known for its lovely brick or clapboard homes and structures. Those along **Federal Street, Park Row,** and on the stately ivy league **Bowdoin College** campus make up the **Federal Street Historic District.** Poet Henry Wadsworth Longfellow attended Bowdoin and a plaque is displayed outside his window. Another literary notable, Harriet Beecher Stowe, came to Brunswick and wrote *Uncle Tom's Cabin.*

In the center is Brunswick's business district, Pleasant Street, and—at the end of Pleasant Street—**Maine Street,** which claims to be the widest (198 ft across) in the state.

Maine Street takes you to the 110-acre campus of **Bowdoin College,** an enclave of distinguished architecture, gardens, and grassy quadrangles in the middle of town. Campus tours (☎ 207/725–3000) depart every day but Sunday from the admissions office in Chamberlain Hall. Among the historic buildings are Massachusetts Hall, a stout, sober, hip-roofed brick structure dating from 1802, which once housed the entire college. Hubbard Hall, an imposing 1902 neo-Gothic building, is home to Maine's only gargoyle and to the **Peary-MacMillan Arctic Museum.** The museum contains photographs, navigational instruments, and artifacts from the first successful expedition to the North

Pole, in 1909, by two of Bowdoin's most famous alumni, Admiral Robert E. Peary and Donald B. MacMillan. *Museum:* ☎ *207/ 725–3416.* ✉ *Free.* ☼ *Tues.–Sat. 10–5, Sun. 2–5.*

Don't miss the **Bowdoin College Museum of Art,** in a splendid Renaissance Revival–style building, with seven galleries radiating from a rotunda. Designed in 1894 by Charles F. McKim, the building stands on a rise, its facade adorned with classical statues and the entrance set off by a triumphal arch. The collections encompass Assyrian and classical art and that of the Dutch, Italian, French, and Flemish old masters; a superb gathering of Colonial and Federal paintings, notably Gilbert Stuart portraits of Madison and Jefferson; and a Winslow Homer Gallery of engravings, etchings, and memorabilia (open summer only). The museum's collection also includes 19th- and 20th-century American painting and sculpture, with works by Mary Cassatt, Andrew Wyeth, and Robert Rauschenberg. ✉ *Walker Art Bldg.,* ☎ *207/725–3275.* ✉ *Free.* ☼ *Tues.–Sat. 10–5, Sun. 2–5.*

Civil War buffs will want to visit the **General Joshua L. Chamberlain Museum.** The museum documents the hero's life and contains Civil War memorabilia. ✉ *226 Main St,* ☎ *207/729–6606.* ✉ *$3.* ☼ *Tues.–Sat. 10–4.*

OFF THE
BEATEN PATH

THE HARPSWELLS – A side trip from Bath or Brunswick on Route 123 or Route 24 takes you to the peninsulas and islands known collectively as the Harpswells. The numerous small coves along Harpswell Neck shelter the boats of local lobstermen, and summer cottages are tucked away amid the birch and spruce trees.

The Arts

Bowdoin Summer Music Festival (✉ Bowdoin College, ☎ 207/725–3322 for information or ☎ 207/725–3895 for tickets) is a six-week concert series featuring performances by students, faculty, and prestigious guest artists. **Maine State Music Theater** (✉ Pickard Theater, Bowdoin College, ☎ 207/725–8769) stages musicals from mid-June through August. **Theater Project of Brunswick** (✉ 14 School St., ☎ 207/729–8584) performs semi-professional, children's, and community theater.

Dining and Lodging

$–$$ ✕ **The Great Impasta.** This small, storefront restaurant is a great spot for lunch, tea, or dinner. Try the seafood lasagna, or match your favorite pasta and sauce to create your own dish. ✉ *42 Maine St.,* ☎ *207/729–5858. Reservations not accepted. AE, D, DC, MC, V.*

$$$$ ✕▦ **Captain Daniel Stone Inn.** This Federal inn overlooks the Androscoggin River. While no two rooms are furnished identically, all offer executive-style comforts and many have whirlpool baths and pullout sofas in addition to queen-size beds. A guest parlor, 24-hour breakfast room, and excellent service in the Narcissa Stone Restaurant (no lunch Saturday) make this an upscale escape from college-town funk. ✉ *10 Water St., 04011,* ☎ FAX *207/725–9898. 34 rooms. Restaurant. CP. AE, DC, MC, V.*

$$$–$$$$ ▦ **Harpswell Inn.** The stately dormered white clapboard Harpswell Inn is surrounded by spacious lawns and neatly pruned shrubs. The living room has a view of Middle Bay and Birch Island from its position on Lookout Point. Half the rooms also have water views. The carriage house in back has two luxury suites, one with a whirlpool. The 1761 no-smoking inn welcomes children over 10. ✉ *141 Lookout Point Rd.,*

S. Harpswell 04079, ☎ 207/833–5509 or 800/843–5509. 12 rooms, 5 with bath; 3 suites. Full breakfast. MC, V.

Shopping

Brunswick's Maine Street offers a number of specialty shops and galleries. Foremost of these is the **O'Farrell Gallery** (⌧ 58 Maine St., ☎ 207/729–8228), which represents artists such as Neil Welliver, Marguerite Robichaux, and Sheila Geoffrion. **Connections: Objects & Images Gallery** (⌧ 56 Maine St., ☎ 207/6725–1399) offers fine crafts and art. Nearby **ICON Contemporary Art** (⌧ 19 Mason St., ☎ 207/725–8157) specializes in modern art. Chocoholics will want to stop in at **Tontine Fine Candies** (⌧ Tontine Mall, 149 Maine St., ☎ 207/729–4462) in the downtown Tontine Mall.

Tuesdays and Fridays from May through October see a fine **farmers' market** on the town mall, between Maine Street and Park Row.

Outdoor Activities and Sports

SEA KAYAKING

H2Outfitters (⌧ Orr's Island, ☎ 207/833–5257) offers instruction, rentals, and half-day through multi-day trips.

Bath

18 *11 mi east of Brunswick, 38 mi northeast of Portland.*

Bath, east of Brunswick on Route 1, has been a shipbuilding center since 1607. Today, the Bath Iron Works turns out guided-missile frigates for the U.S. Navy and merchant container ships. It's a good idea to avoid Bath and Route 1 here weekdays between 3:15 and 4:30 PM, when BIW's major shift change occurs. The massive exodus can tie up traffic for miles.

The **Maine Maritime Museum and Shipyard** in Bath has ship models, journals, photographs, and other artifacts to stir the nautical dreams of salts old and young. The 142-ft Grand Banks fishing schooner *Sherman Zwicker,* one of the last of its kind, is on display when in port. You can watch boatbuilders wield their tools on classic Maine boats at the restored Percy & Small Shipyard and Boat Shop. The outdoor shipyard is open May–November; during these months visitors may take scenic tours of the Kennebec River on the *Linekin II.* During off-season, the Maritime History Building has indoor exhibits, videos, and activities. ⌧ *243 Washington St., ☎ 207/443–1316. ▨ $7.50. ☉ Daily 9:30–5.*

OFF THE
BEATEN PATH

POPHAM – Follow Route 209 south from Bath to Popham, site of the short-lived 1607 Popham Colony, where the *Virginia,* the first European ship built in the New World, was launched. Benedict Arnold set off from Popham on his ill-fated march against the British in Québec. Here also are granite-walled Ft. Popham (Phippsburg, ☎ 207/389–1335), built in 1607, and Popham Beach (☞ *below*).

Beaches

Popham Beach State Park (Phippsburg, ☎ 207/389–1335), at the end of Route 209, south of Bath, has a good sand beach, a marsh area, bathhouses, and picnic tables; admission is charged.

Reid State Park (☎ 207/371–2303), on Georgetown Island, off Route 127, has 1½ mi of sand on three beaches. Facilities include bathhouses, picnic tables, fireplaces, and snack bar. Parking lots fill by 11 AM on summer Sundays and holidays, and admission is charged.

The Arts

Chocolate Church Arts Center (✉ 804 Washington St., ☎ 207/442–8455) hosts folk, jazz, and classical concerts, theater productions, and performances for children. The Gallery offers changing exhibits by Maine artists in a variety of media, including textiles, photography, painting, and sculpture.

Dining and Lodging

$$$$ ✕ **Robinhood Free Meetinghouse.** Chef Michael Gagne, one of Maine's
★ best, finally has a restaurant that complements his classic and creative multiethnic cuisine. The 1855 Greek Revival–style meeting house has large-paned windows and is decorated simply: cream-colored walls, pine floorboards, cherry Shaker-style chairs, white table linen. Begin with the artichoke strudel, move onto a classic veal saltimbocca or a confit of duck, and finish up with Gagne's signature, "Obsession in Three Chocolates." ✉ *Robinhood Rd., Georgetown,* ☎ *207/371–2188. D, MC, V. No lunch. Reduced hrs mid-Oct.–mid-May.*

$$ ✕ **Kristina's Restaurant & Bakery.** This frame house turned restaurant, with a front deck built around a huge maple tree, turns out some of the finest pies, pastries, and cakes on the coast. A satisfying dinner of New American cuisine may include fresh seafood and grilled meats. All meals can be packed to go. ✉ *160 Centre St.,* ☎ *207/442–8577. D, MC, V. Closed Jan. No dinner Sun. Call ahead in winter.*

$$$–$$$$ ⊞ **Fairhaven Inn.** This cedar-shingle house built in 1790 is set on 16 acres of pine woods and meadows sloping down to the Kennebec River. Guest rooms are furnished with handmade quilts and mahogany four-poster beds with pineapple finials. The Tavern Room offers a place to relax and socialize. ✉ *North Bath Rd., 04530,* ☎ *207/443–4391. 8 rooms, 6 with bath. Hiking, cross-country skiing. Full breakfast. D, MC, V.*

En Route The **Montsweag Flea Market** on Route 1 in Woolwich, midway between Bath and Wiscasset, is a roadside attraction with a bounty of trash and treasures. ☎ *207/443–2809.* ☺ *Weekends May–Oct., also Wed. (antiques) and Fri. during peak season.*

Wiscasset

⑲ *10 mi northeast of Bath, 21 mi east of Brunswick, 46 mi northeast of Portland.*

Settled in 1663 on the banks of the Sheepscot River, Wiscasset fittingly bills itself as "Maine's Prettiest Village." Take a walking tour by the elegant sea captains' homes (many now antique shops or galleries), old cemeteries, churches, and public buildings.

The **Nickels-Sortwell House** is an outstanding example of Federal architecture maintained by the Society for the Preservation of New England Antiquities. ✉ *Main St.,* ☎ *207/882–6218.* ⊡ *$4.* ☺ *June–Sept., Wed.–Sun. 11–5; tours on the hr, 11–4.*

The 1807 **Castle Tucker** is known for its extravagant architecture, Victorian decor, and free-standing elliptical staircase. ✉ *Lee St. at High St.,* ☎ *207/882–7364.* ⊡ *$4.* ☺ *July–Aug., Tues.–Sat. noon–5.*

Those who appreciate both music and antiques will enjoy a visit to the **Musical Wonder House** to see and hear the vast collection of antique music boxes from around the world. ✉ *18 High St.,* ☎ *207/882–7163.* ⊡ *1-hr presentation on main floor $10; 3-hr tour of entire house $30 or $50 for 2 people.* ☺ *Mid-May–mid-Oct., daily 10–6; last tour usually at 4; call ahead for 3-hr tours.*

Travel from Wiscasset to Newcastle in restored 1930s coaches on the **Maine Coast Railroad.** ⊠ *Rte. 1,* ☎ *207/882–8000.* ▨ *$10.*

Dining and Lodging

$$$$ ✕▣ **Squire Tarbox.** The Federal-style Squire Tarbox is equal parts inn, restaurant, and working goat farm. Its quiet, country setting toward the end of Westport Island, midway between Bath and Wiscasset, is far removed from the rushing traffic of Route 1, yet all area attractions are easily accessible. Rooms are simply furnished with antiques and country pieces; four have fireplaces. The dining room offers a fixed menu that changes nightly and always includes a vegetarian entrée and a sampling of the inn's own goat cheese. Reservations are required for dinner. ⊠ *Rte. 144 (Box 1181, Westport 04578),* ☎ *207/882–7693. 11 rooms. Restaurant. Full breakfast; MAP available. AE, D, MC, V. Open mid-May–late Oct.*

Shopping

The Wiscasset area rivals Searsport as a destination for antiquing. Shops line Wiscasset's main and side streets and spew over the bridge into Edgecomb.

The **Wiscasset Bay Gallery** (⊠ Water St., ☎ 207/882–7682) specializes in 19th- and 20th-century American and European artists. The **Maine Art Gallery** (⊠ Warren St., ☎ 207/882–7511) carries the works of local artists. The **Butterstamp Workshop** (⊠ Middle St., ☎ 207/882–7825) carries handcrafted folk art designs from antique molds.

Boothbay

⑳ *60 mi northeast of Portland, 50 mi southwest of Camden.*

When Portlanders want to take a brief respite from what they know as city life, many come north to the Boothbay region, which comprises Boothbay proper, East Boothbay, and Boothbay Harbor. This part of the near mid-coast shoreline is a craggy stretch of inlets where pleasure crafts anchor alongside trawlers and lobster boats. Commercial Street, Wharf Street, the By-Way, and Townsend Avenue are lined with shops, galleries, and ice cream parlors. Excursion boats (☞ Outdoor Activities and Sports, *below*) leave from the piers off Commercial Street. From the harbor visitors may elect to catch a boat to Monhegan Island or be content visiting the little shops, waterfront restaurants, and inns.

At the **Boothbay Railway Village,** about a mile north of Boothbay, you can ride 1½ mi on a narrow-gauge steam train through a re-creation of a turn-of-the-century New England village. Among the 24 village buildings is a museum with more than 50 antique automobiles and trucks. ⊠ *Rte. 27,* ☎ *207/633–4727.* ▨ *$6.* ⊙ *Memorial Day–mid-Oct., weekends 9:30–5; early-June–Columbus Day, daily 9:30–5; special Halloween schedule. Closed Columbus Day–Memorial Day.*

Dining and Lodging

$$–$$$ ✕ **Black Orchid.** The classic Italian fare includes fettuccine Alfredo with fresh lobster and mushrooms, and fillets of Angus steak with marsala sauce. The upstairs and downstairs dining rooms have a Roman-trattoria ambience, with frilly leaves and fruit hanging from the rafters and little else in the way of decor. In the summer there is a raw bar outdoors. ⊠ *5 By-Way, Boothbay Harbor,* ☎ *207/633–6659. AE, MC, V. No lunch. Closed Nov.–Apr.*

$–$$ ✕ **Lobstermen's Co-op.** Lobster lovers and landlubbers alike will find something at this dockside working lobster pound. Lobster, steamers, seafood, hot dogs, hamburgers, sandwiches, and desserts are on the menu. Eat indoors or outside while watching the lobstermen at work. ⊠ *Atlantic Ave., Boothbay Harbor,* ☎ *207/633–4900. Closed mid-Oct.–mid-May.*

$$$$ ✕⊡ **Spruce Point Inn.** Escape the busyness of Boothbay Harbor at this sprawling resort, which is a short shuttle to town yet a world away. There are guest rooms in the main inn, family cottages, and condominiums. Most rooms are comfortably but not fancifully decorated, and have ocean views. The dining room has an unparalleled view of the outer harbor and open ocean and serves such entrées as roasted maple duck and the chef's signature dish, lobster cioppino made with local shellfish and served over cappellini. ⊠ *Atlantic Ave. (Box 237), Boothbay Harbor 04538,* ☎ *207/633–4152 or 800/553–0289,* FAX *207/633–7138. 37 rooms, 24 suites, 7 family cottages, 4 condominiums. Lounge, saltwater pool, freshwater pool, tennis, dock. MAP. AE, MC, V. Closed mid-Oct.–mid May.*

$$$$ ⊡ **Anchor Watch.** This country Colonial on the water overlooks the outer harbor and lies within easy walking distance of town. Guest rooms are decorated with quilts and stenciling and are named for the Monhegan ferries that ran in the 1920s. Breakfast may include apple-puff pancake, muffins, fruit, omelets, blueberry blintzes, and more. The owners also operate the *Balmy Days* motorcraft to Monhegan. ⊠ *3 Eames Rd., Boothbay Harbor 04538,* ☎ *207/633–7565. 4 rooms. Dock. Full breakfast. MC, V. Closed Jan.*

$$$–$$$$ ⊡ **Fisherman's Wharf Inn.** All rooms overlook the water at this Colonial-style motel built 200 ft out over the harbor. The large dining room has floor-to-ceiling windows, and several day-trip cruises leave from this location. ⊠ *42 Commercial St., Boothbay Harbor 04538,* ☎ *207/633–5090 or 800/628–6872,* FAX *207/633–5092. 54 rooms. Restaurant. AE, D, DC, MC, V. Closed late Oct.–mid-May.*

$$–$$$$ ⊡ **Kenniston Hill Inn.** The oldest inn in Boothbay (circa 1786), this classic center-chimney Colonial with its white clapboards and columned porch offers comfortably old-fashioned accommodations on 4 acres of land only minutes from Boothbay Harbor. Five guest rooms have fireplaces, and some have four-poster beds and rocking chairs. ⊠ *Rte. 27 (Box 125, 04537),* ☎ FAX *207/633–2159 or 800/992–2915. 10 rooms. Full breakfast. D, MC, V.*

Outdoor Activities and Sports

BOAT TRIPS

Balmy Day Cruises (☎ 207/633–2284 or 800/298–2284) has day trips to Monhegan Island and tours of the harbor and nearby lighthouses. **Cap'n Fish's Boat Trips** (☎ 207/633–3244) offers sightseeing cruises throughout the region, including puffin cruises, lobster-hauling and whale-watching rides, and trips to Damariscove Harbor, Pemaquid Point, and up the Kennebec River to Bath, departing from Pier 1.

Shopping

BOOTHBAY HARBOR

Boothbay Harbor, and Commercial Street in particular, is chockablock with gift shops, T-shirt shops, and other seasonal emporia catering to visitors. **Maine Trading Post** (⊠ 80 Commercial St., ☎ 207/633–2760) sells antiques and fine reproductions that include rolltop desks able to accommodate personal computers, as well as gifts and decorative accessories. **House of Logan** (⊠ Townsend Ave., ☎ 207/633–2293) sells clothing for men and women; children's clothes can be found next door at the **Village Store**.

EDGECOMB

Edgecomb Potters (⊠ Rte. 27, ☎ 207/882–6802) sells glazed porcelain pottery and other crafts at rather high prices; some discontinued items or seconds are discounted. These potters have an excellent reputation and have a store in Freeport if you miss this one. **Sheepscot River Pottery** (⊠ Rte. 1, ☎ 207/882–9410) has original hand-painted pottery as well as a large collection of American-made crafts, including jewelry, kitchenware, furniture, and home accessories. The **Gil Whitman Gallery** (⊠ Rte. 1, Edgecomb, ☎ 207/882–7705) exhibits the work of bronze sculptor Gil Whitman in a barn gallery and an outdoor sculpture garden, where giant metal flowers bloom amidst the real thing. The studio and workshop areas also are open to visitors.

Pemaquid Point

㉑ *8 mi southeast of Wiscasset.*

Here's a good spot to have a reliable Maine-coast map handy—not because getting to Pemaquid Point is so difficult, it's just nice to have a confirmation that the circuitous route you're taking really is getting you somewhere. After all, this is a region filled with river outlets, rocky inlets, and peninsulas. Navigation is a breeze coming from Boothbay or Wiscasset. Follow Route 27 out of Boothbay or Route 1 north from Wiscasset into Damariscotta, then head south on Route 129 and 130 into Pemaquid Point.

At the **Colonial Pemaquid Restoration,** on a small peninsula jutting into the Pemaquid River, English mariners established a fishing and trading settlement in the early 17th century. The excavations at **Ft. William Henry,** begun in the mid-1960s, have turned up thousands of artifacts from the Colonial settlement, including the remains of an old customs house, tavern, jail, forge, and homes, and from even earlier Native American settlements. The state operates a museum displaying many of the artifacts. ⊠ *Rte. 130,* ☎ *207/677–2423.* ☞ *$2.* ☉ *Memorial Day–Labor Day, daily 9:30–5.*

Route 130 terminates at the **Pemaquid Point Light,** which looks as though it sprouted from the ragged, tilted chunk of granite that it commands. The former lighthouse-keeper's cottage is now the **Fishermen's Museum,** with photographs, models, and artifacts that explore commercial fishing in Maine. Here, too, is the **Pemaquid Art Gallery,** which mounts changing exhibitions from July 1 through Labor Day. ⊠ *Rte. 130,* ☎ *207/677–2494.* ☞ *Donation requested.* ☉ *Memorial Day–Columbus Day, Mon.–Sat. 10–5, Sun. 11–5.*

En Route   Return to Route 1 via Route 32 through the charming fishing villages of New Harbor and Round Pond.

The Arts

Round Top Center for the Arts (⊠ Business Rte. 1, Damariscotta, ☎ 207/563–1507) has exhibits, concerts, shows, and classes.

Beach

Pemaquid Beach Park (⊠ Off Rte. 130, New Harbor, ☎ 207/677–2754) has a good sand beach, snack bar, changing facilities, and picnic tables overlooking John's Bay; admission is charged.

Dining and Lodging

$ ✕ **Round Pond Lobstermen's Coop.** Lobster doesn't get much rougher, any fresher, or any cheaper than that served at this no-frills dockside take-out. The best deal is the dinner special: a 1-pound lobster, steamers, and corn-on-the-cob, with a bag of chips (regulars often bring beer, wine, bread, and/or salads). Settle in at a picnic table and breathe in the fresh salt air while you drink in the view over dreamy Round Pond Harbor. ⊠ *Round Pond Harbor, off Rte. 32, Round Pond,* ☎ *207/529–5725. MC, V.*

$$$$ ✕⛱ **Bradley Inn.** Within walking distance of the Pemaquid Point lighthouse, beach, and fort, the 1900 Bradley Inn has comfortable and uncluttered rooms; ask for one of the cathedral-ceiling, waterside rooms on the third floor, for breathtaking views of the sunset over the water. The Ship's Restaurant serves a variety of fresh seafood dishes; there's light entertainment in the pub on weekends. ⊠ *Rte. 130 (H. C. 61, Box 361, New Harbor 04554),* ☎ *207/677–2105,* FAX *207/677–3367. 12 rooms, 1 cottage, 1 carriage house. Restaurant, pub, croquet, bicycles. CP. AE, D, MC, V.*

$$$$ ✕⛱ **Newcastle Inn.** This classic country inn with a riverside location and an excellent dining room attracts guests year-round. Renovations, ongoing at press time, will have enlarged rooms, which are filled with country pieces and antiques, and some with added fireplaces and whirlpool tubs. Guests spread out in the cozy pub, comfortable living room, and spacious sunporch overlooking the river. A full breakfast is served on the back deck in fine weather. The dining room, open to the public for dinner by reservation, emphasizes Maine seafood such as local Pemaquid oysters, lobster, and Atlantic salmon. Choose from three-or five-course dinners. ⊠ *River Rd., Newcastle 04553,* ☎ *207/563–5685 or 800/832–8669. 14 rooms. 2 dining rooms, pub, TV room. Full breakfast; MAP available. AE, MC, V.*

$$ ⛱ **Briar Rose.** Round Pond is a sleepy harborside village with a old-fashioned country store, two lobster coops, a nice restaurant, and a handful of antiques and craft shops. The mansard-roofed Briar Rose commands a ship-captain's view over it all. Guest rooms are large, airy, and decorated with antiques and whimsies. ⊠ *Rte. 32, Round Pond 04556,* ☎ *207/529–5478. 2 rooms, 1 suite. Full breakfast. MC, V.*

Portland to Pemaquid Point A to Z

Getting Around

BY BUS

Greater Portland's **Metro** (☎ 207/774–0351) runs seven bus routes in Portland, South Portland, and Westbrook. The fare is $1 for adults, 50¢ for senior citizens and people with disabilities, and children (under 5 free); exact change ($1 bills accepted) is required. Buses run from 5:30 AM to 11:45 PM.

BY CAR

The Congress Street exit from I–295 takes you into the heart of Portland. Numerous city parking lots have hourly rates of 50¢ to 85¢; the Gateway Garage on High Street, off Congress, is a convenient place to leave your car while exploring downtown. North of Portland, I–95 takes you to Exit 20 and Route 1, Freeport's Main Street, which continues on to Brunswick and Bath. East of Wiscasset you can take Route 27 south to the Boothbays, where Route 96 is a good choice for further exploration.

Contacts and Resources

CAR RENTAL

Alamo (⊠ Rear 9 Johnson St., ☎ 207/775–0855 or 800/327–9633 in Portland). **Avis** (⊠ Portland International Jetport, ☎ 207/874–7501 or 800/331–1212). **Budget** (⊠ Portland International Jetport, ☎ 207/772–6789 or 800/527–0700). **Hertz** (⊠ 1049 Westbrook St., Portland International Jetport, ☎ 207/774–4544 or 800/654–3131).

Thrifty (✉ 1000 Westbrook St., Portland International Jetport, ☎ 207/772–4628 or 800/367–2277).

Maine Medical Center (✉ 22 Bramhall St., Portland, ☎ 207/871–0111). **Mid Coast Hospital** (✉ 1356 Washington St., Bath, ☎ 207/443–5524; ✉ 58 Baribeau Dr., Brunswick, ☎ 207/729–0181). **St. Andrews Hospital** (✉ 3 St. Andrews La., Boothbay Harbor, ☎ 207/633–2121). **Miles Memorial Hospital** (✉ Bristol Rd., Damariscotta, ☎ 207/563–1234).

Off-season, most information offices are open weekdays 9–5; the hours below are for summer only.

Boothbay Harbor Region Chamber of Commerce (✉ Box 356, Boothbay Harbor, ☎ 207/633–2353) is open weekdays 8–5, Saturday 11–4, Sunday noon–4. **Chamber of Commerce of the Bath Brunswick Region** (✉ 45 Front St., Bath, ☎ 207/443–9751; ✉ 59 Pleasant St., Brunswick, ☎ 207/725–8797) is open weekdays 8:30–5. **Convention and Visitors Bureau of Greater Portland** (✉ 305 Commercial St., ☎ 207/772–5800) is open June–Columbus Day, weekdays 8–6 and weekends 10–6. **Freeport Merchants Association** (✉ Box 452, Freeport, ☎ 207/865–1212) is open weekdays 9–5. **Greater Portland Chamber of Commerce** (✉ 145 Middle St., Portland, ☎ 207/772–2811) is open weekdays 8–5. **Maine Publicity Bureau** (✉ Rte. 1, Exit 17 off I–95, Yarmouth, ☎ 207/846–0833) is open daily 9–5.

PENOBSCOT BAY

Purists hold that the Maine coast begins at Penobscot Bay, where the vistas over the water are wider and bluer; the shore a jumble of broken granite boulders, cobblestones, and gravel punctuated by small sand beaches; and the water numbingly cold. Port Clyde in the southwest and Stonington in the southeast are the outer limits of Maine's largest bay, 35 mi apart across the bay waters but separated by a drive of almost 100 mi on scenic but slow two-lane highways. From Pemaquid Point at the western extremity of Muscongus Bay to Port Clyde at its eastern extent, it's less than 15 mi across the water, but it's 50 mi for the motorist, who must return north to Route 1 to reach the far shore.

Rockland, the largest town on the bay, is Maine's major lobster distribution center and the port of departure for trips to Vinalhaven, North Haven, and Matinicus islands. The Camden Hills, looming green over Camden's fashionable waterfront, turn bluer and fainter as one moves on to Castine, the elegant small town across the bay. In between Camden and Castine is the flea-market mecca of Searsport. Deer Isle is connected to the mainland by a slender, high-arching bridge, but Isle au Haut, accessible from Deer Isle's fishing town of Stonington, can be reached by passenger ferry only: More than half of this steep, wooded island is wilderness, the most remote section of Acadia National Park.

The most promising shopping areas are Main Street in Rockland, Main and Bay View streets in Camden, Main Street in Blue Hill, and Main Street in Stonington. Antiques shops are clustered in Searsport and scattered around the outskirts of villages, in farmhouses and barns; yard sales abound in summertime.

Tenants Harbor

㉒ *13 mi south of Thomaston.*

In and around Tenants Harbor you'll see waterside fields, spruce woods, ramshackle barns, and trim houses. Tenants Harbor is a quintessential Maine fishing town, its harbor dominated by lobster boats, its shores rocky and slippery, its center a scattering of clapboard houses, a church, a general store. The fictional Dunnet Landing of Sarah Orne Jewett's classic book *The Country of the Pointed Firs* is based on this region.

Dining and Lodging

$$–$$$ ✕🛏 **East Wind Inn & Meeting House.** On a knob of land overlooking the harbor and the islands, the East Wind offers simple hospitality, a wraparound porch, and unadorned but comfortable guest rooms, suites, and apartments in three buildings; some have fireplaces. The inn is open to the public for dinner, breakfast, and Sunday brunch. Dinner options include prime rib, boiled lobster, and baked stuffed haddock. ✉ *Rte. 131 (10 mi off Rte. 1), Box 149, 04860, ☎ 800/241–8439 or 207/372–6366,* 🆑 *207/372–6320. 21 rooms, 10 with bath; 3 suites; 4 apartments. Restaurant. CP. AE, D, MC, V. Closed Jan.–Mar.*

Monhegan Island

㉓ *East of Pemaquid Point, south of Port Clyde.*

Tiny, remote Monhegan Island, with its high cliffs fronting the open sea, was known to Basque, Portuguese, and Breton fishermen well before Columbus "discovered" America. About a century ago Monhegan was discovered again by some of America's finest painters, including Rockwell Kent, Robert Henri, A. J. Hammond, and Edward Hopper, who sailed out to paint the savage cliffs, the meadows, the wild ocean views, and the shacks of fishermen. Tourists followed, and today Monhegan is overrun with visitors in summer.

Port Clyde, a fishing village at the end of Route 131, is the point of departure for the *Laura B.* (☎ 207/372–8848 for schedules), the mailboat that serves Monhegan Island. The *Balmy Days* (☎ 207/633–2284 or 800/298–2284) sails from Boothbay Harbor to Monhegan on daily trips in summer, and Hardy Boat Cruises (☎ 207/677–2026 or 800/278–3346) leaves daily from Shaw's Wharf in New Harbor.

Day visitors should bring a picnic lunch, as restaurants can have long waits at lunchtime. Overnight visitors have limited lodging choices, including the simply appointed Island Inn (☎ 207/596–0371) with a commanding view over the harbor and a good dining room that serves breakfast, lunch, and dinner. Reservations are essential.

The **Monhegan Museum,** contained in an 1824 lighthouse, has wonderful views of Manana Island and the Camden Hills in the distance. Inside are displays depicting island life and local flora and birds in addition to artwork. The volunteer on duty at the door does not charge admission, although a donation is appreciated and suggested. ✉ *White Head Rd., no phone.* ☾ *July–mid-Sept., 11:30–3:30.*

Beach

Swim Beach, a five-minute walk from the ferry, is rather rocky but rarely has more than a few sun worshipers in sight, a few with kids in tow.

Outdoor Activities and Sports

WALKING

Everyone who comes to Monhegan comes either to paint or to walk the trails. In all, there are 17 mi of paths crisscrossing the island, lead-

Penobscot Bay

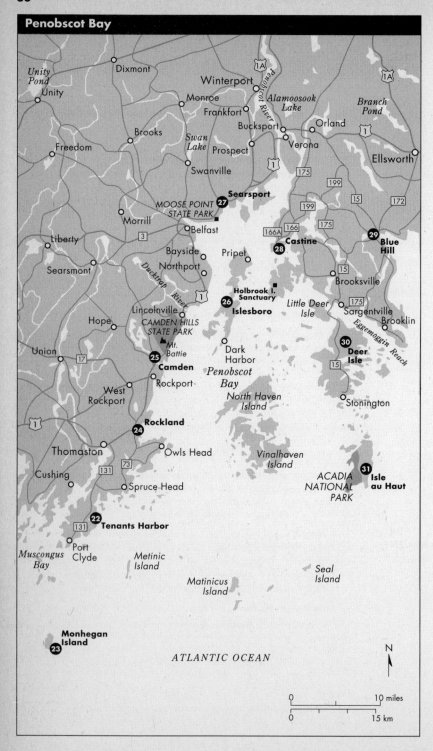

ing from the village, with shops and artists' studios, to the lighthouse, through the woods and to the cliffs.

Rockland

24 *27 mi south of Belfast, 53 mi northeast of Brunswick.*

Rockland earned its reputation as a large fishing port and the commercial hub of the coast, with working boats moored alongside a flotilla of cruise schooners. Although Rockland retains its working-class flavor, the expansion of the Farnsworth Museum, combined with additional boutiques, restaurants, and bed-and-breakfasts, has made it a good stop for coastal travelers. This also is a base for some windjammers and is the point of departure for popular day trips to Vinalhaven and North Haven islands and distant Matinicus. The outer harbor is bisected by a nearly mile-long granite breakwater, which begins on Samoset Road and ends with a **lighthouse** that was built in 1888. This is one of the best places in the area to watch the windjammers sail in and out of Rockland Harbor. Another good location to do so is **Owl's Head Lighthouse** off Route 73.

★ In downtown Rockland is the **William A. Farnsworth Library and Art Museum,** an excellent small museum specializing in American art with a focus on Maine-related art. Artists represented in strength in the museum's permanent collection include Andrew, N. C., and Jamie Wyeth, Fitz Hugh Lane, George Bellows, Frank W. Benson, Edward Hopper, Louise Nevelson, Fairfield Porter, and Neil Welliver. In 1998, as part of its 50th anniversary celebration, the museum plans to open a new gallery and study center devoted to the Maine work of Andrew Wyeth and other members of the Wyeth family. It will be located in the circa 1870 Pratt Memorial Methodist Church on the museum's campus and will exhibit works from the personal collection of Andrew and Betsy Wyeth. This collection includes Andrew Wyeth paintings such as *The Patriot, Adrift, Maiden Hair, Dr. Syn, The Clearing, Geraniums,* and *Watch Cap.* Many festivities and programs are planned in conjunction with the anniversary and opening; call for up-to-date information. Between the museum and the new gallery is the **Farnsworth Homestead,** a handsome circa 1852 Greek Revival dwelling that retains its original lavish Victorian furnishings. (For admission information, *see* Olson House, *below.*)

OFF THE **CUSHING –** The William A. Farnsworth Library and Art Museum also op-
BEATEN PATH erates the **Olson House,** which was made famous by Andrew Wyeth's painting *Christina's World.* ⊠ *352 Main St., Cushing (14 mi southwest of Rockland),* ☎ *207/596-6457.* ⊠ *Museum and homestead $5; Olson House $3.* ☉ *Museum Mon.–Sat. 10–5, Sun. 1–5, closed Mon. Oct.–May; Olson House Wed.–Sun. 11–4, closed Oct.–May.*

☉ **Owls Head Transportation Museum** displays antique aircraft, cars, and engines and stages weekend air shows. ⊠ *Rte. 73, Owls Head (2 mi south of Rockland),* ☎ *207/594–4418.* ⊠ *$6.* ☉ *May–Oct., daily 10–5; Nov.–Apr., weekdays 10–4, weekends 10–3.*

☉ **Shore Village Museum** is a must for lighthouse buffs. It contains the largest collection of lighthouse and Coast Guard artifacts on display in the country as well as permanent exhibits of maritime and Civil War memorabilia. ⊠ *104 Limerock St.,* ☎ *207/594–0311.* ☉ *June–mid-Oct., daily 10–4.*

Dining and Lodging

$$ ✕ **Jessica's.** Perched on a hill at the extreme southern end of Rock-
★ land, Jessica's occupies four cozy dining rooms in a tastefully renovated

Victorian home. Billed as a European bistro, this restaurant lives up to its Continental label with creative entrées that include veal Zurich, paella, and pork Portofino; other specialties of the Swiss chef are focaccia with a selection of toppings and a half-dozen pastas and risottos. ⊠ *2 S. Main St. (Rte. 73),* ☎ *207/596–0770. D, MC, V. Closed Tues. in winter.*

$–$$ ✕ **Water Works.** This brick building just off Main Street serves light
★ pub-style fare, including soups and home-style suppers such as turkey and meat loaf. There's a good variety of Maine microbrews, as well as an excellent selection of single malt scotch and bourbon. A wall of water decorates the small dining room, while a massive stone fireplace dominates the pub. A children's menu is available. ⊠ *Lindsey St.,* ☎ *207/596–7950. MC, V.*

$$$$ 🏨 **Samoset Resort.** Next to the breakwater, on the Rockland–Rockport town line, is this sprawling oceanside resort with excellent facilities. ⊠ *Warrenton St., Rockport,* ☎ *207/594–2511 or 800/341–1650 outside ME,* 🅵🅰🆇 *207/594–0722. 132 rooms, 18 suites. Restaurant, indoor and outdoor pools, golf, tennis, racquetball, fitness center, children's programs. AE, D, DC, MC, V.*

$$$–$$$$ 🏨 **Limerock Inn.** You can walk to the Farnsworth and the Shore Vil-
★ lage museums from this magnificent Queen Anne–style Victorian on a quiet residential street. Meticulously decorated rooms include Island Cottage, with a whirlpool tub and doors that open onto a private deck overlooking the backyard garden, and Grand Manan, which has a fireplace, whirlpool tub, and a four-poster king-size bed. ⊠ *96 Limerock St., 04841,* ☎ *207/594–2257 or 800/546–3762. 8 rooms. Croquet, bicycles. Full breakfast. MC, V.*

Outdoor Activities and Sports

BOAT TRIPS
North End Shipyard Schooners (⊠ Box 482, ☎ 800/648–4544) operates three- and six-day cruises on the schooners *American Eagle, Isaac H. Evans,* and *Heritage.* **Vessels of Windjammer Wharf** (⊠ Box 1050, ☎ 207/236–3520 or 800/999–7352) organizes three- and six-day cruises on the *Pauline,* a 12-passenger motor yacht, and the *Stephen Taber,* a windjammer. *Victory Chimes* is a 132-ft, three-masted schooner, the largest in Maine's windjammer fleet, that offers three- and six-day trips. **Bay Island Yacht Charters** (⊠ 120 Tillison Ave., ☎ 207/236–2776 or 800/421–2492) offers bareboat and charters, daysailer rentals, and sailing lessons.

Shopping

The **Personal Bookstore** (⊠ 78 Main St, Thomaston, ☎ 207/354–8058 or 800/391–8058) is a book lover's treasure. Maine authors frequently do book-signings; browsers will find some autographed copies on the shelves. **Reading Corner** (⊠ 408 Main St., ☎ 207/596–6651) carries an extensive inventory of cookbooks, children's books, Maine titles, best-sellers, and one of the area's best newspaper and magazine selections. The **Store** (⊠ 435 Main St., ☎ 207/594–9246) has top-of-the-line cookware, table accessories, and an outstanding card selection.

Camden

㉕ *8 mi north of Rockland, 19 mi south of Belfast.*

"Where the mountains meet the sea" is an apt description of Camden, as you will discover when you step out of your car and look up from the harbor. Camden is famous not only for geography but for its large fleet of windjammers—relics and replicas from the age of sail. At just about any hour during the warmer months you're likely to see at least one windjammer tied up in the harbor, and windjammer cruises are a superb way to explore the ports and islands of Penobscot Bay. Downtown Camden offers the best shopping in the region, and its compact size makes it perfect for exploring on foot: Shops, restaurants, and galleries line Main and Bayview streets and side streets and alleys around the harbor.

The entrance to the 5,500-acre **Camden Hills State Park** (☎ 207/236–3109) is 2 mi north of Camden on Route 1. If you're accustomed to the Rockies or the Alps, you may not be impressed with heights of not much more than 1,000 ft, yet the Camden Hills are landmarks for miles along the low, rolling reaches of the Maine coast. The park contains 20 mi of trails, including the easy Nature Trail up Mount Battie. Hike or drive to the top for a magnificent view over Camden and island-studded Penobscot Bay. The 112-site camping area, open mid-May through mid-October, has flush toilets and hot showers. ⌦ *Trails and auto road up Mount Battie $2.*

Dining and Lodging

$$–$$$ ✕ **Chez Michel.** This unassuming restaurant, serving up a fine rabbit pâté, mussels marinière, steak au poivre, and boeuf bourguignon, might easily be on the Riviera instead of Lincolnville Beach. Chef Michel Hetuin creates bouillabaisse as deftly as he whips up New England fisherman chowder, and he welcomes special requests. ✉ *Rte. 1, Lincolnville Beach,* ☎ *207/789–5600. AE, D, MC, V. Closed Nov.–mid-Apr.*

$$ ✕ **Waterfront Restaurant.** A ringside seat on Camden Harbor can be had here; the best view is from the outdoor deck, open in warm weather. The fare is primarily seafood: boiled lobster, scallops, bouillabaisse, seafood risotto. Lunchtime highlights include Tex-Mex dishes and lobster and crabmeat rolls. ✉ *Bay View St.,* ☎ *207/236–3747. Reservations not accepted. AE, MC, V. Closed winter.*

$$$$ ✕▥ **Whitehall Inn.** One of Camden's best-known inns, just north of town, is an 1843 white clapboard, wide-porch ship captain's home with a turn-of-the-century wing. Just off the main lobby with its faded Oriental rugs, the Millay Room preserves memorabilia of the poet Edna St. Vincent Millay, who grew up in the area. Rooms are sparsely furnished, with dark-wood bedsteads, white bedspreads, and clawfoot tubs. The dining room, serving traditional and creative American cuisine, is open to the public for dinner. ✉ *52 High St. (Rte. 1), Box 558, 04843,* ☎ *207/236–3391 or 800/789–6565,* ℻ *207/236–4427. 49 rooms. Restaurant, golf privileges, tennis courts, shuffleboard. CP and MAP available. AE, MC, V. Closed mid-Oct.–late May.*

$$$$ ▥ **Inn at Sunrise Point.** For comfort and location, you can't beat this
★ fine B&B perched on the water's edge, with magnificent views over Penobscot Bay. Travel writer Jerry Levitin built his dream getaway here. Three rooms in the main house and four cottages are simply but tastefully decorated. Each room has a television and VCR, fireplace, terry-cloth robes, and telephone. The cottages also have whirlpool tubs and private decks. A full breakfast is served in the solarium; guests take high tea in the paneled library with stone fireplace. ✉ *Off Rte. 1 (Box 1344, 04843), Lincolnville Beach,* ☎ ℻ *207/236–7716 or* ☎ *800/435–6278. 7 rooms. Closed winter.*

$$$$ ▥ **Norumbega.** This stone castle, built in 1886 amid Camden's ele-
★ gant clapboard houses, was obviously the fulfillment of a fantasy. The public rooms have gleaming parquet floors, oak and mahogany paneling, richly carved wood mantels over fireplaces, gilt mirrors, and Em-

pire furnishings. At the back of the house, several decks and balconies overlook the garden, the gazebo, and the bay. The view improves as you ascend; the penthouse suite has a small deck, private bar, and a skylight in the bedroom. ⊠ *61 High St., 04843,* ☎ *207/236–4646,* FAX *207/236–0824. 12 rooms. Full breakfast. AE, MC, V.*

$$–$$$$
★ 🔲 **Camden Maine Stay.** Within walking distance to shops and restaurants, this 1802 clapboard inn is on the National Register of Historic Places. The grounds are classic and inviting, from the waving flag and colorful flowers lining the granite walk in summer to the snow-laden bushes in winter. Rooms are equally colorful and fresh with lots of Eastlake furniture. ⊠ *22 High St., 04842,* ☎ *207/236–9636,* FAX *207/236–0621. 7 rooms, 5 with bath; 1 suite. Full breakfast. AE, MC, V.*

Nightlife and the Arts

NIGHTLIFE

Peter Ott's Tavern (⊠ 16 Bay View St., ☎ 207/236–4032) is a steak house with a lively bar scene. **Sea Dog Tavern & Brewery** (⊠ 43 Mechanic St., ☎ 207/236–6863) is a popular brew pub serving locally made lagers and ales in a retrofitted woolen mill.

THE ARTS

Bay Chamber Concerts (⊠ Rockport Opera House, 6 Central St., Rockport, ☎ 207/236–2823) offers chamber music every Thursday night and some Friday nights during July and August; concerts are given once a month September through May.

Outdoor Activities and Sports

Maine Sport (⊠ Rte. 1, Rockport, ☎ 207/236–8797), the best sports outfitter north of Freeport, rents bikes, camping and fishing gear, canoes, kayaks, cross-country skis, ice skates, and snowshoes. It also offers skiing and kayaking clinics and trips.

Windjammers create a stir whenever they sail into Camden harbor, and a voyage around the bay on one of them, whether for an afternoon or a week, is unforgettable. The season for the excursions is from June through September. Excursion boats, too, provide a great opportunity for getting afloat on the waters of Penobscot Bay. Eggemoggin Reach is a famous cruising ground for yachts, as are the coves and inlets around Deer Isle and the Penobscot Bay waters between Castine and Camden.

Appledore (⊠ 0 Lily Pond Dr., ☎ 207/236–8353 or 800/233–7437) has two-hour day sails as well as private charters on an 86-ft schooner. The **Maine Windjammer Association** (⊠ Box 1144, Blue Hill 04614, ☎ 800/807–9463) represents the Camden-based windjammers *Angelique, Grace Bailey, J & E Riggin, Lewis R. French, Mary Day, Mercantile, Nathaniel Bowditch, Roseway,* and *Timberwind,* which offer three- to eight-day cruises.

Shopping

Shops and galleries line Camden's Bay View and Main streets and the alleys that lead to the harbor. Exploring is best done on foot. **Maine's Massachusetts House Galleries** (⊠ Rte. 1, Lincolnville, ☎ 207/789–5705) has a broad selection of regional art, including bronzes, carvings, sculptures, and landscapes and seascapes in pencil, oil, and watercolor. The **Pine Tree Shop & Bayview Gallery** (⊠ 33 Bay View St., ☎ 207/236–4534) specializes in original art, prints, and posters—almost all with Maine themes. The **Owl and Turtle Bookshop** (⊠ 8 Bay View St., ☎ 207/236–4769) sells a thoughtfully chosen selection of books, CDs, cassettes, and cards, including Maine-published works. The two-story shop has special rooms devoted to marine books and children's books. The **Windsor Chairmakers** (⊠ Rte. 1, Lincolnville, ☎ 207/789–5188

30%*
more
charming.

(*depending on the exchange rate)

Air Canada can't take credit for the very generous exchange rate on American currency. But, in all modesty, we do pride ourselves on getting a lot of other things right. *Like more nonstops* between the USA and Canada than any other airline. Not to mention convenient connections to our vast global network. We even offer you your choice of Mileage Plus[1], OnePass[2] or our own Aeroplan[3] miles.

So to say that we are eager to please would be a remarkable understatement. However, this may help to explain why Americans polled by Business Traveler International Magazine declared Air Canada *The Best Airline to Canada*. For the fifth year in a row (wow, thanks guys). And why more people fly Air Canada from the USA to Canada than any other airline. Air Canada. We're like a regular airline, only nicer.

For more details, please call your travel agent or Air Canada at **1-800-776-3000.** For great holiday packages, call **Air Canada's Canada** at 1-800-774-8993 (ext. 8045). And feel free to visit us on our Internet site at this address: http://www.aircanada.ca

[1]Mileage Plus is a registered trademark of United Airlines. [2]OnePass is a registered trademark of Continental Airlines. [3]Aeroplan is a registered trademark of Air Canada.

Pick up the phone.
Pick up the miles.

Now when you sign up with MCI you can receive up to 8,000 bonus frequent flyer miles on one of seven major airlines.

Then earn another 5 miles for every dollar you spend on a variety of MCI services, including MCI Card® calls from virtually anywhere in the world.*

You're going to use these services anyway. Why not rack up the miles while you're doing it?

Is this a great time, or what? :-)

or 800/789–5188) sells custom-made, handcrafted beds, chests, china cabinets, dining tables, highboys—and, of course, chairs.

Skiing

Camden Snowbowl. No other ski area can boast a view over island-studded Penobscot Bay. ⊠ *Box 1207, Camden 04843,* ☎ *207/236–3438.*

DOWNHILL

In a Currier & Ives setting there's a 950-ft-vertical mountain, a small lodge with cafeteria, a ski school, and ski and toboggan rentals. Camden Snowbowl has 11 trails accessed by one double chair and two T-bars. It also has night skiing.

CROSS-COUNTRY

There are 16 km (10 mi) of cross-country skiing trails at the **Camden Hills State Park** (☎ 207/236–9849) and 20 km (12½ mi) at the **Tanglewood 4-H Camp** in Lincolnville (☎ 207/789–5868), about 5 mi away.

OTHER ACTIVITIES

Camden Snowbowl has a small lake that is cleared for ice-skating, a snow-tubing park, and a 400-ft toboggan run that shoots sledders out onto the lake.

En Route The lovely community of **Bayside,** a section of Northport that is off Route 1 on the way to Belfast, is dotted with 150-year-old Queen Anne cottages that have freshly painted porches and exquisite architectural details. Some of these homes line the main one-lane thoroughfare of George Street; others are clustered on bluffs with water views around town greens complete with flagpoles and swings; yet others are on the shore.

Islesboro

● *4 mi east of Lincolnville.*

Islesboro, reached by car-and-passenger ferry (Maine State Ferry Service, ☎ 207/734–6935 or 800/491–4883) from Lincolnville Beach, on Route 1 north of Camden, has been a retreat of wealthy, very private families for more than a century. The long, narrow, mostly wooded island has no real town to speak of; there are scatterings of mansions as well as humbler homes at Dark Harbor (where celebrity couple John Travolta and Kelly Preston live) and at Pripet near the north end. Since the amenities on Islesboro are quite spread out, you don't want to come on foot. If you plan to spend the night here, you should make a reservation well in advance.

Dining and Lodging

$$$$ ✕🛏 **Dark Harbor House.** The yellow-clapboard, 1896 neo-Georgian summer "cottage" has a stately portico and a dramatic hilltop setting. An elegant double staircase curves from the ground floor to the spacious bedrooms; some have balconies, five have fireplaces, two have four-poster beds. The dining room, open to the public for dinner by reservation, emphasizes seafood. ⊠ *Main Rd. (Box 185, 04848),* ☎ *207/734–6669,* ℻ *207/734–6938. 10 rooms. Restaurant. Full breakfast. MC, V. Closed mid-Oct.–mid-May.*

En Route Belfast has a lively waterfront and a charming Main Street beckoning architecture buffs to do the 1-mi self-guided walking tour of period sea captains' homes, reminders of the town's heyday in the 1800s. Belfast was once home to more sea captains than any other port in the world. You can also explore the galleries and shops along Main Street or take a train ride along the water or through fall foliage on the **Belfast & Moosehead Lake Railroad** ⊠ *One Depot Sq., Unity 04988,* ☎ *207/948–5500* *or 800/392–5500.* ▦ *$14.* ⊙ *May–Oct.; call for schedule information and directions.*

Sailing schedules of the 150-passenger **Voyageur** (☎ 800/392–5500), a former Mississippi riverboat, coordinate with that of the Belfast & Moosehead Lake Railroad; a discount applies if you travel on both. The *Voyageur* leaves Belfast twice daily in season for 1½-hour narrated tours of the bay.

Searsport

㉗ *38 mi north of Rockland, 57 mi east of Augusta.*

Searsport, Maine's second-largest deepwater port (after Portland)—bills itself as the antiques capital of Maine. The town's stretch of Route 1 has many antiques shops and a large weekend flea market in summer.

Searsport preserves a rich nautical history at the **Penobscot Marine Museum,** where nine historic and two modern buildings document the region's seafaring way of life. Included are display photos of 284 sea captains, artifacts of the whaling industry (lots of scrimshaw), hundreds of paintings and models of famous ships, navigational instruments, and treasures collected by seafarers. ⊠ *Church St.,* ☎ *207/548–2529.* ▦ *$5.* ⊙ *Memorial Day weekend–mid-Oct., Mon.–Sat. 10–5, Sun. noon–5.*

Dining and Lodging

$$–$$$ ✕ **Nickerson Tavern.** Built in 1838 by a sea captain, this restaurant has three dining rooms, all decorated in a nautical motif; the Searsport Room is the most intimate. The menu changes seasonally—appetizers may include crab cakes or shrimp satay, and raspberry hazelnut chicken or veal picata milanese might show up as entrées. ⊠ *Rte. 1,* ☎ *207/548–2220. D, MC, V. No lunch.* ⊙ *Mid-June–Labor Day, daily; reduced hrs off season. Closed Jan.–Apr.*

$–$$ ✕ **90 Main.** This family-run restaurant with an outdoor patio in the back is helmed by young chef and owner Sheila Costello. Using Pemaquid oysters, Maine blueberries, organic vegetables grown on a nearby farm, and other fresh, local ingredients, Costello creates flavorful dishes that delight all the senses. Choose from a chalkboard full of specials that always includes a macrobiotic option, or start with the smoked seafood and pâté sampler or the spinach salad topped with sautéed chicken, sweet peppers, hazelnuts, and a warm raspberry vinaigrette. Entrées include ribeye steak and seafood linguine fra Diablo. ⊠ *90 Main St., Belfast,* ☎ *207/338–1106. AE, MC, V.*

$$–$$$ ▥ **Homeport Inn.** This 1861 inn, a former sea captain's home, provides an opulent Victorian environment that puts you in the mood to rummage through the nearby antiques and treasure shops. The back rooms downstairs have private decks and views of the bay. Families prefer the two-bedroom housekeeping cottages. ⊠ *Rte. 1,* ☎ *207/548–2259 or 800/742–5814. 6 rooms with bath, 4 rooms share bath, 2 2-bedroom cottages. Full breakfast. AE, D, MC, V.*

$$ ▥ **Inn on Primrose Hill.** Built in 1812 and once the home of a navy admiral, this inn near the waterfront is the most elegant in the area. The 2 acres that surround it have formal gardens, a brick terrace with wrought-iron furniture, and croquet. Ionic columns belie the inn's original Federal architecture. Owners Pat and Linus Heinz have restored authentic details such as ornate Waterford chandeliers, a mahogany dining set, and a black marble fireplace. There are several spacious public rooms including double parlors, a library with a large-screen TV, and a sunny conservatory with wicker and plump upholstered furniture. Guest rooms, which are less elaborate than the public spaces, have either partial bay views or garden views. ⊠ *212 High St.,* ☎ *207/338–6982 or 888/338–6982. 3 rooms with bath, 1 room shares bath. Croquet. Full breakfast, afternoon tea. No credit cards.*

State Park

Moose Point State Park (⊠ Rte. 1, between Belfast and Searsport, ☎ 207/548–2882) is ideal for easy hikes and picnics overlooking Penobscot Bay.

Castine

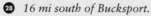 28 *16 mi south of Bucksport.*

Historic Castine, over which the French, the British, the Dutch, and the Americans fought from the 17th century to the War of 1812, has two museums and the ruins of a British fort, but the finest aspect of Castine is the town itself: the lively, welcoming town landing; the serene Federal and Greek Revival houses; and the town common. Castine invites strolling, and you would do well to start at the town landing, where you can park your car, and walk up Main Street past the two inns and on toward the white Trinitarian Federated Church with its tapering spire.

The town common is ringed by a collection of white clapboard buildings that includes the Ives House (once the summer home of the poet Robert Lowell), the Abbott School, and the Unitarian Church, capped by a whimsical belfry that suggests a gazebo. This makes an ideal walk in summer or fall and it takes on a special glow at Christmas.

Dining and Lodging

$$–$$$$ ✕▣ **Castine Inn.** Light, airy rooms, upholstered easy chairs, and fine
★   prints and paintings are typical of the guest-room furnishings here. The third floor has the best views: the harbor over the handsome formal gardens on one side, the village on the other. The dining room, decorated with a wraparound mural of Castine and its harbor, is open to the public for breakfast and dinner; the menu includes traditional New England fare plus creative entrées such as sweetbreads with hazelnut butter and roast duck with peach chutney. There's a snug, English-style pub off the lobby. ⊠ *Main St. (Box 41, 04421),* ☎ *207/326–4365,* FAX *207/326–4570. 17 rooms, 3 suites. Restaurant, pub. Full breakfast. MC, V. Closed Nov.–Apr.*

Nightlife and the Arts

NIGHTLIFE

Dennett's Wharf (⊠ Sea St., ☎ 207/326–9045) draws a crowd every lunchtime for a terrific view and every evening for drinking and dancing. It's open from May to October.

THE ARTS

Cold Comfort Productions (⊠ Box 259, no phone), a community theater, mounts plays in July and August.

Shopping

Chris Murray Waterfowl Carver (⊠ Upper Main St., ☎ 207/326–9033) sells award-winning wildfowl carvings and offers carving instruction.

Blue Hill

 29 *19 mi southeast of Bucksport.*

Castine may have the edge over Blue Hill in charm, for its Main Street is not a major thoroughfare and it claims a more dramatic perch over its harbor, yet Blue Hill is certainly appealing and has a better selection of shops and galleries. Blue Hill, renowned for its pottery, has two good shops in town.

The Arts

Kneisel Hall Chamber Music Festival (⊠ Kneisel Hall, Rte. 15, ☎ 207/374–2811) has concerts on Sunday and Friday in summer. **Left Bank Bakery and Café** (⊠ Rte. 172, ☎ 207/374–2201) rates a gold star for bringing notable musical talent from all over the country to sleepy Blue Hill. **Surry Opera Co.** (⊠ Morgan Bay Road, Surry, ☎ 207/667–2629) stages operas throughout the area in summer.

Dining and Lodging

$$–$$$ ✕ **The Firepond.** The Firepond attracts customers from all over the re-
★   gion. The upstairs dining room has the air of an English country house's library, with built-in bookshelves, antiques, and Oriental carpets; a street-level dining area increases the seating capacity to 120. The kitchen delivers old favorites like lobster Firepond—with three cheeses, served over pasta—and veal, pork, and scallop specialties. ⊠ *Main St., ☎ 207/374–9970. AE, D, MC, V. Closed Jan.–Apr.*

$$ ✕ **Jonathan's.** The downstairs room has captain's chairs, linen tablecloths, and local art; in the post-and-beam upstairs, there's wood everywhere, plus candles with hurricane globes and high-back chairs. The menu may include pan-seared medallions of venison with sweet-potato pancakes and several fresh-fish entrées. The wine list has 150 selections from French, Italian, and Californian, and local vineyards. ⊠ *Main St., ☎ 207/374–5226. MC, V. No lunch. Closed Mar.*

$$$$ ✕🏠 **Blue Hill Inn.** This rambling, antiques-filled inn is a comforting place to relax after exploring nearby shops and galleries; four rooms have fireplaces. The inn is equally renowned for its dining room, which serves hearty breakfasts and multicourse, candlelit dinners featuring fresh, organically raised produce and herbs, local meats, and seafood. An hors d'oeuvres hour precedes dinner in the garden or by the living-room fireplace. ⊠ *Union St. (Box 403, 04614), ☎ 207/374–2844 or 800/826–7415, FAX 207/374–2829. 11 rooms. Restaurant. Full break-fast; MAP available. MC, V. Closed Dec.–mid-May.*

$$$$ 🏠 **John Peters Inn.** The John Peters is unsurpassed for the privacy of
★   its location and the good taste in the decor of its guest rooms. The living room has two fireplaces and a baby grand piano. Huge breakfasts include the famous lobster omelet, served with lobster-claw shells as decoration. The Surry Room has a king-size bed, a fireplace, curly-maple chest, and six windows. The large rooms in the carriage house have dining areas, cherry floors and woodwork, and wicker and brass accents. ⊠ *Peters Point (Box 916, 04614), ☎ 207/374–2116. 7 rooms and 1 suite in inn; 6 suites in carriage house. Pool, boating. Full break-fast. MC, V. Closed Nov.–Apr.*

Outdoor Activities and Sports

BOATING

The **Phoenix Centre** (⊠ Rte. 175, Blue Hill Falls, ☎ 207/374–2113) gives sea-kayaking tours of Blue Hill Bay and Eggemoggin Reach.

STATE PARK

Holbrook Island Sanctuary (⊠ Penobscot Bay, Brooksville, ☎ 207/326–4012) has a gravelly beach with a splendid view and hiking trails.

Shopping

Old Cove Antiques (⊠ Rte. 15, Sargentville, ☎ 207/359–2031) has folk art, quilts, hooked rugs, and folk carvings. **Leighton Gallery** (⊠ Parker Point Rd., ☎ 207/374–5001) shows oil paintings, lithographs, watercolors, and other contemporary art in the gallery, and sculpture in its garden. **Handworks Gallery** (⊠ Main St., ☎ 207/374–5613) carries unusual crafts, jewelry, and clothing. **North Country Textiles** (⊠ Main St., ☎ 207/374–2715) specializes in fine woven shawls, place mats, throws, baby blankets, and pillows in subtle patterns and color schemes.

Rackliffe Pottery (⊠ Rte. 172, ☎ 207/374–2297) is famous for its vivid blue pottery, including plates, tea and coffee sets, pitchers, casseroles, and canisters. **Rowantrees Pottery** (⊠ Union St., ☎ 207/374–5535) has an extensive selection of styles and patterns in dinnerware, tea sets, vases, and decorative items.

En Route The scenic Route 15 south from Blue Hill passes through Brooksville and on to the graceful suspension bridge that crosses Eggemoggin Reach to Deer Isle. The turnout and picnic area at Caterpillar Hill, 1 mi south of the junction of Routes 15 and 175, commands a fabulous view of Penobscot Bay, the hundreds of dark green islands, and the Camden Hills across the bay, which from this perspective look like a range of mountains dwarfed and faded by an immense distance—yet they are less than 25 mi away.

Deer Isle

③⓪ *8 mi south of Blue Hill.*

Deer Isle has a mostly sparsely settled landscape of thick woods opening to tidal coves, shingled houses with lobster traps stacked in the yards, and dirt roads that lead to summer cottages.

Haystack Mountain School of Crafts attracts internationally renowned glassblowers, potters, sculptors, jewelers, blacksmiths, printmakers, and weavers to its summer institute. You can attend evening lectures or visit the studios of artisans at work (by appointment only). ⊠ *South of Deer Isle Village on Rte. 15, turn left at Gulf gas station and follow signs for 6 mi,* ☎ *207/348–2306.* ⊡ *Free.* ☉ *June–Sept.*

Dining and Lodging

$$$$ ✕⊞ **Goose Cove Lodge.** The heavily wooded property at the end of a back road has a fine stretch of ocean frontage, a sandy beach, and a long sandbar that leads to a nature preserve. Cottages and suites are in either secluded woodlands or on the shore. Some are attached, some have a single large room, and still others have one or two bedrooms. All but three units have fireplaces. The restaurant's prix-fixe four-course repast (always superb and always including at least one vegetarian entrée; reservations essential) is preceded by complimentary hors d'oeuvres. Friday night, there's a lobster feast on the inn's private beach. ⊠ *Goose Cove Rd. (Box 40), Sunset 04683,* ☎ *207/348–2508,* ℻ *207/348–2624. 12 suites, 13 cottages. Restaurant, hiking, volleyball, beach, boating. MAP. MC, V. Closed mid-Oct.–mid-May.*

$$$$ ✕⊞ **Pilgrim's Inn.** The deep red, four-story, gambrel-roof house dat-
★ ing from about 1793 overlooks a mill pond and harbor in Deer Isle Village. The library has wing chairs and Oriental rugs; a downstairs taproom has a huge brick fireplace and pine furniture. Guest rooms have English fabrics and carefully selected antiques. The dining room (reservations essential, no lunch) is in the attached barn, an open space both rustic and elegant, with farm implements, French oil lamps, and tiny windows. The five-course, single-entrée menu changes nightly; it might include rack of lamb or fresh local seafood. ⊠ *Rte. 15A, 04627,* ☎ *207/348–6615. 13 rooms, 10 with bath; 2 seaside cottages. Restaurant, bicycles. Full breakfast, afternoon hors d'oeuvres; MAP available. MC, V. Closed mid-Oct.–mid-May.*

Shopping

Old Deer Isle Parish House Antiques (⊠ Rte. 15, Deer Isle Village, ☎ 207/348–9964) is a place for poking around in the jumbles of old kitchenware, glassware, books, and linen. **Blue Heron Gallery & Studio** (⊠ Church St., Deer Isle Village, ☎ 207/348–6051) sells the work of the Haystack Mountain School of Crafts faculty. **Deer Isle Artists Association** (⊠ Rte. 15, Deer Isle Village, no phone) has group exhibits of prints, drawings, and sculpture from mid-June through Labor Day.

Isle au Haut

③ *14 mi south of Stonington.*

Isle au Haut thrusts its steeply ridged back out of the sea south of Stonington. Accessible only by passenger mailboat (☎ 207/367–5193), the island is worth visiting for the ferry ride alone, a half-hour cruise amid the tiny, pink-shore islands of Merchants Row, where you may see terns, guillemots, and harbor seals. More than half the island is part of **Acadia National Park**: 17½ mi of trails extend through quiet spruce and birch woods, along cobble beaches and seaside cliffs, and over the spine of the central mountain ridge. (For more information on Acadia National Park, *see* Bar Harbor and Acadia, *below*). From late June to mid-September, the mailboat docks at **Duck Harbor** within the park. The small campground here, with five Adirondack-type lean-tos, is open mid-May–mid-October and fills up quickly; reservations are essential, and they can be made after April 1 by writing to Acadia National Park (⊠ Box 177, Bar Harbor 04609).

Dining and Lodging

$$$$ 🍽 **The Keeper's House.** This converted lighthouse-keeper's house is on a rock ledge surrounded by thick spruce forest. There is no electricity, but every guest receives a flashlight at registration; guests dine by candlelight on seafood or chicken and read in the evening by kerosene lantern. Trails link the historic inn with Acadia National Park's Isle au Haut trail network, and you can walk to the village. The five guest rooms are spacious, airy, and simply decorated with painted wood furniture and local crafts. A separate cottage, the Oil House, has no indoor plumbing. Access to the island is via the daily (except Sunday and holidays) mailboat from Stonington—a scenic, 40-minute trip. ⊠ *Box 26, 04645,* ☎ *207/367–2261. 4 rooms share 2 baths, 1 cottage. Dock, bicycles. AP. No credit cards. BYOB. Closed Nov.–Apr.*

Penobscot Bay A to Z

Getting Around

BY CAR

Route 1 follows the west coast of Penobscot Bay, linking Rockland, Rockport, Camden, Belfast, and Searsport. On the east side of the bay, Route 175 (south from Route 1) takes you to Route 166A (for Castine) and Route 15 (for Blue Hill, Deer Isle, and Stonington). A car is essential for exploring the bay area.

Contacts and Resources

B&B RESERVATION AGENCY

Camden Accommodations, (⊠ 77 Elm St., Camden, ☎ 207/236–6090 or 800/236–1920, ℻ 207/236–6091) provides assistance for reservations in and around Camden.

EMERGENCIES

Blue Hill Memorial Hospital (⊠ Water St., Blue Hill, ☎ 207/374–2836). **Island Medical Center** (⊠ Airport Rd., Stonington, ☎ 207/367–2311). **Penobscot Bay Medical Center** (⊠ Rte. 1, Rockport,

☎ 207/596–8000). **Waldo County General Hospital** (✉ 56 Northport Ave., Belfast, ☎ 207/338–2500).

VISITOR INFORMATION

Belfast Area Chamber of Commerce (✉ Box 58, Belfast 04915, ☎ 207/ 338–5900); information booth on Main Street is open May–October, daily 10–6. **Blue Hill Chamber of Commerce** (✉ Box 520, Blue Hill 04614, no phone). **Castine Town Office** (✉ Emerson Hall, Court St., Castine 04421, ☎ 207/326–4502). **Rockland–Thomaston Area Chamber of Commerce** (✉ Harbor Park, Box 508, Rockland 04841, ☎ 207/ 596–0376) is open daily 9–5 in summer, weekdays 9–5 in winter. **Rockport-Camden-Lincolnville Chamber of Commerce** (✉ Public Landing, Box 919, Camden 04843, ☎ 207/236–4404 or 800/223–5459) is open summer weekdays 9–5, Saturday 10–5, Sunday noon–4; winter weekdays 9–5, Saturday 10–4. **Waldo County Regional Chamber of Commerce** (✉ School St., Unity, ☎ 207/948–5050 or 800/870–9934) is open off-season 9–3 and in summer 9–5.

MOUNT DESERT ISLAND

East of Penobscot Bay, Acadia is the informal name for the area that includes Mount Desert Island (pronounced "dessert") and its surroundings: Blue Hill Bay; Frenchman Bay; and Ellsworth, Hancock, and other mainland towns. Mount Desert, 13 mi across, is Maine's largest island, and it harbors most of Acadia National Park, Maine's principal tourist attraction, with more than 4 million visitors a year. The 40,000 acres of woods and mountains, lake and shore, footpaths, carriage roads, and hiking trails that make up the park extend to other islands and some of the mainland. Outside the park, on Mount Desert's east shore, Bar Harbor has become a busy tourist town. An upper-class resort town of the 19th century, Bar Harbor serves park visitors with a variety of inns, motels, and restaurants.

Bar Harbor

③② *160 mi northeast of Portland, 22 mi southeast of Ellsworth. Coastal Rte. 1 passes through Ellsworth, where Rte. 3 turns south to Mount Desert Island and takes you into Bar Harbor.*

Most of Bar Harbor's grand mansions were destroyed in a mammoth fire that devastated the island in 1947, but many of the surviving estates have been converted to attractive inns and restaurants. Motels abound, yet the town retains the beauty of a commanding location on Frenchman Bay. Shops, restaurants, and hotels are clustered along Main, Mt. Desert, and Cottage streets.

Bar Harbor Historical Society Museum, on the lower level of the Jesup Memorial Library, displays photographs of Bar Harbor from the days when it catered to the very rich. Other exhibits document the great fire of 1947. ✉ *34 Mt. Desert St.,* ☎ *207/288–4245.* ⊠ *Free.* ☉ *Mid-June–mid-Oct., Mon.–Sat. 1–4 or by appointment.*

☺ **Acadia Zoo** has pastures, streams, and woods that shelter about 40 species of wild and domestic animals, including reindeer, wolves, monkeys, and a moose. A barn has been converted to a rain-forest habitat for monkeys, birds, reptiles, and other Amazon creatures. ✉ *Rte. 3, Trenton, north of Bar Harbor,* ☎ *207/667–3244.* ⊠ *$6.* ☉ *May–Dec., daily 9:30–dusk.*

The Arts

Arcady Music Festival (☎ 207/288–3151) schedules concerts (primarily classical) at a number of locations around Mount Desert Island,

Mount Desert Island

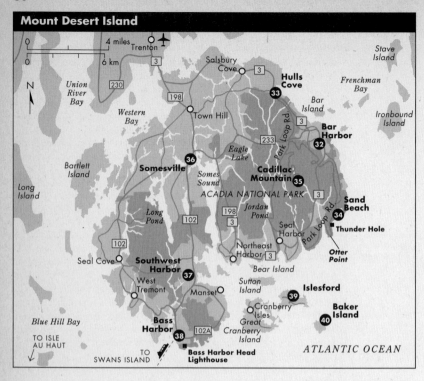

as well as at selected off-island sites, year-round. **Bar Harbor Festival** (✉ 59 Cottage St., Bar Harbor, ☎ 207/288–5744) programs recitals, jazz, chamber music, string-orchestra, and pop concerts by up-and-coming young professionals from mid-July to mid-August. **Pierre Monteux School for Conductors and Orchestra Musicians** (✉ Rte. 1, Hancock, ☎ 207/422–3931) presents public concerts by faculty and students during the term (late June–late July). Symphonic concerts are Sunday at 5 and chamber-music concerts are Wednesday at 8—all held in the Pierre Monteux Memorial Hall.

Dining, Lodging, and Camping

$$$ ✕ **Porcupine Grill.** Named for a cluster of islets in Frenchman Bay, this two-story restaurant has earned culinary fame for its cornbread-stuffed pork chops, crabmeat terrine made with local goat cheese, salmon with citrus relish, fresh pastas, and a Caesar salad tossed with Parmesan and fried shrimp. Soft green walls, antique furnishings, and Villeroy & Boch porcelain create an ambience that complements the cuisine. There's also a wine bar with a lighter menu. ✉ *123 Cottage St.,* ☎ *207/288–3884. AE, DC, MC, V. No lunch. Closed Mon.–Thurs. Jan.–June.*

$$–$$$ ✕ **George's.** Candles, flowers, and linens grace the tables of the four
★ small dining rooms in this old house. The menu shows a distinct Mediterranean influence in the phyllo-wrapped lobster; the lamb and wild game entrées are superb. ✉ *7 Stephen's La.,* ☎ *207/288–4505. AE, D, DC, MC, V. No lunch. Closed Nov.–mid-June.*

$$$$ ✕▥ **Le Domaine.** This inn, on 100 acres 9 mi east of Ellsworth, has
★ seven rooms done in French country style, with chintz and wicker, simple desks, and window seats; five of them have balconies or porches over the gardens. The elegant but not intimidating dining room (no lunch) has polished wood floors; copper pots hanging from the mantel; and silver, crystal, and linen on the tables. A screened-in dining area

overlooks the gardens in back. Owner Nicole Purslow, who trained at Cordon Bleu in her native France, prepares such specialties as *lapin pruneaux* (rabbit in a rich brown sauce), sweetbreads with lemon and capers, and coquilles St-Jacques. ✉ *Rte. 1 (Box 496, Hancock 04640),* ☎ *207/422–3395, 207/422–3916, or 800/554–8498;* FAX *207/422– 2316. 7 rooms. Restaurant, badminton, hiking, boating, fishing. MAP. AE, D, MC, V. Closed Nov.–mid-May.*

$$$ ✕▥ **Bar Harbor Inn.** The roots of this genteel inn date to the 1880s. The large yet cozy lobby, where breakfast and tea are served daily, has a fireplace and wing chairs. Guest rooms in the Oceanfront Lodge are larger than those in the main building and have balconies with ocean views. The formal waterfront dining room, **The Reading Room,** serves a mostly Continental menu but has some Maine specialties like lobster pie and a scrumptious Indian pudding. ✉ *Newport Dr., 04609,* ☎ *207/288–3351 or 800/248–3351,* FAX *207/288–5296. 153 rooms. 2 restaurants, no-smoking rooms, pool, business services. AE, D, DC, MC, V.*

$$$$ ▥ **Cleftstone Manor.** Attention, lovers of Victoriana! This inn was made in high Victorian heaven expressly for you. Ignore the fact that it is set amid sterile motels just off Route 3, the road along which traffic roars into Bar Harbor. Inside this rambling brown house, a deeply plush mahogany-and-lace world awaits. The parlor is cool and richly furnished with red velvet and brocade-trim sofas with white doilies, grandfather and mantel clocks, and oil paintings hanging on powderblue walls. Guest rooms are similarly ornate, and five rooms have fireplaces. ✉ *Rte. 3, Eden St., 04609,* ☎ *207/288–4951 or 800/962–9762. 14 rooms, 2 suites. Full breakfast, afternoon and evening refreshments. D, MC, V. Closed late-Oct.–early-May.*

$$$–$$$$ ▥ **Wonder View Inn.** Although the rooms here are standard motel accommodations, with two double beds and nondescript furniture, this establishment is distinguished by its extensive grounds and imposing view of Frenchman Bay. Redecorating and modernization occurred early in 1997. The woods muffle the sounds of traffic on Route 3. ✉ *Rte. 3 (Box 25), Bar Harbor 04609,* ☎ *207/288–3358 or 888/439–8439,* FAX *207/288–2005. 79 rooms. Restaurant, pool. AE, D, MC, V. Closed late Oct.–mid-May.*

$ ⚐ **Lamoine State Park.** Off Mount Desert Island, but convenient to it, this 61-site campground is open mid-May–mid-October; the 55-acre park has a splendid front-row seat on Frenchman Bay as well as a boat launching ramp, saltwater fishing pier, and children's playground. ✉ *Rte. 184, Lamoine,* ☎ *207/667–4778.*

Outdoor Activities and Sports

BICYCLING

Bikes can be rented at **Acadia Bike & Canoe** (✉ 48 Cottage St., ☎ 207/ 288–9605) and **Bar Harbor Bicycle Shop** (✉ 141 Cottage St., ☎ 207/ 288–3886).

BOATING

For canoe rentals try **Acadia Bike & Canoe** (☞ Bicycling, *above*). For guided kayak tours, try **National Park Kayak Tours** (✉ 137 Cottage St., ☎ 207/288–0342) or **Coastal Kayaking Tours** (✉ 48 Cottage St., ☎ 207/288–9605).

Acadian Whale Watcher (✉ Golden Anchor Pier, West St., ☎ 207/288– 9794 or 800/421–3307) runs 3½-hour whale-watching cruises June–mid-October. ***Chippewa*** (✉ Bar Harbor Inn Pier, ☎ 207/288–4585 or

207/288–2373) is a 65-ft classic motor vessel that cruises past islands and lighthouses three times a day (including sunset) in summer. **Natalie Todd** (✉ Bar Harbor Inn Pier, ☎ 207/288–4585 or 207/288–2373) offers two-hour cruises on a three-masted windjammer mid-May–mid-October. **Frenchman Bay Company** (✉ Harbor Place, ☎ 207/288–3322 or 800/508–1499) operates the windjammer *Bay Lady,* the nature-sight-seeing cruise vessel *Acadian,* and the 300-passenger *Whale Watcher* in summer.

CARRIAGE RIDES

Wildwood Stables (✉ Park Loop Rd., near Jordan Pond House, ☎ 207/276–3622) gives romantic tours in traditional horse-drawn carriages on the 51-mi network of carriage roads designed and built by philanthropist John D. Rockefeller, Jr. There are three two-hour trips and three one-hour trips daily, including a "tea-and-popover ride" that stops at Jordan Pond House (☞ Dining, Lodging, and Camping *in* Acadia National Park, *below*) and a sunset ride to the summit of Day Mountain.

Shopping

Bar Harbor in summer is prime territory for browsing for gifts, T-shirts, and novelty items; for bargains, head for the outlets that line Route 3 in Ellsworth, which have good discounts on shoes, sportswear, cookware, and more.

Acadia Shops (✉ 45 and 85 Main St., Bar Harbor; Inside the park at Cadillac Mountain summit; Thunder Hole on Ocean Dr.; Jordan Pond House on Park Loop Rd.) sell crafts and Maine foods and books. **Island Artisans** (✉ 99 Main St., ☎ 207/288–4214) is a crafts cooperative. The **Lone Moose–Fine Crafts** (✉ 78 West St., ☎ 207/288–4229) has art glass and works in clay, pottery, wood, and fiberglass. The **Eclipse Gallery** (✉ 12 Mt. Desert St., ☎ 207/288–9048) carries handblown glass, ceramics, art photography, and wood furniture.

OFF THE
BEATEN PATH

BARTLETT MAINE ESTATE WINERY – Enjoy tours, tastings, and gift packs at this winery, where wines are produced from locally grown apples, pears, blueberries, and other fruit. ✉ *Rte. 1, Gouldsboro, northeast of Bar Harbor (via Ellsworth),* ☎ *207/546-2408.* ☽ *June–mid-Oct., Mon.–Sat. 10-5.*

Acadia National Park

㉝ The **Hulls Cove** approach to Acadia National Park is 4 mi northwest of Bar Harbor on Route 3. Even though it is often clogged with traffic in summer, the **Park Loop Road** provides the best introduction to the park. At the start of the loop at Hulls Cove, the **visitor center** shows a free 15-minute orientation film. Also available at the center are books, maps of the hiking trails and carriage roads in the park, the schedule for naturalist-led tours, and cassettes for drive-it-yourself park tours.

En Route Traveling south on the Park Loop Road, you'll reach a small ticket booth where you pay the $5-per-vehicle entrance fee to Acadia National Park. Take the next left to the parking area for Sand Beach.

㉞ **Sand Beach** is a small stretch of pink sand backed by the mountains of Acadia and the odd lump of rock known as the Beehive. The **Ocean Trail,** which runs alongside the Park Loop Road from Sand Beach to the Otter Point parking area, is a popular and easily accessible walk with some of the most spectacular scenery in Maine: huge slabs of pink granite heaped at the ocean's edge, ocean views unobstructed to the horizon, and **Thunder Hole,** a natural seaside cave into which the ocean rushes and roars.

③⑤ **Cadillac Mountain,** at 1,532 ft, is the highest point on the eastern seaboard. From the smooth, bald summit you have a 360-degree view of the ocean, islands, jagged coastline, and the woods and lakes of Acadia and its surroundings. You can drive, as well as hike, to the summit.

Dining, Lodging, and Camping

$$ ✕ **Jordan Pond House.** Oversize popovers (with homemade strawberry jam) and tea are a century-old tradition at this rustic restaurant in the park, where in fine weather you can sit on the terrace or the lawn and admire the views of Jordan Pond and the mountains. Take tea or stay for a dinner of lobster stew or seafood. ⊠ *Park Loop Rd.,* ☎ *207/276–3316. Reservations essential. AE, D, MC, V. Closed late Oct.–mid-May.*

$$$$ 🏠 **Inn at Canoe Point.** Seclusion and privacy are bywords of this snug,
★ 100-year-old Tudor-style house on the water at Hulls Cove, 2 mi from Bar Harbor and ¼ mi from Acadia National Park's Hulls Cove Visitor Center. The Master Suite, a large room with a gas fireplace, is a favorite for its size and for its French doors, which open onto a waterside deck. The inn's large living room has huge windows on the water, a granite fireplace, and a waterfront deck where a full breakfast is served on summer mornings. ⊠ *Rte. 3 (Box 216), Bar Harbor 04609,* ☎ *207/ 288–9511. 3 rooms, 2 suites. Full breakfast. D, MC, V.*

$ 🏕 **Blackwoods and Seawall.** In Acadia National Park, **Blackwoods** (⊠ Rte. 3, Northeast Harbor, ☎ 800/365–2267), open year-round, and **Seawall** (⊠ Rte. 102A, Northeast Harbor, ☎ 207/244–3600), open late May to late September, fill up quickly during the summer season, even though they have a total of 530 campsites. Space at Seawall is allocated on a first-come, first-served basis, starting at 8 AM. Between mid-June and mid-September, reserve a Blackwoods site within eight weeks of a visit. No reservations are required off-season.

Outdoor Activities and Sports

BIKING

The network of carriage roads that wind through the woods and fields of Acadia National Park is ideal for biking and jogging when the ground is dry and for cross-country skiing in winter. The Hulls Cove Visitor Center has a carriage-road map.

HIKING

Acadia National Park maintains nearly 200 mi of foot and carriage paths, ranging from easy strolls along flatlands to rigorous climbs that involve ladders and handholds on rock faces. Among the more rewarding hikes are the Precipice Trail to Champlain Mountain, the Great Head Loop, the Gorham Mountain Trail, and the path around Eagle Lake. The Hulls Cove Visitor Center has trail guides and maps.

Around Acadia

On completing the 27-mi Park Loop Road, you can continue your auto tour of the island by heading west on Route 233 for the villages on Somes Sound, a true fjord—the only one on the East Coast—which
③⑥ almost bisects Mount Desert Island. **Somesville,** the oldest settlement on the island (1621), is a carefully preserved New England village of white clapboard houses and churches, neat green lawns, and bits of blue water visible behind them.

③⑦ Route 102 south from Somesville takes you to **Southwest Harbor,** which combines the rough, salty character of a working port with the refinements of a summer resort community. From the town's Main Street (Route 102), turn left onto Clark Point Road to reach the harbor.

Mount Desert Oceanarium has exhibits in two locations on the fishing and sea life of the Gulf of Maine, a live seal program, and lobster hatchery as well as hands-on exhibits such as a "touch tank." ⊠ *Clark Point Rd., Southwest Harbor,* ☎ *207/244–7330;* ⊠ *Rte. 3, Thomas Bay, Bar Harbor,* ☎ *207/288–5005.* ☑ *Call for admission fees (combination tickets available for both sites).* ☉ *Mid-May–mid-Oct., Mon.–Sat. 9–5.*

Wendell Gillery Museum of Bird Carving features bird carvings by Gillery, offers carving demonstrations and workshops and natural history programs, and exhibits wildlife art. ⊠ *Main St., Southwest Harbor,* ☎ *207/244–7555.* ☑ *$3.* ☉ *June–Oct., Tues.–Sun. 10–4; May and Nov.–Dec., Fri.–Sat. 10–4.*

En Route From Southwest Harbor, continue south on Route 102, following Route 102A where the road forks and passing through the communities of Manset and Seawall on your way to Bass Harbor.

38 In **Bass Harbor,** 4 mi south of Southwest Harbor, visit the **Bass Harbor Head lighthouse,** which clings to a cliff at the eastern entrance to Blue Hill Bay and was built in 1858. This tiny lobstering village has cottages for rent, inns, a restaurant, a gift shop, and the **Maine State Ferry Service**'s car-and-passenger ferry to Swans Island. ☎ *207/244–3254.* ☉ *5 daily runs June–mid-Oct.; fewer trips rest of yr.*

Dining and Lodging

$$$$ ✕▥ **Claremont Hotel.** Built in 1884 and operated continuously as an inn, the Claremont calls up memories of long, leisurely vacations of days gone by. The yellow-clapboard structure commands a view of Somes Sound, croquet is played on the lawn, and cocktails and lunch are served at the Boat House in midsummer. The cottages have not been updated as much as the inn's rooms, and their facilities have garnered some complaint. The large, old-style dining room, open to the public for breakfast and dinner, has picture windows. The menu changes weekly and always includes fresh fish and at least one vegetarian entrée; reservations are essential, and a jacket is required for dinner. ⊠ *Off Clark Point Rd. (Box 137) Southwest Harbor 04679,* ☎ *207/244–5036 or 800/244–5036,* ☏ *207/244–3512. 24 rooms, 12 cottages, 2 guest houses. Restaurant, tennis court, croquet, dock, boating, bicycles. MAP. No credit cards. Hotel and restaurant closed mid-Oct.–mid-June; cottages closed Nov.–late May.*

$$–$$$ ▥ **Island House.** This sweet B&B on the quiet side of the island has simply decorated bedrooms in the main house as well as a carriage house suite, complete with sleeping loft and kitchenette. ⊠ *Box 1006, Southwest Harbor 04679,* ☎ *207/244–5180. 4 rooms share 2 baths, 1 suite. Full breakfast. No credit cards.*

Nightlife

Acadia has relatively little nighttime activity. A lively boating crowd frequents the lounge at the **Moorings Restaurant** (⊠ Shore Rd. Manset, ☎ 207/244–7070), which is accessible by boat and car, and stays open until after midnight from mid-May through October.

Outdoor Activities and Sports

BICYCLING

You can rent bikes at **Southwest Cycle** (⊠ Main St., Southwest Harbor, ☎ 207/244–5856).

BOATING

National Park Canoe Rentals (⊠ Pretty Marsh Rd., Somesville, at the head of Long Pond, ☎ 207/244–5854) rents canoes. **Manset Yacht Service** (⊠ Shore Rd., ☎ 207/244–4040) rents sailboats.

Bass Harbor Cruises (⊠ Bass Harbor Ferry Dock, Bass Harbor, ☎ 207/244–5365) operates two-hour nature cruises (with an Acadia naturalist) twice daily in summer. *Blackjack* (⊠ Town Dock, Northeast Harbor, ☎ 207/276–5043 or 207/288–3056), a 33-ft Friendship sloop, makes four trips daily, mid-June–mid-October.

Shopping
ANTIQUES
Marianne Clark Fine Antiques (⊠ Main St., Southwest Harbor, ☎ 207/244–9247) has an eclectic array of formal and country furniture, American paintings, and accessories from the 18th and 19th centuries.

BOOKS
Port in a Storm Bookstore (⊠ Main St., Somesville, ☎ 207/244–4114) is a book lover's nirvana.

Island Excursions

Off the southeast shore of Mount Desert Island at the entrance to Somes Sound, the five **Cranberry Isles**—Great Cranberry, Islesford (or Little Cranberry), Baker Island, Sutton Island, and Bear Island—escape the hubbub that engulfs Acadia National Park in summer. Great Cranberry and Islesford are served by the **Beal & Bunker passenger ferry** (☎ 207/244–3575) from Northeast Harbor and by **Cranberry Cove Boating Company** (☎ 207/244–5882) from Southwest Harbor. Baker Island is reached by the summer cruise boats of the **Islesford Ferry Company** (☎ 207/276–3717) from Northeast Harbor; Sutton and Bear islands are privately owned.

㊴ **Islesford** comes closest to having a village: a collection of houses, a church, a fishermen's co-op, a market, and a post office near the ferry dock. The **Islesford Historical Museum,** run by Acadia National Park, has displays of tools, documents relating to the island's history, and books and manuscripts of the poet Rachel Field (1894–1942), who summered on Sutton Island. ⊠ *Islesford Historical Museum,* ☎ 207/288–3338. 🎫 *Free.* ☉ *Mid-June–Sept. 10:30–noon and 12:30–4:30.*

㊵ The 123-acre **Baker Island,** the most remote of the group, looks almost black from a distance because of its thick spruce forest. The Islesford Ferry cruise boat from Northeast Harbor offers a 4½-hour narrated tour, during which you are likely to see ospreys nesting on a sea stack off Sutton Island, harbor seals basking on ledges, and cormorants flying low over the water. Because Baker Island has no natural harbor, the tour boat ties up off-shore, and you take a fishing dory to get to shore.

Mount Desert Island A to Z

Getting Around
BY CAR
North of Bar Harbor, the scenic 27-mi Park Loop Road takes leave of Route 3 to circle the eastern quarter of Mount Desert Island, with one-way traffic from Sieur de Monts Spring to Seal Harbor and two-way traffic between Seal Harbor and Hulls Cove. Route 102, which serves the western half of Mount Desert, is reached from Route 3 just after it crosses onto the island or from Route 233 west from Bar Harbor.

All of these island roads pass in, out, and through the precincts of Acadia National Park.

Contacts and Resources

CAR RENTAL

Avis (✉ 99 Godfrey Blvd., Bangor International Airport, ☎ 207/947–8383 or 800/331–1212). **Budget** (✉ Hancock County Airport, ☎ 207/667–1200 or 800/527–0700). **Hertz** (✉ 299 Godfrey Blvd., Bangor International Airport, ☎ 207/942–5519 or 800/654–3131). **Thrifty** (✉ 357 Odlin Rd., Bangor International Airport, ☎ 207/942–6400 or 800/367–2277).

EMERGENCIES

Mount Desert Island Hospital (✉ 10 Wayman La., Bar Harbor, ☎ 207/288–5081). **Maine Coast Memorial Hospital** (✉ 50 Union St., Ellsworth, ☎ 207/667–5311). **Southwest Harbor Medical Center** (✉ Herrick Rd., Southwest Harbor, ☎ 207/244–5513).

GUIDED TOURS

Bar Harbor Taxi and Tours (☎ 207/288–4020) conducts half-day historic and scenic tours of the area.

National Park Tours (☎ 207/288–3327) operates a 2½-hour bus tour of Acadia National Park, narrated by a local naturalist. The bus departs twice daily, May–October, across from Testa's Restaurant at Bayside Landing on Main Street in Bar Harbor.

Acadia Air (☎ 207/667–5534), on Route 3 in Trenton, between Ellsworth and Bar Harbor at Hancock County Airport, offers aircraft rentals and seven different aerial sightseeing itineraries, from spring through fall.

VISITOR INFORMATION

Acadia National Park (✉ Box 177, Bar Harbor 04609, ☎ 207/288–3338). **Hulls Cove Visitor Center,** (✉ Off Rte. 3, at start of Park Loop Rd.) is open May–June and September–October, daily 8–4:30; July–August, daily 8–6. **Bar Harbor Chamber of Commerce** (✉ 93 Cottage St., Box 158, Bar Harbor 04609, ☎ 207/288–3393, 207/288–5103, or 800/288–5103) is open summer weekdays 8–5, winter weekdays 8–4:30.

4 New Brunswick

With the highest tides in the world carving a rugged coast and feeding more whales than you can imagine, New Brunswick can be a phenomenal adventure. White sandy beaches, lobsters in the pot, and cozy inns steeped in history make it easy to have a relaxing interlude, too. And with fine art galleries, museums, and a dual Acadian and Loyalist heritage, the province is an intriguing cultural destination.

NEW BRUNSWICK IS WHERE the great Canadian forest, sliced by sweeping river valleys and modern
highways, meets the sea. It's an old place in New
World terms, and the remains of a turbulent past are still evident in
some of its quiet nooks. Near Moncton, for instance, wild strawber-
ries perfume the air of the grassy slopes of Fort Beausejour, where, in
1755, one of the last battles for possession of Acadia took place—the
English finally overcoming the French. The dual heritage of New
Brunswick (35% of its population is Acadian French) provides added
spice. Other areas of the province were settled by the British and by
Loyalists, American colonists who chose to live under British rule after
the American Revolution. If you stay in both Acadian and Loyalist regions, a trip to New Brunswick can seem like two vacations in one.

Updated by
Ana Watts

More than half the province is surrounded by coastline—the rest nes-
tles into Québec and Maine, creating slightly schizophrenic attitudes
in border towns. The dramatic Bay of Fundy, which has the highest
tides in the world, sweeps up the coast of Maine, around the en-
chanting Fundy Isles at the southern tip of New Brunswick and on up
the province's rough and intriguing south coast. To the north and
east, the gentle, warm Gulf Stream washes quiet beaches.

New Brunswick is still largely unsettled—85% of the province is
forested. Inhabitants have chosen the easily accessible area around rivers,
ocean, and lakes, leaving most of the interior to the pulp companies.
For years this Cinderella province has been somewhat ignored by
tourists who whiz through to better-known Atlantic destinations. New
Brunswick's residents can't seem to decide whether this makes them
unhappy or not. The government, however, sees tourism as a culturally and economically friendly way of helping the province toward economic self-sufficiency. Money is important in the economically depressed
maritime area, where younger generations have traditionally left home
for higher-paying jobs in Ontario and "the West." But no one wishes
to lose the special characteristics of this still unspoiled province.

This attitude is a blessing in disguise to motorists who do leave the major
highways to explore 2,240 km (1,389 mi) of spectacular seacoast,
pure inland streams, pretty towns, and historical cities. The custom of
hospitality is so much a part of New Brunswick nature that tourists
are perceived more as welcome visitors than paying guests. Even cities
often retain a bit of naïveté. It makes for a charming vacation, but don't
be deceived by ingenuous attitudes. Most residents are products of excellent school and university systems, generally travel widely, live in
modern cities, and are well versed in world affairs.

Pleasures and Pastimes

Beaches

There are two kinds of saltwater beaches in New Brunswick: warm-
m-m-m-m and c-c-c-c-cold. The warm beaches are along the Northumberland Strait and Gulf of St. Lawrence on the east coast. Here, it's
sand castles, sunscreen, and a little beach volleyball on the side. If sand
and solitude are more your style, try Kouchibouguac National Park
and its 26 km (16 mi) of beaches and dunes.

The cold beaches are on the Bay of Fundy, on the province's southern
coast. The highest tides in the world (a *vertical* difference of as much
as 48 ft) have carved some spectacular caves, crevices, and cliffs. There
are some sandy beaches, and hardy souls do swim in the "invigorat-
ing" salt water. But the Fundy beaches are more for adventurers who

want to investigate aquatic wildlife on the flats at low tide, hound rocks, or hunt fossils.

Dining

Cast your line just about anywhere in New Brunswick and you catch fish 'n chips, clams 'n chips, and scallops 'n chips. If you want the seafood but not the batter, you'll need a longer line. New Brunswick has never been famous for sophisticated dining, but Saint John, Moncton, and some communities along the Acadian Peninsula offer some interesting options, and resort communities like St. Andrews and Caraquet have consistently good catches.

Silver salmon, once a spring staple when set nets were allowed, is still available but quite costly. Most salmon served in restaurants is farm-reared. Lobster is available in most restaurants but is not always cheap. Residents buy it fresh from the fishermen or shore outlets and devour it in huge quantities. New Brunswick shellfish is especially tasty: Look for oysters, scallops, clams, crab, and mussels. And be sure to try the purple seaweed called dulse, which the natives eat like potato chips. To be truly authentic, accompany any New Brunswick–style feast with hearty Moosehead beer, brewed in Saint John.

In the spring, fiddlehead ferns—a provincial delicacy—are picked from the banks of rivers and streams. Eaten as a vegetable (boiled, drenched with lemon, butter, salt, and pepper), fiddleheads have something of an artichoke taste.

CATEGORY	COST*
$$$$	over $30
$$$	$20–$30
$$	$10–$20
$	under $10

per person, excluding drinks, service, and 15% harmonized sales tax (HST).

Lodging

Among its more interesting options, New Brunswick has a number of officially designated Heritage Inns. These historically significant establishments run the gamut from elegant to homey; many have antique china and furnishings. Hotels and motels in and around Saint John and Fredericton are adequate and friendly. Accommodations in Saint John are at a premium in summer, so reserve ahead.

CATEGORY	COST*
$$$$	over $140
$$$	$85–$140
$$	$50–$85
$	under $50

All prices are for a standard double room, excluding 15% harmonized sales tax (HST).

Outdoor Activities and Sports

BIKING

Byroads, lanes, and rolling secondary highways run through small towns, along the ocean, and into the forest. Set out on your own, or try a guided adventure.

FISHING

Dotted with freshwater lakes, crisscrossed with fish-laden rivers, and bordered by 1,129 km (700 mi) of seacoast, this province is one of Canada's natural treasures. Sports people are drawn by the bass fishing and such world-famous salmon rivers as the Miramichi. Commercial fishermen often take visitors line fishing for groundfish.

GOLF

There are 45 excellent golf courses in New Brunswick. Many provide sparkling views of the sea.

WHALE-WATCHING

Whether you yearn to see a humpback, finback, or minke whale, outfitters along the Bay of Fundy can take you where the action is. Most trips run May through September.

WINTER SPORTS

New Brunswick can get as much as 16 ft of snow each year, so winter fun often lasts well into spring. Dogsledding is taking off, ice-fishing communities pop up on many rivers, and you can always find someone to go tobogganing, skating, or snowshoeing with you. Snowmobiling has boomed: There are more than 9,000 km (5,580 mi) of groomed, marked, and serviced snowmobile trails and dozens of snowmobile clubs hosting special events.

For cross-country skiers, New Brunswick has groomed trails at such parks as Mactaquac Provincial Park near Fredericton, Fundy National Park in Alma, and Kouchibouguac National Park between Moncton and Bathurst. Many communities and small hotels offer groomed trails, but it's also possible to set off on your own. New Brunswick downhill ski areas usually operate from mid-December through April. There are four ski hills—Farlagne, Crabbe, Poley, and Sugarloaf.

Shopping

Fine art galleries proudly display and sell local artists' paintings and sculptures. Craft galleries, shops, and fairs brim with beautiful jewelry, glass, pottery, clothing, furniture, and leather goods. Some of the province's better bookstores even have sections devoted to New Brunswick authors, both literary and popular. You'll find a number of intriguing shopping areas in Saint John, as well as the Old City Market. Fredericton has the Saturday morning Boyce Farmers' Market and shops with crafts, treasures, and a bit of haute couture. The resort town of St. Andrews has some appealing craft stores and shops.

Exploring New Brunswick

In recent years high-tech companies in New Brunswick have helped lead much of the world onto the Information Highway, but all that has done little to change its settlement patterns. The population still clings to the original highways—rivers and oceans. In fact, the Saint John River in the west and the Fundy and Acadian Coasts in the south and east essentially encompass the province.

The Saint John River valley scenery is panoramic—gently rolling hills and sweeping forests, with just enough rocky gorges to keep it interesting. The French, English, Scots, and Danes who settled along the river have ensured its culture is equally intriguing. Here you'll find Fredericton, capital of the province.

The Fundy Coast is phenomenal. Yachts, fishing boats, and tankers bob on the waves at high tide, then sit high and dry on the ocean floor when it goes out. The same tides force the mighty Saint John River to reverse its flow in the old city of Saint John. The southwestern shores have spawned more than their share of world-class artists, authors, actors, and musicians. Maybe it's the Celtic influence; maybe it's the fog.

Along the Acadian Coast the water is warm, the sand is fine, and the accent is French—except in the middle. Where the Miramichi River meets the sea, there is an island of English, Irish, and Scottish tradition that is unto itself, rich in folklore and legend. Many people here find their livelihood in the forests, in the mines, and on the sea.

Numbers in the text correspond to numbers in the margin and on the New Brunswick, Fredericton, Downtown Saint John, and Greater Saint John maps.

Great Itineraries

IF YOU HAVE 3 DAYS

Plan to concentrate on one region if you only have a few days. Otherwise, because distances are so great, you'll spend all your time driving, and you'll have no time to enjoy the scenery, history, and culture. The Saint John River valley is best seen by following the well-marked River Valley Scenic Drive from **Edmundston** ⑦ to **Saint John** ⑪–㉓— a trip of about 380 km (236 mi).

This journey begins in the botanical gardens in **St-Jacques,** just outside Edmundston. The drive from Edmundston to 🚉 **Fredericton** ①– ⑤ is about 275 km (171 mi) of panoramic pastoral and river scenery. With its Gothic cathedral, Victorian architecture, museums, theater company, and riverfront pathways, Fredericton is both beautiful and culturally rich. Don't miss nearby **Kings Landing Historical Settlement** ⑥, a faithful depiction of life on the river in the last century.

The drive from Fredericton to 🚉 **Saint John** ⑪–㉓ is just over 100 km (62 mi) and passes through the village of **Gagetown** ⑩, a must-see for those who love art and history. Saint John is Canada's oldest incorporated city and celebrates its impressive heritage with enthusiasm.

IF YOU HAVE 6 DAYS

You can easily explore two regions of the province in six days. To the Saint John River valley region (with one night in 🚉 **Fredericton** ①–⑤ and the next in 🚉 **Saint John** ⑪–㉓) you can add the Fundy Coastal area: Here again it is easily seen by following the well-marked Fundy Coastal Drive. Visit 🚉 **St. Andrews by-the-Sea** ㉕, where art, history, nature, and seafood abound. A whale-watching tour, which might entail a ferry ride to either **Grand Manan** ㉖ or **Deer Island** ㉘, is well worth the time and distance.

The Fundy Coastal Drive winds about 100 km (62 mi) along the coast past Saint John to the fishing village of **St. Martins** on Route 111. Follow the Fundy Coastal Route signs inland, over hill and dale to Hampton (back on Route 1) and up the Kennebecasis River Valley to Sussex. The Fundy Coastal Route soon heads back for the bay through Fundy National Park, but travelers would do better to stay on the Trans-Canada Highway for another 75 km (47 mi) and stop in 🚉 **Moncton** ㉛ for two nights. This city is a microcosm of New Brunswick in that English and French flow with equal ease. It is also a center of Acadian French culture and education and has several attractions for children.

Moncton is a good starting point for touring the rest of the Bay of Fundy. Drive 80 km (50 mi) down the coast to Alma, the entrance to magnificent **Fundy National Park** ㉚. On the way back to Moncton are **Cape Enrage** and **Hopewell Cape,** where the Fundy Tides have sculpted gigantic flowerpots that turn into islands at high tide.

IF YOU HAVE 10 DAYS

With up to 10 days to explore New Brunswick you can see it all—much of the Acadian Coast as well as the Saint John River valley and the Bay of Fundy coast. For this tour you'll follow the Acadian Coastal Drive, another officially designated provincial tourist route that is well marked from Aulac to Campbellton, a distance of about 400 km (248 mi). But 🚉 **Shediac,** about 30 km (19 mi) north of Moncton, is

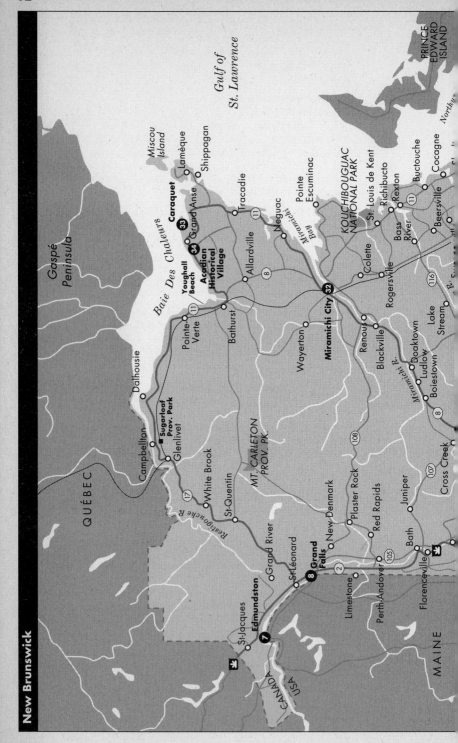

one place to start. Shediac is famous for lobsters and Parlee Beach. Another 65 km (40 mi) north is unspoiled **Kouchibouguac National Park,** which protects beaches, forests, and peat bogs. The coastal drive from the national park to 🏞 **Miramichi City** ㉜, about 75 km (47 mi), follows a fascinating network of fishing villages. Most of the communities are Acadian, but as you approach Miramichi City, English dominates again. Here a variety of cultural influences have created a rich history and tradition. A stopover in one of the city's motels will position you perfectly to begin your exploration of the Acadian Peninsula.

It is only about 120 km (74 mi) from Miramichi City to 🏞 **Caraquet** ㉝, but it might as well be a million. The entire peninsula is so different from the rest of the province it is like a trip to a foreign country: This is a romantic land with a dramatic history and an artistic flair. The **Acadian Historical Village** ㉞ is a faithful re-creation of the traditional Acadian way of life.

When to Tour New Brunswick

Late spring through fall are lovely times to visit, although lovers of winter sports have plenty of options, too. Whales are more plentiful in the Bay of Fundy after the first of August. Festivals celebrating everything from jazz to salmon are held from late spring until early fall.

FREDERICTON

The small inland city of Fredericton spreads itself on a broad point of land jutting into the Saint John River. Its predecessor, the early French settlement of St. Anne's Point, was established in 1642, during the reign of the French governor Villebon, who made his headquarters at the junction of the Nashwaak and the Saint John rivers. Settled by Loyalists and named for Frederick, second son of George III, the city serves as the seat of government for New Brunswick's 723,900 residents. Wealthy and scholarly Loyalists set out to create a gracious and beautiful place, and thus even before the establishment of the University of New Brunswick, in 1785, the town served as a center for liberal arts and sciences. It remains a gracious and beautiful place as well as a center of education, arts, and culture. The river, once the only highway to Fredericton, is now a focus of recreation, and the streets are shaded by leafy plumes of ancient elms.

Exploring Fredericton

Downtown Queen Street runs parallel with the river, and its blocks enclose historic sites and attractions. Most major sites are within walking distance of each other. An excursion to Kings Landing Historical Settlement (☞ Side Trip from Fredericton, *below*), a reconstructed village, can bring alive the province's history.

Dressed in 18th-century costume, actors from the Calithumpians theater company (☎ 506/457–1975) offer free historical walks from City Hall in July and August. Other tours can be arranged.

A Good Walk

Start at City Hall on Phoenix Square, at the corner of York and Queen streets. Once a farmers' market and opera house, its modern council chambers are decorated with tapestries that illustrate Fredericton's history. Walk down (as the river flows) Queen Street to Carleton Street to the **Military Compound** ①, which also contains the New Brunswick Sports Hall of Fame. If you arrive in Officers' Square at lunchtime in summer, you'll be treated to outdoor theater (☞ Nightlife and the Arts, *below*). On a rainy day the show goes on in the nearby College of Craft and Design. In Officers' Square, the **York-Sunbury Museum** ② occupies what were the Officers' Quarters. Next stop down the river side of Queen Street is the **Beaverbrook Art Gallery** ③, with its sculpture garden outside. Turn right on Church Street and walk to **Christ Church Cathedral** ④, with gleaming new copper on its renovated steeple. Once you have had your fill of its exquisite architecture and stained glass, turn right and start walking back up Queen. The **Provincial Legislature** ⑤ is on your left. Restaurants and cafés along Queen Street provide plenty of opportunities for refreshment. If you make your way back to **York Street** (across from where you started at City Hall), turn left to visit a chic block of interesting shops.

One variation to this walk: If you're touring on Saturday, start in the morning with the **Boyce Farmers' Market** to get a real taste of the city.

TIMING

The distances are not long, so the time you spend depends on how much you like sports, history, art, and churches. You could do it all in an afternoon, but start at the Boyce Farmers' Market on Saturday.

Sights to See

❸ **Beaverbrook Art Gallery.** One of the gifts the late Lord Beaverbrook, former New Brunswick resident and multimillionaire British peer and newspaper magnate, showered upon his native province is this museum, with its collections of historic and contemporary art and the McCain "gallery-within-a-gallery" devoted to Atlantic Canadian artists. Salvador Dalí's gigantic canvas *Santiago el Grande* is here as well as canvasses by Reynolds, Turner, Hogarth, Gainsborough, and the Canadian Group of Seven. The gallery has a major collection of the works of Cornelius Krieghoff, famed Canadian landscape painter of the early 1800s. ⊠ *703 Queen St.,* ☎ *506/458–8545.* ☞ *$3.* ☉ *Mid-June–early-Sept., weekdays 9–6, weekends 10–5; mid-Sept.–mid-June, Tues.–Fri. 9–5, Sat. 10–5, Sun. noon–5.*

Boyce Farmers' Market. You can't miss this Saturday morning market; just follow the crowds. There's lots of local meat and produce, as well as baked goods, craft items, and seasonal items from wreaths to maple syrup. Look for good ready-to-eat food, whether it's German sausages or tasty sandwiches. ⊠ *Bounded by Regent, Brunswick, and George Sts.*

❹ **Christ Church Cathedral.** One of Fredericton's prides, this gray stone building, completed in 1853, is an excellent example of decorated Gothic architecture and the first new cathedral foundation built on British soil since the Norman Conquest. Inside you'll see a clock known as "Big Ben's little brother," the test run for London's famous timepiece, designed by Lord Grimthorpe. ⊠ *Church St.,* ☎ *506/450–8500.* ☉ *Free tours June–Aug., daily 9–9.*

❶ **Military Compound.** The restored buildings of the former British and Canadian post include soldiers' barracks, a guardhouse, and a cell block. It extends two blocks along Queen Street. Redcoats stand guard; in summer a changing-of-the-guard ceremony takes place in Officers' Square at 11 and 7. Within the Military Compound stands the John Thurston Clark Building—an outstanding example of Second Empire architecture that now houses the ☞ **New Brunswick Sports Hall of Fame.** ⊠ *Queen St. at Carleton St.,* ☎ *506/453–2324.* ☞ *Free.*

New Brunswick Sports Hall of Fame. This attraction in the John Thurston Clark Building of the ☞ **Military Compound** celebrates the personalities and events that have shaped New Brunswick's rich sports heritage. Displayed in the main and second-floor galleries are an ex-

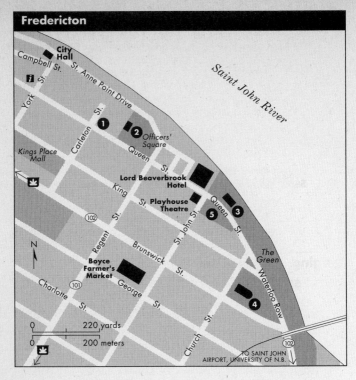

tensive collection of sports memorabilia and the original charcoal portraits of its more than 130 honored members. Special exhibits coincide with national and international sporting events. ⊠ *503 Queen St.,* ☏ *506/453–3747.* ⌑ *Free.* ☉ *Call for hrs of operation.*

❺ **Provincial Legislature.** The interior chamber of the legislature, where the premier and elected members govern the province, reflects the taste of the late Victorians. The chandeliers are brass and the prisms are Waterford. Replicas of portraits by Sir Joshua Reynolds of King George III and Queen Charlotte hang here. There is a free-standing staircase, and a volume of Audubon's *Birds of America* is on display. ⊠ *Queen St.,* ☏ *506/453–2527.* ⌑ *Free.* ☉ *Legislature tours June–Aug., daily 9–6; Sept.–May, weekdays 9–4; library weekdays 8:15–5.*

York Street. This is the city's high-fashion block—trendy shops, a hairdresser cum art dealer, and an incense-burning boutique, to name a few. About the middle of the upriver side of the block is Mazucca's Alley, with more shops and the gateway to several pubs and restaurants.

❷ **York-Sunbury Museum.** Officers' Quarters houses a museum that offers a living picture of the community from the time when only First Nations peoples inhabited the area, through the Acadian and Loyalist days, to the immediate past. Its penny-farthing bicycle looks impossible to ride, and its World War I trench puts you in the thick of battle. It also contains the shellacked remains of a Fredericton legend, the puzzling Coleman Frog. ⊠ *Officers' Sq., Queen St.,* ☏ *506/455–6041.* ⌑ *$2.* ☉ *May–Labor Day, Mon.–Sat. 10–6 (also July–Aug., Mon. and Fri. 10–9, Sun. noon–6); Labor Day–mid-Oct., weekdays 9–5, Sat. noon–4; mid-Oct.–Apr., Mon., Wed., and Fri. 11–3, or by appointment.*

Dining

$$ ✕ **Luna Steakhouse.** Specialties include huge Caesar salads, garlic bread, escargots, brochettes, and Italian food. In fine weather you can dine on an outdoor terrace. Inside, the stucco walls and dark arches make a cozy environment. ⊠ *168 Dundonald St.,* ☎ *506/455–4020. AE, DC, MC, V.*

$$ ✕ **Mei's Chinese Restaurant.** In this family operation downtown, mother Mei does all the cooking. She serves a variety of Chinese cuisine including Szechuan, Cantonese, and Taiwanese; dumplings are a house specialty. Sushi is available if you call a day in advance. The decor is basic. This is a very popular spot for lunch weekdays. ⊠ *73 Carlton St.,* ☎ *506/454–2177. AE, MC, V. No lunch weekends.*

$–$$ ✕ **Bar B Q Barn.** Special children's menus and barbecued ribs and chicken are the standards; the blackboard lists plenty of other daily dinner specials, such as salmon, scallops, and chili. This local favorite has a convenient downtown location and is great for winding down; the bar serves fine martinis. ⊠ *540 Queen St.,* ☎ *506/455–2742. AE, DC, MC, V.*

Lodging

$$$ ⊞ **Howard Johnson Motor Lodge.** This HoJo is on the north side of the river and at the north end of the Princess Margaret Bridge. It has a terrace bar in a pleasant interior courtyard overlooked by the balconies of many of the rooms. Guest-room decor is standard for the chain. ⊠ *Trans-Canada Hwy., Box 1414, E3B 5E3,* ☎ *506/472–0480 or 800/596–4656,* ⅎ𝔸𝕏 *506/472–0170. 116 rooms. Restaurant, bar, indoor pool, driving range, miniature golf, 4 tennis courts, exercise room. AE, D, DC, MC, V.*

$$$ ⊞ **Lord Beaverbrook Hotel.** A central location is this modern, seven-story hotel's main attraction. Some rooms have whirlpools or minibars. A veranda off the main dining room overlooks the river, and the bar is lively. ⊠ *659 Queen St., E3B 5A6,* ☎ *506/455–3371,* ⅎ𝔸𝕏 *506/455–1441. 168 rooms. 2 restaurants, bar, no-smoking rooms, indoor pool. AE, DC, MC, V.*

$$$ ⊞ **Sheraton Fredericton.** Within months of being named Sheraton Inn of the Year for North America in 1996, this property was upgraded to a hotel. The only real difference is some small added amenities. It is still a stately riverside property within walking distance of downtown. The elegant country decor is almost as delightful as the sunset views over the river from the restaurant and many of the modern rooms. The gift shop carries topnotch crafts. ⊠ *225 Woodstock Rd., E3B 2H8,* ☎ *506/457–7000 or 800/325–3535,* ⅎ𝔸𝕏 *506/457–4000. 223 rooms. Restaurant, bar, minibars, indoor pool, outdoor pool, hot tub, sauna, exercise room. AE, D, DC, MC, V.*

$$–$$$ ⊞ **Carriage House Inn.** This Heritage mansion has lovely bedrooms furnished with Victorian antiques. Homemade breakfast, complete with homemade maple syrup for the fluffy pancakes, is served in the solarium. Breakfast is included in the rates. ⊠ *230 University Ave., E3B 4H7,* ☎ *506/452–9924 or 800/267–6068,* ⅎ𝔸𝕏 *506/458–0799. 10 rooms, 6 with bath. AE, MC, V.*

Nightlife and the Arts

The Arts
Theatre New Brunswick (⊠ 686 Queen St., ☎ 506/458–8344) performs in the Playhouse and tours the province. The **Playhouse** (⊠ 686 Queen St.) is the venue for theater and most other cultural performances, including Symphony New Brunswick and traveling ballet and dance companies. **The Calithumpians** offer summer outdoor theater daily—

12:15 weekdays, 2 PM weekends—in Officers' Square. Some top musicians and other performers appear at the larger **Aitken Center** (⊠ Rte. 102, ☏ 506/453–5054) on the University of New Brunswick campus near Fredericton.

Nightlife

Fredericton has lively nightlife, with lots of live music in downtown pubs, especially on the weekends. Just wander down **King Street** until you hear your kind of music. **Dolan's Pub** (⊠ 349 King St., ☏ 506/454–7474) has Celtic and folk-style entertainment. At **The Dock** (⊠ 375 King, ☏ 506/458–1254)), you'll hear rock, blues, folk— anything but country. **The Lunar Rogue** (⊠ 625 King St., ☏ 506/450–2065) has an old-world pub atmosphere and showcases acoustic folk, rock, and Celtic music.

Outdoor Activities and Sports

Rowing

Shells, canoes, and kayaks can be rented by the hour, day, or week at the **Aquatic Center** (☏ 506/462–6021), which also arranges guided tours and instruction.

Skiing

Crabbe Mountain Winter Park (⊠ Box 20187, Kings Place Postal Outlet, Fredericton, E3B 7A2, ☏ 506/463–8311) is in Lower Hainesville (about 55 km, or 34 mi, west of Fredericton). There are 14 trails, a vertical elevation of 853 ft, snowboard and ski rentals, instruction, babysitting, and a lounge and restaurant.

Walking

Fredericton has a fine network of walking trails, one of which follows the river from the Green, past the Victorian mansions on Waterloo Row, behind the Beaverbrook Art Gallery, and along the river bank to the Sheraton. Its total length is over 3 km (2 mi), but you can do shorter pieces. If you have a summer evening, walk it upstream, toward the Sheraton, and bask in the glow of a sunset. The visitor information center has a trail map.

Shopping

New Brunswick is known for its crafts, and mammoth **crafts markets** are held occasionally in Fredericton and every Labor Day weekend in Mactaquac Provincial Park (☞ Saint John River Valley to Saint John, *below*). For sale are pottery, blown glass, pressed flowers, metal flowers, turned wood, leather, quilts, and other fine items, many made by members of the New Brunswick Craft Council.

Aitkens Pewter (⊠ 65 Regent St., ☏ 506/453–9474) specializes in pewter goblets, belt buckles, and jewelry. **Gallery 78** (⊠ 96 Queen St., ☏ 506/454–5192), in a Victorian mansion, has works by local artists. **Mulhouse Country Classics** (⊠ Trans-Canada Hwy., ☏ 506/459–8859) is a gem for crafts, Tilley Endurable clothing, and handmade furniture. Excellent men's shoes can be bought at **Hartt's Shoe Factory** (⊠ 401 York St., ☏ 506/458–8358). **The Linen Closet** (⊠ 397 King St., ☏ 506/450–8393) sells Battenburg lace, exquisite bedding, and bathroom accessories.

Side Trip from Fredericton

West of Fredericton, the Kings Landing Historical Settlement was built by moving period buildings to a new shore. The Trans-Canada Highway takes you past some spectacular river and hill scenery. You'll pass the Mactaquac Dam (turn off here if you want to visit Mactaquac Provincial Park). The drive to Kings Landing takes less than a half hour, but to appreciate New Brunswick's background and history, plan to spend most of a day.

Kings Landing Historical Settlement

★ ☙ ❻ *30 km (19 mi) west of Fredericton.*

This excellent outdoor living history museum on the Saint John River evokes the sights, sounds, and society of rural New Brunswick between 1790 and 1900. The winding country lanes and meticulously restored homes will pull you back a century or more so you can learn firsthand how to forge a nail at the blacksmith's shop or bake bread on an open hearth. There are daily dramas in the theater, barn dances, and strolling minstrels. You'll see how the wealthy owner of the sawmill lived and just how different things were for the lowly immigrant farmer or the storekeeper. You can get a hearty meal from the Kings Head Inn. ✉ *Exit 259, Trans-Canada Hwy. (near Prince William),* ☎ *506/363–5090.* ✉ *$8.75.* ☉ *June–mid-Oct., daily 10–5.*

SAINT JOHN RIVER VALLEY TO SAINT JOHN

The Saint John River forms 120 km (74 mi) of the border with Maine and rolls down to Saint John, New Brunswick's largest, and Canada's oldest, city. Gentle hills of rich farmland and the blue sweep of the water make this a pretty drive. The Trans-Canada Highway (Route 2) follows the banks of the river for most of its winding, 403-km (250-mi) course. At the northern end of the valley, near the border with Québec, is the mythical Republic of Madawaska. In the early 1800s the narrow wedge of land was coveted by Québec and New Brunswick; the United States claimed it as well. To settle the issue, New Brunswick governor Sir Thomas Carleton rolled dice all night with the governor of British North America at Québec. Sir Thomas won at dawn—by one point. Settling the border with the Americans was more difficult; even the lumbermen engaged in combat. Finally, in 1842, the British flag was hoisted over Madawaska county. One old-timer, tired of being asked to which country he belonged, replied, "I am a citizen of the Republic of Madawaska." So began the republic, which exists today with its own flag (an eagle on a field of white) and a coat of arms.

St-Jacques

280 km (174 mi) north of Fredericton.

This town near the Québec border contains Les Jardins de la République Provincial Park, with recreational facilities, the Antique Auto Museum, and a botanical garden. In the **New Brunswick Botanical Garden,** roses, rhododendrons, alpine flowers, and dozens of annuals and perennials bloom in the eight gardens while Mozart, Handel, Bach, or Vivaldi plays in the background. Two arboretums have coniferous and deciduous trees and shrubs. ✉ *Main St.,* ☎ *506/739–6335.* ✉ *$4.75.* ☉ *Mid-May–mid-Oct., daily 9–dusk.*

Skiing

Mont Farlagne (✉ Box 61, Edmundston E3V 3K7, ☎ 506/735–8401) in St-Jacques, near Edmundston, offers 17 trails on a vertical drop of 182 meters (600 ft). Its 4 lifts can handle 4,000 skiers per hour, and there is night skiing on 6 trails. Snowboarding and a tube slide add to the fun. There are equipment rentals, instruction, and a lounge with live music.

Edmundston

❼ *5 km (3 mi) from St. Jacques, 275 km (171 mi) northwest of Fredericton.*

Edmundston, the unofficial capital of Madawaska, has always depended on the wealth of the deep forest around it. Even today, Edmundston looks to the Fraser Company pulp mills as the major source of employment. It was in these woods that the legend of Paul Bunyan was born; tales spread to Maine and even to the West Coast. The **Foire Brayonne** festival (☎ 506/739–6608), held annually during the last week of July, is proud to claim the title of the biggest Francophone festival outside of Québec's Winter Carnival. It is one of the most lively and vibrant cultural events in New Brunswick, offering concerts by acclaimed artists as well as local musicians and entertainers.

Grand Falls

❽ *50 km (31 mi) south of St. Jacques.*

At Grand Falls, the Saint John throws itself over a high cliff, squeezes through a narrow rocky gorge, and emerges as a wider river. The result is a magnificent cascade, whose force has worn strange round wells in the rocky bed—some as much as 16 ft in circumference and 30 ft deep. A **pontoon boat** operates June–October at the lower end of the gorge ($8 adults, $4 children) and offers an entirely new perspective of the cliffs and wells. Tickets are available at the Malabeam Tourist Info Centre (✉ 24 Madawaska Rd., ☎ 506/475–7788).

The **Gorge Walk,** which starts at the tourist information center (✉ 24 Madawaska Rd.) and covers the full length of the gorge, is dotted with interpretation panels and interesting monuments. There is no charge for the walk, unless you descend to the wells ($2). According to Indian legend, a young maiden named Malabeam led her Iroquois captors to their deaths over the foaming cataract rather than guide them to her village.

The **Grand Falls Historical Museum** depicts local history. ✉ 209 Sheriff St., ☎ 506/473–5265. 🎟 Free. ☯ July–Aug., Mon.–Sat. 9–5, Sun. 2–5; Sept.–June, by appointment.

Shopping

The studio and store of the **Madawaska Weavers** (✉ Main St., St-Léonard, north of Grand Falls, ☎ 506/423–6341) has handwoven items known the world over. Handsome skirts, stoles, and ties are some of the items for sale.

En Route About 75 km (47 mi) south of Grand Falls, stop in **Florenceville** for a look at the small but reputable Andrew and Laura McCain Gallery (✉ McCain St., ☎ 506/392–5249), which has launched the career of many New Brunswick artists. The Trans-Canada Highway is intriguingly scenic, but if you're looking for less crowded highways and typical small communities, cross the river to Route 105 at Hartland (about 20 km, or 12 mi, south of Florenceville), via the **longest covered bridge** in the world—1,282 ft in length.

Mactaquac Provincial Park

❾ *197 km (122 mi) south of Grand Falls.*

Within Mactaquac Provincial Park is Mactaquac Pond, whose existence is attributed to the building of the hydroelectric dam that has caused the upper Saint John River to flood as far up as Woodstock. Park facilities include an 18-hole golf course, two beaches with lifeguards, two marinas, supervised craft activities, and a dining room. There are 300 campsites; reservations are advised for high season. A privately operated power boat marina within the park rents canoes, paddleboats, windsurfers, and kayaks. ⊠ *Rte. 105 at Mactaquac Dam,* ☎ *506/363–4747.* ☞ *$3.50 per vehicle in summer, free off-season.* ☉ *Overnight camping mid-May–Thanksgiving.*

En Route From Fredericton to Saint John you have a choice of two routes. Route 7 cuts away from the river to run straight south for its fast 109 km (68 mi). Route 102 leads along the Saint John River through engaging communities. You don't have to decide until you hit Oromocto, the site of the Canadian Armed Forces Base, **Camp Gagetown** (not to be confused with the pretty town of Gagetown farther downriver), the largest military base in Canada. Prince Charles completed his helicopter training here. The base has an interesting military museum. ⊠ *Building A5,* ☎ *506/422–1304.* ☞ *Free.* ☉ *July–Aug., weekdays 9–5, weekends and holidays noon–5; Sept.–June, weekdays noon–4. After-hrs tours can be arranged.*

Gagetown

⑩ *50 km (31 mi) southeast of Fredericton.*

Gagetown, a pleasant historic community, bustles with artisans' studios and the summer sailors who tie up at the marina. The gingerbread-trimmed **Tilley House** takes you back to Canada's beginnings. Once the home of Sir Leonard Tilley, one of the Fathers of the Confederation, it now houses the **Queens County Museum.** ⊠ *Front St.,* ☎ *506/488–2966.* ☞ *$1.* ☉ *Mid-June–mid-Sept., daily 10–5.*

Shopping
Flo Grieg's (⊠ 36 Front St., ☎ 506/488–2074) carries superior pottery made on the premises. **Claremont House B&B** (⊠ Tilley Rd., ☎ 506/488–2825) displays unusual batik items and copper engravings. **Loomcrofters** (⊠ Loomcroft La. off Main St., ☎ 506/488–2400) is a good choice for handwoven items.

OFF THE BEATEN PATH

From Gagetown you can ferry across the river to Jemseg and continue to **Grand Lake Provincial Park** (☎ 506/385-2919), which offers freshwater swimming off the sandy beaches of Grand Lake. At Evandale (30 km, or 19 mi) south of Gagetown, you can ferry to Belleisle Bay and the beautiful **Kingston Peninsula,** with its mossy Loyalist graveyards and pretty churches.

Saint John

70 km (43 mi) south of Gagetown.

Saint John, the first incorporated city (1785) in Canada, has that weather-beaten quality common to so many antique seaport communities. Although the city is sometimes termed a blue-collar town because so many of its residents work for Irving Oil, its genteel Loyalist heritage lingers; you sense it in the grand old buildings, the ladies' teas at the old Union Club, and the lovingly restored redbrick buildings of the downtown harbor district.

In 1604 two Frenchmen, Samuel de Champlain and Sieur de Monts, landed here on Saint John the Baptist Day to trade with the natives. Nearly two centuries later, in May 1785, 3,000 Loyalists escaping from the Revolutionary War poured off a fleet of ships to found a city amid the rocks and forests. From those beginnings, Saint John has emerged as a shipbuilding center and a thriving industrial port.

Up until the early 1980s, the buildings around Saint John's waterfront huddled together in forlorn dilapidation, their facades crumbling and blurred by a century of grime. A surge of civic pride sparked a major renovation project that reclaimed these old warehouses as part of a successful waterfront development.

The city has spawned many of the province's major artists—Jack Humphrey, Millar Brittain, and Fred Ross—along with such Hollywood notables as Louis B. Mayer, Donald Sutherland, and Walter Pidgeon. There's also a large Irish population that emerges in a jubilant Irish Festival every March. In July costumed residents reenact the landing of the Loyalists during the Loyalist City Festival.

Brochures for three good self-guided city tours are available at information centers, including one in Market Square. In July and August, free guided walking tours begin at 10 and 2 in Market Square at Barbour's General Store. For information call the Saint John Tourist and Convention Center (☎ 506/658–2990).

A Good Walk

Saint John is a city on hills, and **King Street** ⑪, its main street, slopes steeply to the harbor. A system of escalators/elevators and skywalks inside buildings means you can climb to the top and take in some of the more memorable spots without effort; you can also walk outside if you wish. Start at the foot of King, **Market Slip** ⑫. This is where the Loyalists landed in 1783 and is the site of **Barbour's General Store** and the Little Red Schoolhouse. Here you'll also find **Market Square,** with its visitor information center, restaurants, shops, and the fine **New Brunswick Museum** ⑬.

From the second level of Market Square, a skywalk crosses Dock Street and an escalator takes you up into the City Hall shopping concourse. Here, if you wish, you can branch off to the Canada Games Aquatic Centre and its pools and fitness facilities; and Harbour Station with a busy schedule of concerts, sporting events, and trade shows. Once you are through City Hall, another skywalk takes you across Chipman Hill and into the **Brunswick Square Complex** of shops, hotel, and office space. To visit historic **Loyalist House** ⑭, exit onto Germain Street and turn left: it's on the corner at the top of the hill. In the flavorful **Old City Market** ⑮, across from Brunswick Square, you'll make your way past fishmongers, farmers, and craftspeople. When you leave by the door at the top of the market, you will be at "the head of King" and right across Charlotte Street from **King Square** ⑯. Take a walk through the square, past the statues and bandstand, to Sydney Street. Cross Sydney and you're in the **Loyalist Burial Grounds** ⑰. Make your way back to Sydney Street at King Street East; across King Street is the **Old Courthouse** ⑱ with its amazing spiral staircase. Continue up Sydney; turn right on King Square South and you're at the gilded and gorgeous Imperial Theatre (☞ Nightlife and the Arts, *below*). Follow King Square South and cross Charlotte Street to reach the back door of historic **Trinity Church** ⑲. You can enter this way or walk back to King Street, turn left, and turn left onto Germain Street for the imposing gates and stairs of Trinity's main entrance.

To end your walk, make your way back to King Street and walk down the hill toward the water. You'll notice a plaque near the corner of Canterbury Street (at 20 King Street) that identifies a site where Benedict Arnold operated a coffeehouse. At the foot of the hill is **Prince William**

Street, just steps from where you began at Market Slip. Turn left for wonderful shops and historic architecture.

TIMING

Allow the better part of a day for this walk, if you include a few hours for the New Brunswick Museum and some time for shopping. You can walk the route in a couple of hours, though. Note that on Sunday some of the indoor walkways will be closed, and so will the City Market.

Sights to See

Barbour's General Store. This 19th-century shop is filled with the mingled aromas of tobacco, pickles, smoked fish, peppermint sticks, and dulse, an edible seaweed. ⊠ *Market Slip,* ☎ *506/658–2939.*

Brunswick Square Complex. Buildings here include the Delta Brunswick Hotel and Brunswick Square, a multilevel mall and office tower. The major office tower tenant is NB Tel, a highly innovative communications company.

16 **King Square.** Laid out in a Union Jack pattern, this green refuge has a two-story bandstand and a number of monuments. In its northeast corner you'll find a strange mass of metal on the ground. It is actually a great lump of melted stock from a neighboring hardware store that was demolished in Saint John's Great Fire of 1877, in which hundreds of buildings were destroyed. ⊠ *Between Charlotte and Sydney Sts.*

11 **King Street.** The steep main street of the city is lined with solid Victorian redbrick buildings filled with a variety of shops.

17 **Loyalist Burial Grounds.** This cemetery, now a landscaped park, is like a history book published in stone. Brick walkways and a beaver-dam fountain make it a delightful spot. ⊠ *Off Sydney St., between King and E. Union Sts.*

14 **Loyalist House.** Daniel David Merritt, a wealthy Loyalist merchant, built this imposing Georgian structure in 1810. It is distinguished by its authentic period furniture and eight fireplaces. ⊠ *120 Union St.,* ☎ *506/652–3590.* ☞ *$2.* ☉ *June–Sept., daily 10–5; Oct.–May, by appointment.*

12 **Market Slip.** This waterfront area at the foot of King Street is where the Loyalists landed in 1783. Today it's the site of the Saint John Hilton, an information center, and restaurants, but you still get a feeling for the city's maritime heritage.

Market Square. Restored buildings on the waterfront have been attractively developed and hold historic exhibits, shops, restaurants, and cafés. Also here are the Saint John Regional Library and the fine **New Brunswick Museum.**

★ ⊙ **13** **New Brunswick Museum.** With three floors of natural history, New Brunswick history, and art galleries, this inviting museum has something for everyone. The full-size suspended right whale model and skeleton are impossible to miss. Hike through time on a geologic trail; encounter the industries that shaped the province, from logging to shipping, in displays that re-create the past; and see fine and decorative art from New Brunswick and around the world. There's also a Family Discovery Gallery and a gift shop. ⊠ *Market Sq.,* ☎ *506/643–2300.* ☞ *$6, free Wed. 6–9.* ☉ *Weekdays 9–9, Sat. 10–6, Sun. noon–5.*

15 **Old City Market.** Built in 1876 with a ceiling like an inverted ship's keel, the handsome market occupies a city block between Germain and Charlotte streets. Its temptations include fresh-cooked lobster, great cheeses, dulse, and tasty, inexpensive snacks, along with plenty of

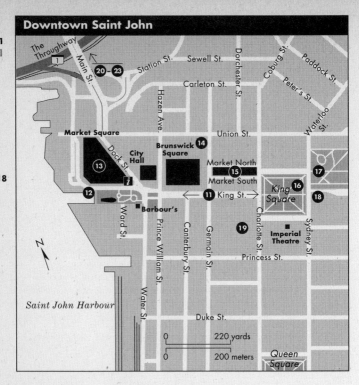

Downtown Saint John

souvenir and craft items. ⊠ *47 Charlotte St.,* ☎ *506/658–2820.*
◯ *Mon.–Thurs. 7:30–6, Fri. 7:30–7, Sat. 7:30–5.*

⑱ Old Courthouse. This 1829 neoclassical building has a spiral staircase,
built of tons of unsupported stones, that ascends seemingly by mira-
cle for three stories. You can see the staircase year-round during business hours, except when court is in session. ⊠ *King St. E and Sydney
St.* ⊠ *Free.*

Prince William Street. South of King Street near Market Slip, this street
is full of historic bank and business buildings. Today they hold interesting shops and galleries. At the foot of the street is the lamp known
as the Three Sisters, which was erected to guide ships into the harbor
in 1848.

⑲ Trinity Church. The church dates from 1880, when it was rebuilt after
the Great Fire. Inside, over the west door, note the coat of arms—a
symbol of the monarchy—rescued from the council chamber in Boston
by a British colonel during the American Revolution. It was deemed a
worthy refugee and given a place of honor in the church. ⊠ *115 Charlotte St.,* ☎ *506/693–8558 for information about hrs.*

A Good Drive

A car can take you to a number of area sights around downtown. The
Reversing Falls ⑳ are a fascinating phenomenon. Any bus headed west
from downtown will also take you there, or take Dock Street over the
viaduct and on to Main Street. For the industrial waterfront route to
the falls, turn left off Main at Keddy's Hotel. For a more scenic route,
keep going up Main and turn left onto Douglas Avenue, with its grand
old homes. A right turn off Douglas Avenue onto Fallsview Drive
takes you to a great Reversing Falls lookout. If you continue down Douglas Avenue, keep right, and cross the Reversing Falls Bridge; the Reversing Falls Tourist Bureau and interpretation center are on your left.

In case you want to see the world.

At American Express, we're here to make your journey a smooth one. So we have over 1,700 travel service locations in over 120 countries ready to help. What else would you expect from the world's largest travel agency?

do more

http://www.americanexpress.com/travel

Travel

In case you want to be welcomed there.

We're here to see that you're always welcomed at establishments everywhere. That's why millions of people carry the American Express® Card – for peace of mind, confidence, and security, around the world or just around the corner.

do more

Cards

In case you're running low.

We're here to help with more than 118,000 Express Cash locations around the world. In order to enroll, just call American Express before you start your vacation.

do more

Express Cash

And just in case.

We're here with American Express® Travelers Cheques and Cheques *for Two.*® They're the safest way to carry money on your vacation and the surest way to get a refund, practically anywhere, anytime.

Another way we help you ...

do more®

Travelers Cheques

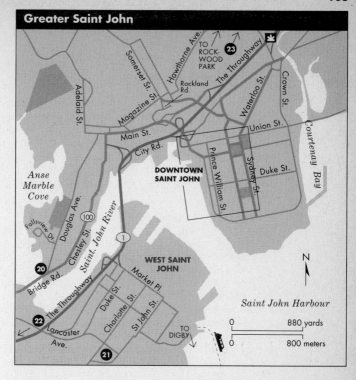

Also west of the city is the historic **Carleton Martello Tower** ㉑. Turn left from the Reversing Falls Tourist Bureau, past the Simms Brush Factory, and bear left when the road splits. The rest of the way is well marked. Off Route 1 at Catherwood Drive, the **Irving Nature Park** ㉒, 600 acres of volcanic rock and forest along the Bay of Fundy shore, has walking trails that make you feel far from the city. If you have children, you may want to visit **Cherry Brook Zoo** ㉓, to the north of downtown Saint John.

TIMING

To fully appreciate the Reversing Falls takes time; you need to visit at high, slack, and low tides. Check with any visitor information office for these times to help you plan a visit.

Sights to See

㉑ **Carleton Martello Tower.** This is a great place to survey the harbor. The tower was built during the war of 1812 as a precaution against American attack. The guides will tell you about the spartan life of a soldier living in the stone fort, and an audiovisual presentation outlines its role in the defense of Saint John during World War II. ✉ *Whipple St. at Fundy Dr.* ☎ *506/636–4011.* ▭ *$2.25.* ◷ *June–mid-Oct., daily 9–5.*

㉓ **Cherry Brook Zoo.** An entertaining monkey house, wildebeests, and other exotic species are highlights of this small zoo. It's at the northern end of **Rockwood Park** (☎ 506/658–2829), which has plenty of activities. ✉ *R.R. 1, Sandy Point Rd.,* ☎ *506/634–1440.* ▭ *$4.75.* ◷ *Daily 10– dusk.*

㉒ **Irving Nature Park.** At this lovely 600-acre reserve on a peninsula close to downtown you can experience the ecosystems of the southern New Brunswick coast. Roads and seven walking trails up to several miles long make bird- and nature-watching easy. From downtown take

Route 1 west to Exit 107 (Catherwood Rd.) south; follow Sand Cove Road 4½ km (3 mi) to the park. ⊠ *Sand Cove Rd,* ☎ *506/634–7135 for seasonal access.* ☑ *Free.*

㉒ Reversing Falls. Twice daily at the Reversing Falls rapids, the strong Fundy tides rise faster than the river can empty, and the tide water attempts to push the river water back upstream. When the tide ebbs, the river once again pours over the rock ledges and the rapids appear to reverse themselves. To learn more about the phenomenon, watch the film shown at the **Reversing Falls Tourist Bureau.** There's a restaurant here, too. You can also ride a jet boat (☞ Outdoor Activities and Sports, *below*) for a closer (and wetter) look. A pulp mill on the bank is less scenic, and the stench it occasionally sends out is one of the less-than-charming parts of a visit. ⊠ *Rte. 100, Reversing Falls Bridge,* ☎ *506/658–2937.*

Dining and Lodging

$$$ ✕ **Top of the Town.** This dining room at Keddy's Fort Howe Hotel has a spectacular view of the harbor and city as well as a sophisticated menu. Local seafood is creatively prepared; Fundy scallops are a specialty, and the Maritime Mix—mussels, herring, and lobster—is a favorite. ⊠ *Main and Portland Sts.,* ☎ *506/657–7320, 506/657–7325 direct line after 5 PM. Reservations essential. AE, DC, MC, V.*

$$ ✕ **Mexicali Rosa's.** For a franchise this restaurant has a lot of character. The decor is essentially Santa Fe style, with adobe arches and so forth. The specialty is California-Mexican food, which is heavy on sauces, as opposed to Tex-Mex, which concentrates more on meats. Guests waiting to be seated can order a fine margarita in the large lounge. The chimichangas are with good reason the most popular dish. ⊠ *88 Prince William St.,* ☎ *506/652–5252. AE, MC, V.*

$–$$ ✕ **Grannan's.** Seafood brochette with scallops, shrimp, and lobster tail, sautéed at your table in a white-wine and mushroom sauce, is a favorite in this nautically decorated restaurant, but there are abundant choices. The desserts, including bananas Foster flambéed at your table, are memorable. Dining spills over onto the sidewalk in summer. ⊠ *1 Market Sq.,* ☎ *506/634–1555. AE, DC, MC, V.*

$–$$ ✕ **Incredible Edibles.** Here you can enjoy down-to-earth food—biscuits, garlic-laden hummus, salads, pastas, and desserts—in cozy rooms or, in summer, on the outdoor terrace. The menu also includes beef and chicken dishes. ⊠ *42 Princess St.,* ☎ *506/633–7554. AE, DC, MC, V. Closed Sun.*

$$–$$$ ✕🏨 **Saint John Hilton.** Part of the Market Square complex, this Hilton is furnished in Loyalist decor; guest rooms overlook the harbor or the town. Mellow antiques furnish corners of the Turn of the Tide dining room and the medieval-style Great Hall, which hosts banquets. A pedestrian walkway system connects the 12-story property to uptown shops, restaurants, a library, museum, an aquatic center, and a civic center. The large Turn of the Tide restaurant has terrific views of the harbor. Although the dining is pleasant at all times, with seafood and meat choices, the best meal is the Sunday brunch, with a long table full of dishes from the exotic to the tried-and-true. ⊠ *1 Market Sq., E2L 4Z6,* ☎ *506/693–8484 or 800/561–8282 (Canada only),* FAX *506/657–6610. 197 rooms. Restaurant, bar, pool, exercise room. AE, D, DC, MC, V.*

$$–$$$ ✕🏨 **Shadow Lawn Country Inn.** This charming inn is in an affluent
★ suburb, with tree-lined streets and palatial houses, 10 minutes from Saint John. Tennis, golf, horseback riding, and a yacht club are nearby. The inn has antique-furnished bedrooms, some with fireplaces; one suite has a whirlpool bath. The dining room is open to the public for three

meals a day; seafood is a specialty. Continental breakfast is included in the room rate. ⊠ *3180 Rothesay Rd., Rothesay E2E 5V7,* ☎ *506/ 847–7539 or 800/561–4166,* FAX *506/849–9238. 9 rooms, 2 suites. Restaurant. AE, D, DC, MC, V.*

Nightlife and the Arts

THE ARTS

The **Imperial Theatre** (⊠ King Sq., ☎ 506/633–9494 for box office), a beautifully restored 1913 vaudeville theatre, is home to Saint John's theater, opera, ballet, and symphony productions as well as road shows. **Aitken Bicentennial Exhibition Centre (ABEC)** (⊠ 20 Hazen Ave., ☎ 506/633–4870), in a former Carnegie library, has several galleries displaying the work of local artists and artisans, a hands-on science gallery for children, and a spring/fall Listen and Lunch series. Admission is free.

NIGHTLIFE

Taverns and lounges, usually with music of some kind, provide lively nightlife. Top musical groups, noted professional singers, and other performers regularly appear at **Harbour Station** (⊠ 99 Station St., ☎ 506/ 657–1234). **O'Leary's Pub** (⊠ 46 Princess St., ☎ 506/634–7135) is in the middle of the Trinity Royal Preservation Area and specializes in old-time Irish fun complete with Celtic performers; on Wednesday, Brent Mason, a well-known neo-folk artist, starts the evening with a set and then turns the mike over to the audience.

Outdoor Activities and Sports

BOAT TOURS

The **Reversing Falls Jet Boat** ride (⊠ 55 Fallsview Dr., 1 Market Sq., (☎ 506/634–8987 or 506/634–8824) could be the 20-minute thrill of a lifetime as you view the Reversing Falls close up. At complete low tide passengers must be 16 years or older; at other times children are welcome. Cost is $20 per person. **Harbor tours** are offered by Partridge Island Tours (☎ 506/693–2598) and DMK Marine Tours (☎ 506/ 635–4150).

KAYAKING

Kayaking along the Fundy coast has become very popular. **Eastern Outdoors** (⊠ Brunswick Sq., ☎ 506/634–1530 or 800/565–2925) has single and double kayaks, lessons, tours, and white-water rafting on the world-famous Reversing Falls Rapids and other river systems.

Shopping

Prince William Street provides interesting browsing in antiques shops and crafts boutiques. **House of Tara** (⊠ 72 Prince William St., ☎ 506/ 634–8272) is wonderful for fine Irish linens and woolens. **Brunswick Square** (⊠ King and Germain Sts., ☎ 506/658–1000), a vertical mall, has many top-quality boutiques. **Old City Market,** between Charlotte and Germain streets, bustles Monday–Saturday and stocks delicious local specialties, such as maple syrup and lobster.

THE FUNDY COAST

Bordering the chilly and powerful tidal Bay of Fundy is some of New Brunswick's loveliest coastline. A tour of the region will take you from the border town of St. Stephen and the lovely resort village of St. Andrews, past tiny fishing villages and rocky coves, to Fundy National Park, where the world's most extreme tides rise and fall twice daily. The Fundy Isles—Grand Manan Island, Deer Island, and Campobello—are havens of peace that have lured harried mainlanders for generations.

St. Stephen

㉔   *107 km (66 mi) west of Saint John.*

St. Stephen is over the St. Croix River from Calais, Maine. There's a provincial visitor information center (☎ 506/466–7390) on King Street. The town is a mecca for chocoholics, who converge on the small town during the Chocolate Festival held early in August. "Choctails," chocolate puddings and cakes, and even complete chocolate meals should come as no surprise when you realize that it was here that the chocolate bar was invented. Sample Ganong's famed, hand-dipped chocolates at the factory store, the **Ganong Chocolatier.** ✉ *73 Mill-town Blvd.,* ☎ *506/465–5611.* ۞ *July–Aug., weekdays 9–8, weekends 9–5; Sept.–Dec., daily 9–5; Jan.–June, Mon.–Sat. 9–5.*

Crocker Hill Studios and Gardens, on the banks of the St. Croix River, is a lovely oasis 3 km (2 mi) east of downtown. Walk down the path to the artists' studio of Steve Smith and his wife, Gail, with its watercolor bird paintings and carved decoys. It is surrounded by a fragrant, tranquil garden with hundreds of herbs and flowers. Relax on one of the comfortable garden benches and watch the osprey and eagles soar over the river. There is a gift shop. ✉ *R.R. 3, Ledge Rd.,* ☎ *506/466–4251.* 🎟 *$3.* ۞ *June–Sept., daily 10–5; Oct.–May, by appointment or chance.*

St. Andrews by-the-Sea

★ **㉕**   *29 km (18 mi) southeast of St. Stephen.*

On Passamaquoddy Bay, St. Andrews by-the-Sea is one of North America's prettiest and least-spoiled resort towns. Long the summer place of the affluent (mansions ring the town), St. Andrews retains its year-round population of fishermen, and little has changed in the past two centuries. Of the town's 550 buildings, 280 were erected before 1880; 14 have survived from the 1700s. Some Loyalists even brought their homes with them piece by piece from Castile, Maine, across the bay, when the American Revolution didn't go their way.

Pick up a walking-tour map at the tourist information center at 46 Reed Avenue (next to the arena) and follow it through the pleasant streets. A particular gem is the **Court House** (✉ 123 Frederick St., ☎ 506/529–4248), which is still active. Within these old stone walls is the **Old Gaol,** home of the county's archives. Tours are given weekdays 9–5. **Greenock Church,** at the corner of Montague and Edward streets, owes its existence to a remark someone made at an 1822 dinner party about the "poor" Presbyterians not having a church of their own. Captain Christopher Scott, who took exception to the slur, spared no expense on the building, which is decorated with a carving of a green oak tree in honor of Scott's birthplace, Greenock, Scotland. Take time to stroll along **Water Street** down by the harbor, with its assortment of eateries, gift and craft shops, and artists' studios.

The **Ross Memorial Museum** is a monument to an American family, summer residents of St. Andrews, who really appreciated beautiful things. ✉ *188 Montague St.,* ☎ *506/529–1824.* 🎟 *Free.* ۞ *Late May–June and early October, Mon.–Sat. 10–4:30; July–Sept., Mon.–Sat. 10–4:30, Sun. 1:30–4:30; shoulder seasons, Tues.–Sat. 10–4:30.*

Kingsbrae Gardens, a horticultural garden complete with mazes, is scheduled to open in spring 1998 on 27 acres of a historic estate. At press time no specific information was available on admission prices and hours. ✉ *220 King St.,* ☎ *506/529–3335.*

The **Huntsman Aquarium and Museum** houses marine life and displays, including some very entertaining seals fed at 11 and 4 daily. ⊠ *Brandy Cove Rd.,* ☎ *506/529–1202.* ⊠ *$4.50.* ⊗ *May–June, daily 10–4:30; July–Aug., daily 10–6; Sept.–Oct., Mon.–Tues. noon–4:30, Wed.–Sun. 10–4:30.*

OFF THE
BEATEN PATH

MINISTERS ISLAND – Besides being a huge estate, complete with an ocean-fed swimming pool, the house (not fully restored) and buildings on this island retreat are historically significant. Covenhoven was the summer home of Sir William Van Horne, chairman of the Canadian Pacific Railway, who presided over the railroad's push through the Rocky Mountains. Getting here is an adventure: Line up on the Bar Road at low tide (check local schedules), and you drive across the sand bar to the island for a tour. ⊠ *Bar Rd., 5 km (3 mi) north of St. Andrews,* ☎ *506/ 529-5081 for tour information.* ⊠ *$5.* ⊗ *Open June–Oct., daylight hrs at low tide.*

Dining and Lodging

$$–$$$ ✕ **The Gables.** Salads, lobster rolls, fish and seafood fried or grilled, and fresh-made desserts are served in this casual harborside eatery. You can eat outside on the deck in summer. ⊠ *143 Water St.,* ☎ *506/529– 3440. MC, V.*

$$$ ✕🏠 **The Algonquin.** The wraparound veranda of this grand old resort
★ hotel overlooks wide lawns and lush gardens, and the bellmen wear kilts, setting a mood of relaxed elegance. Rooms, especially those in a new wing, are comfortable and attractively decorated. The excellent dining room is noted for its buffets and seafood. In good weather, meals are served on the veranda. There are fewer services in winter, so call if you plan to visit then. ⊠ *Rte. 127, E0G 2X0,* ☎ *506/529–8823 or 800/563–4299,* ⅎⅩ *506/529–4194. 250 rooms. 2 restaurants, 2 bars, pool, 9-hole and 18-hole golf course, tennis courts, health club, bicycles, children's program. AE, DC, MC, V.*

$$$–$$$$ 🏠 **Kingsbrae Arms.** This restored 1897 estate (the first of its kind to receive five stars from the Canada Select rating agency) is an experience as much as it is a property. The many antique furnishings are both eclectic and entertaining. The decor is classy but full of pampering touches, the garden magnificent, and the owners gregarious. Breakfast is included. ⊠ *219 King St., E0G 2X0,* ☎ *506/529–1897,* ⅎⅩ *506/529– 1197. 6 rooms, 3 suites. Pool. MC, V.*

$$$ 🏠 **Pansy Patch.** A visit to this B&B, a Normandy-style farmhouse built in 1912, is a bit like a close encounter with landed gentry who are patrons of the arts and who like their gardens as rich and formal as their meals. There's an art gallery. Breakfast is included in the price. Nonguests are welcome for lunch and dinner. ⊠ *59 Carleton St., E0G 2X0* ☎ *506/529–3834. 5 rooms. Restaurant. D, MC, V.*

Outdoor Activities and Sports

GOLF
Algonquin Golf Club (☎ 506/529–3062) has a lovely setting.

WATER SPORTS
At the **Adventure Destination Center** on Market Wharf downtown, you can arrange to explore Passamaquoddy Bay on various kinds of boats. **Fundy Tide Runners** (⊠ Market Wharf, ☎ 506/529–4481) uses a 24-ft Zodiac to search for whales, seals, and marine birds. **Seascape Kayak Tours** (⊠ Market Wharf, ☎ 506/529–4866) provides instruction as well as trips around the area from a half day to a week.

Shopping

The Sea Captain's Loft (⊠ Water St., ☎ 506/529–3190) specializes in English and New Brunswick woolens, English bone china, and marvelous wool yarn. **Cottage Craft** (⊠ Town Sq., ☎ 506/529–3190) employs knitters year-round to make mittens and sweaters from their specially dyed wool. **Tom Smith's Studio** (⊠ Water St., ☎ 506/529–4234) is highly regarded for Asian *raku* pottery.

Grand Manan Island

㉖ *2 hrs by car ferry from Black's Harbour.*

Grand Manan, the largest of the three Fundy Islands, is also the farthest away from the mainland; you might see spouting whales, sunning seals, or a rare puffin on the way over. Circular herring weirs dot the island's coastal waters, and fish sheds and smokehouses lie beside long wharfs that reach out to bobbing fishing boats. Place names are romantic—Swallowtail, Southern Head, Seven Days Work, and Dark Harbour. It's easy to get around—only about 32 km (20 mi) of road lead from the lighthouse at Southern Head to the one at Northern Head. Grand Manan attracted John James Audubon, that human encyclopedia of birds, in 1831. The puffin is the island's symbol. Whale-watching expeditions can be booked at the Marathon Inn and the Compass Rose (☞ Dining and Lodging *and* Whale-Watching, *below*), and scuba diving to old wrecks is popular. You can make a day trip here or plan a longer stay and really relax. Ferry service is provided by **Coastal Transport** (☎ 506/662–3724).

Lodging

$$–$$$ ▥ **Marathon Inn.** Perched on a hill overlooking the harbor, this gracious mansion built by a sea captain has guest rooms furnished with antiques. Whale- and bird-watching cruises can be arranged. The dining room specializes in seafood; it does not serve lunch. ⊠ *Box 129, North Head E0G 2M0,* ☎ *506/662–8488. 28 rooms, half with bath. Restaurant, 2 lounges, pool, tennis court. MC, V.*

$$ ▥ **Compass Rose.** A couple from Montréal fell in love with the lovely guest rooms and comfortable turn-of-the-century furnishings in the two old houses that have been combined into this small, English-style country inn. They bought the inn and upgraded the dining room that overlooks the harbor, where they serve morning and afternoon teas as well as lunch and dinner. A full English breakfast is included in the rate. ⊠ *North Head E0G 2M0,* ☎ *506/662–8570. 8 rooms. Restaurant. MC, V.*

Outdoor Activities and Sports

TOURS

More than 240 species of seabirds nest on Grand Manan Island, which draws painters, nature photographers, hikers, and whale-watchers. Any of these activities can be arranged by calling **Tourism New Brunswick** (⊠ Box 12345, Fredericton E3B 5C3, ☎ 506/453–2170 or 800/561–0123).

WHALE-WATCHING

One New Brunswick experience that is difficult to forget is the sighting of a huge humpback, right whale, finback, or minke. Grand Manan boasts several whale-watching operators: **Ocean Search** (⊠ Marathon Inn, North Head, ☎ 506/662–8488); **Sea Land Adventure** (⊠ Box 86, Castalia E0G 1K0, ☎ 506/662–8997); **Island Coast Boat Tours** (⊠ Box 59, Castalia E0G 1L0, ☎ 506/662–8181); **Sea Watch Tours** (⊠ Box 48, Seal Cove E0G 3B0, ☎ 506/662–8552); **Surfside Boat Tours** (⊠ Box 147, Castalia E0G 1L0, ☎ 506/662–8156).

Campobello Island

★ ㉗ *45 min ferry ride from Deer Island. By road, drive to St. Stephen, cross the border to Maine, drive about 80 km (50 mi) down Rte. 1, then Rte. 190 to Lubec, Maine, and a bridge.*

Neatly manicured, preening itself in the bay, Campobello Island has always had a special appeal to the wealthy and the famous. It was here that the Roosevelt family spent their summers. The 34-room rustic summer cottage of the family of President Franklin Delano Roosevelt is now part of a nature preserve, **Roosevelt International Park,** a joint project of the Canadian and American governments. You can walk miles of trails here. President Roosevelt's boyhood home was also the setting for the movie *Sunrise at Campobello.* ⊠ *Roosevelt Park Rd.,* ☎ *506/752–2922.* 🎫 *Free.* ☉ *House late May–mid-Oct., daily 10–6; grounds daily.*

The island's **Herring Cove Provincial Park** (⊠ Welshpool, ☎ 506/752–7010) has camping facilities and a nine-hole golf course.

Dining and Lodging

$$ ✕🏠 **Lupine Lodge.** Originally a vacation home built by the Adams family (friends of the Roosevelts) around the turn of the century, these three attractive log buildings set on a bluff overlooking the Bay of Fundy are now a modern guest lodge. Nature trails connect it to Herring Cove Provincial Park. Two of the cabins comprise the guest rooms; the third houses the dining room, which specializes in simple but well-prepared local seafood. ⊠ *Box 2, Welshpool E0G 3H0,* ☎ *506/752–2555. 10 rooms, 1 suite. Restaurant, lounge. MC, V.*

$$ 🏠 **Owen House.** Mellow with history, this 200-year-old home, now a bit worn, was built by Admiral Owen, who fancied himself ruler of the island. Its gracious old rooms have hosted such luminaries as actress Greer Garson. Breakfasts are wonderful—pancakes come topped with local berries. ⊠ *Welshpool E0G 3H0,* ☎ *506/752–2977. 3 rooms. MC, V.*

Deer Island

㉘ *40 min by free car ferry from Letete, 13 km (8 mi) south of St. George.*

On Deer Island you'll enjoy exploring the fishing wharves, such as those at Chocolate Cove. Exploring the island takes only a few hours; it's 12 km (7 mi) long, varying in width from almost 5 km (3 mi) to a few hundred feet at some points. At **Deer Point** you can walk through a small nature park while waiting for the ferry to Campobello Island. If you listen carefully, you may be able to hear the sighing and snorting of **"the Old Sow,"** the second largest whirlpool in the world. If you can't hear it, you'll be able to see it, just a few feet offshore.

Lodging

$–$$ 🏠 **West Isles World B&B.** This white frame house overlooks the cove and offers three snug rooms with an informal country feel; the big upstairs bedroom has a water view. A full breakfast is included. The owners will arrange whale-watching cruises for you. ⊠ *Lord's Cove E0G 2J0,* ☎ *506/747–2946. 3 rooms. No credit cards.*

$ 🏠 **45th Parallel Motel and Restaurant.** Deer Island has only one motel—fortunately, it's clean and comfortable. A full breakfast is complimentary, and everything from lobster to hot sandwiches is available at the informal restaurant. Three of the rooms have kitchenettes. Pets are welcome. ⊠ *Fairhaven E0G 1R0,* ☎ *506/747–2231. 10 rooms. Restaurant. AE, MC, V.*

Whale-Watching

Cline Marine Tours (☎ 506/529–2287) offers scenic and whale-watching tours.

St. George

㉙ *40 km (25 mi) east of St. Stephen, 60 km (37 mi) west of Saint John.*

St. George is a pretty town with some excellent bed-and-breakfasts, one of the oldest Protestant graveyards in Canada, and a fish ladder running up the side of a dam. Water runs through this concrete staircase, allowing fish to jump, step by step, to the top and then jump back in the river.

Lodging

$$ ▦ **Granite Town Hotel.** This hotel, built in 1990, has an old-country-inn feeling to it. The decor is subtle, with pine and washed-birch woodwork. Light blues and pinks dominate in the rooms. One side of the building overlooks an apple orchard; the other sits atop the bank of the Maguadavic River. A Continental breakfast is available but is not included in the rate; there is a barbecue available in summer. Two rooms have whirlpool baths. ⊠ *79 Main St., E0G 2Y0,* ☎ *506/755–6415,* ℻ *506/755–6009. 32 rooms. Restaurant, bar, boating, bicycles. AE, D, DC, MC, V.*

Sailing

Fundy Yacht Sales and Charter (⊠ Rte. 2, Dipper Harbour, Lepreau E0G 2H0, ☎ 506/634–1530 or 800/565–2925) charters sailboats.

OFF THE   **ST. MARTINS –** About 45 km (28 mi) east of Saint John on Route 111, the
BEATEN PATH fishing village of St. Martins has a rich shipbuilding heritage, whispering caves, miles of lovely beaches, spectacular tides, and a cluster of covered bridges. If you're tempted to linger, try the **St. Martins Country Inn** (☎ 506/833–4534).

Alma

135 km (84 mi) northeast of Saint John.

Alma is the small seaside town that services Fundy National Park. Here you'll find some motels, great lobster, and the local specialty, sticky buns.

★ ㉚ **Fundy National Park** is an awesome 206-square-km (80-square-mi) microcosm of New Brunswick's inland and coastal climates. Stand on a sandstone ledge above a dark-sand beach and watch the bay's phenomenal tide rise or fall. The park has 110 km (68 mi) of varied hiking and biking trails, as well as some gravel-surface auto trails. There's also golf, tennis, and a restaurant. ⊠ *Hwy. 114, Box 40, E0A 1B0,* ☎ *506/887–6000.* ▭ *$3.50 in summer.*

Outdoor Activities and Sports

GOLF

The **Fundy National Park Golf Club** (☎ 506/887–2970) is nestled near cliffs overlooking the restless Bay of Fundy; deer grazing on the course are one of its hazards.

SKIING AND SNOWMOBILING

Poley Mountain Ski Area (⊠ Box 1097, Sussex E0E 1P0, ☎ 506/433–3230) is 10 km (6 mi) from Sussex. Its 13 trails and snowboard park mean there's fun for everyone on this 660-ft vertical drop. Poley is also on the groomed Fundy Snowmobile Trail between Saint John and Moncton.

Cape Enrage

15 km (9 mi) from Alma.

Route 915 takes you to the wild driftwood-cluttered beach at Cape Enrage, which juts out into the bay. There's a lighthouse and some spectacular views. You can arrange for rappelling and other adventures here.

Outdoor Activities and Sports

Cape Enrage Adventures (⊠ Site 5-5, R.R. 1, Moncton, ☎ 506/856–6081 off-season, 506/887–2273 mid-May–mid-Sept.) arranges rappelling; fee is $40 per person for 3 hours. Canoeing, kayaking, and hiking are other options.

Hopewell Cape

40 km (25 mi) from Alma.

The coast road (Route 114) from Alma to Moncton winds through covered bridges and along rocky coasts. **The Rocks Provincial Park** (⊠ Rte. 114, ☎ 506/734–2026 or 506/734–3429 in season) is home of the famous Giant Flowerpots—rock formations carved by the Bay of Fundy tides. They're topped with vegetation and are uncovered only at low tide, when you can climb down for a closer study.

MONCTON AND THE ACADIAN PENINSULA

The white sands and gentle tides of the Northumberland Strait and Baie des Chaleurs are as different from the rocky cliffs and powerful tides of the Bay of Fundy as the Acadians are from the Loyalists. This tour takes you from the burgeoning city of Moncton with its high-tech industries, past sandy dunes, and through Acadian fishing villages.

Moncton

③ *80 km (50 mi) north of Alma.*

A friendly town, often called the Gateway to Acadia because of its mix of English and French and its proximity to the Acadian shore, Moncton has a renovated downtown, where wisely placed malls do a booming business. You can pick up a walking tour brochure and see the city's historic highlights, too.

This city has long touted two natural attractions: the Tidal Bore and the Magnetic Hill. You may be disappointed if you've read too much tourist hype, though. In days gone by, before the harbor mouth filled with silt, the **Tidal Bore** was an incredible sight, a high wall of water that surged in through the narrow opening of the river to fill red mud banks to the brim. It still moves up the river, and the moving wave is worth waiting for, but it's nowhere near as lofty as it used to be, except sometimes in the spring. Bore Park on Main Street is the best vantage point; viewing times are posted there.

Magnetic Hill creates a bizarre optical illusion. If you park your car in neutral at the designated spot, you'll seem to be coasting uphill without power. Shops, an amusement park, a zoo, a golf course, and a small railroad are part of the larger complex here; there are extra charges for the attractions. ⊠ *North of Moncton off Trans-Canada Hwy. (watch for signs).* ☉ *May–Labor Day, daily 8–8.* ⌑ *2$.*

An excellent family water-theme park, **Magic Mountain,** is adjacent to Magnetic Hill. ⊠ *North of Moncton off Trans-Canada Hwy.,*

☎ *506/857–9283.* 🎫 *$17.25.* ⊘ *Mid-June–July 1 and mid-Aug.–Labor Day, daily 10–6; July 2–mid-Aug., daily 10–8.*

Among Moncton's notable attractions is the **Acadian Museum,** at the University of Moncton, whose remarkable collection of artifacts reflects 300 years of Acadian life in the Maritimes. ⊠ *Clement Cormier Bldg., Archibald St.,* ☎ *506/858–4088.* 🎫 *Free.* ⊘ *June–Sept., weekdays 10–5, weekends 1–5; Oct.–May, Tues.–Fri. 1–4:30, weekends 1–4.*

Dining and Lodging

$$ ✕ **Cy's Seafood Restaurant.** This restaurant, decorated in dark wood
★   and brass, has been serving generous portions for decades. Though renowned for its seafood casserole, the restaurant also offers reliable scallop, shrimp, and lobster dishes. You can see the Tidal Bore from the windows. ⊠ *170 Main St.,* ☎ *506/857–0032. AE, DC, MC, V.*

$$ ✕ **Fisherman's Paradise.** In spite of the enormous dining area, which seats more than 350 people, this restaurant serves memorable à la carte seafood dishes in an atmosphere of candlelight and wood furnishings. ⊠ *375 Dieppe Blvd.,* ☎ *506/859–4388. AE, DC, MC, V.*

$$–$$$ ✕🏨 **Chez Françoise.** This lovely old mansion with a wraparound ve-
★   randa has been decorated in Victorian style. There are 9 guest rooms (six with private bath) in this house; another building across the street houses 10 (four with bath). Front rooms in the main house have water views. The dining room, open to the public for dinner, serves excellent traditional French cuisine with an emphasis on seafood. ⊠ *93 Main St., Shediac (30 km/19 mi northeast of Moncton),* ☎ *506/532–4233. 19 rooms, 10 with bath. Restaurant, bar. AE, D, DC, MC, V. Closed Jan.–May 1.*

$$$ 🏨 **Best Western Crystal Palace.** Moncton's newest hotel has theme rooms (want to be Ali Baba or Elvis for a night?) and, for families, an indoor pool and a miniature wonderland of rides, midway stalls, and coin games. Champlain Mall is just across the parking lot. ⊠ *499 Paul St.,* ☎ *506/ 858–8584,* 𝔉𝔄𝔛 *506/858–5486. 115 rooms. Restaurant, indoor pool. AE, D, DC, MC, V.*

$$$ 🏨 **Hotel Beausejour.** Moncton's finest hotel, conveniently located
★   downtown, has friendly service. The decor of the guest rooms echoes the city's Loyalist and Acadian roots. L'Auberge, the main hotel restaurant, has a distinct Acadian flavor. The Windjammer dining room is more formal, modeled after the opulent luxury liners of the turn of the century, and reservations are required. ⊠ *750 Main St.,* ☎ *506/854– 4344, 800/441–1414 in Canada and the U.S., 800/561–2328 in the Maritimes and Québec,* 𝔉𝔄𝔛 *506/858–0957. 314 rooms. 2 restaurants, bar, café, indoor pool, exercise room. AE, DC, MC, V.*

$$$ 🏨 **Victoria B & B.** This heritage home in the heart of downtown has antique-furnished rooms, with terry robes and aromatic bath gels. The full breakfast, served in the dining room and included in the rate, often features chocolate pecan and orange brandy French toast. ⊠ *71 Park St., E1C 2B2,* ☎ *506/389–8296,* 𝔉𝔄𝔛 *506/389–8296. 3 rooms. Dining room, in-room VCRs. MC, V.*

$$ 🏨 **Marshlands Inn.** In this white clapboard inn, a welcoming double
★   living room with fireplace sets the informal country atmosphere. Bed-rooms are furnished with sleigh beds or four-posters, and all have tele-phones. ⊠ *Box 1440, Sackville (53 km/33 mi east of Moncton) E0A 3C0,* ☎ *506/536–0170, 800/561–1256 in Canada,* 𝔉𝔄𝔛 *506/536– 0721. 19 rooms. Restaurant. AE, DC, MC, V.*

Nightlife and the Arts

THE ARTS

Top musicians and other performers appear at the **Colosseum** (☎ 506/857–4100).

NIGHTLIFE

Moncton's downtown really rocks at night. **Au Deuxième** (✉ 837 Main St., ☎ 506/383–6192) has live music on the weekends, mostly Francophone artists. **Ziggy's** (✉ 730 Main St., ☎ 506/858–8844) offers dance music and fun promotions. **Club Cosmopolitan** (✉ 700 Main St., ☎ 506/857–9117) is open Wednesday through Saturday for dancing, rock, jazz, or the blues. It's billed as one cool club with four different atmospheres. **Chevy's** (✉ 939 Mountain Rd., ☎ 506/858–5861) has comedy, rock and roll, and traditional music.

Shopping

Five spacious malls and numerous pockets of shops make Moncton and Dieppe the best places to shop in New Brunswick.

En Route   Along the coast from Moncton on Route 11 you'll find **Shediac,** a resort town with the warm waters of Parlee Beach and lots of good lobster feeds.

Kouchibouguac National Park

100 km (62 mi) north of Moncton.

★   The white, dune-edged beaches of **Kouchibouguac National Park** are some of the finest on the continent. Kellys Beach and Callander's Beach are supervised and have facilities. The park also protects forests and peat bogs. You can bicycle, canoe, boat, and picnic. There are 311 campsites; reservations are accepted. ✉ *Off Rtes. 11 and 134, Kent County,* ☎ *506/876–2443.* ☞ *$3.50.*

Miramichi City

32   *150 km (93 mi) north of Moncton.*

The fabled Miramichi region is one of lumberjacks and fishermen. Celebrated for salmon rivers that reach into some of the province's richest forests, and the ebullient nature of its residents (Scottish, English, Irish, and a smattering of native and French), this is a land of stories, folklore, and lumber kings.

Sturdy wood homes dot the banks of Miramichi Bay at newly formed Miramichi City, which in 1995 incorporated the former towns of Chatham and Newcastle and several small villages. This is also where the politician and British media mogul Lord Beaverbrook grew up and is buried.

The **Miramichi Salmon Museum** provides a look at the endangered Atlantic salmon and at life in noted fishing camps along the rivers. ✉ *297 Main St., Doaktown, 80 km (50 mi) southwest of Miramichi City,* ☎ *506/365–7787.* ☉ *June–Sept. daily 9–5.* ☞ *$4.*

The **Woodmen's Museum,** with artifacts that date from the 1700s to the present, is in what looks like two giant logs set on more than 60 acres of land. The museum portrays a lumberman's life through displays, but its tranquil grounds are excuse enough to visit. There are picnic facilities and camping sites. ✉ *Rte. 8, Boiestown, 110 km (68 mi) southwest of Miramichi City,* ☎ *506/369–7214.* ☞ *$5.* ☉ *May–Sept., daily 9–5.*

Lodging

$$ ⊡ **Pond's Chalet Resort.** You'll get a traditional fishing-camp experience in this lodge and the chalets set among trees overlooking a salmon river. The accommodations in Ludlow, 15 km (9 mi) northwest of Boiestown, are comfortable but not luxurious. You can canoe and bicycle here, too. The dining room turns out reliable but undistinguished food. ⊠ *Ludlow E0C 1N0 (watch for signs on Rte. 8),* ☎ *506/369–2612,* ℻ *506/369–2293. 10 guest rooms, a 5-bedroom lodge, and 14 cabins. Bar, dining room, tennis court, volleyball, snowmobiling. AE, DC, MC, V.*

$$ ⊡ **Wharf Inn.** Here, in Miramichi country, the staff is friendly and the restaurant serves excellent salmon dinners. This low-rise modern building has two wings; guest rooms in the executive wing have extra amenities. ⊠ *Jane St.,* ☎ *506/622–0302,* ℻ *506/622–0354. 70 rooms. Restaurant, bar, patio lounge, no-smoking rooms, indoor pool. AE, DC, MC, V.*

Outdoor Activities and Sports

In winter **Miramichi Four Seasons Outfitters** (⊠ Box 705, R.R. 2, ☎ 506/622–0089) offers custom dogsledding packages for all levels. In summer the outfitter leads hiking tours of the rocky coastline and inland highland tours for both experienced and casual trekkers.

Caraquet

㉝ *118 km (73 mi) north of Miramichi City.*

Caraquet, on the Acadian Peninsula, is perched along the Baie des Chaleurs, with Québec's Gaspé Peninsula beckoning across the inlet. The town is rich in French flavor and hosts an **Acadian Festival** (☎ 506/727–6515) each August. Beaches are another draw here.

★ ☾ ㉞ A highlight of the Acadian Peninsula is the **Acadian Historical Village,** 10 km (6 mi) west of Caraquet. The more than 40 original buildings re-create an early Acadian community between 1780 and 1890. Summer days are wonderfully peaceful: the chapel bell tolls, ducks waddle and quack under a footbridge, wagons creak, and the smell of hearty cooking wafts from cottage doors. Costumed staff act as guides and demonstrate trades; a restaurant serves old-Acadian dishes. ⊠ *Rte. 11,* ☎ *506/726–2600.* ☞ *$8.75.* ☉ *June–Labor Day, daily 10–6; some buildings open in Sept., daily 10–5.*

Dining and Lodging

$–$$ ✕⊡ **Hotel Paulin.** The word *quaint* really fits this property. Each pretty room has its own unique look, with old pine dressers and brass beds, and the colors are as bright and cheerful as the seaside town. An excellent small dining room specializes in fresh fish cooked to perfection, Acadian style. ⊠ *143 blvd. St-Pierre W, E1W 1B6,* ☎ *506/727–9981. 9 rooms, 4 with bath, 1 suite. Dining room. MC, V.*

Skiing

Sugarloaf Provincial Park (⊠ Box 629, Atholville E0K 1A0, ☎ 506/789–2366) is in Atholville, 180 km (112 mi) north of Caraquet. The eight trails on this 507-ft vertical drop accommodate all levels. There are also 25 km (16 mi) of cross-country ski trails. Instruction and equipment rentals are available; the park has a lounge and cafeteria.

NEW BRUNSWICK A TO Z

Arriving and Departing

By Plane

Air Canada and its regional carrier **Air Nova** (☎ 800/776–3000 in the U.S., 800/661–3936 in Canada) serve New Brunswick in Saint John, Moncton, Fredericton, Bathurst, and St-Léonard, and fly to the Atlantic provinces from Montréal, Toronto, and Boston.

Canadian Airlines International operates through **Air Atlantic** (☎ 800/426–7000 in the U.S., 800/665–1177 in Canada) in Saint John, Fredericton, Moncton, Charlo, and Miramichi, and serves the Atlantic provinces, Montréal, Ottawa, and Boston.

By Train

VIA Rail (☎ 800/562–3952) offers passenger service six times a week from Moncton to Montréal and Halifax.

Getting Around

By Bus

SMT Eastern Ltd. (☎ 506/859–5100 or 800/567–5151) runs buses within the province and connects with most major bus lines.

By Car

New Brunswick has an excellent highway system with numerous facilities. The Trans-Canadian Highway, marked by a maple leaf, is the same as Route 2. The only map you'll need is the one available at the tourist information centers listed below. Major entry points are at St. Stephen, Houlton, Edmundston, and Cape Tormentine from Prince Edward Island, and Aulac from Nova Scotia.

Contacts and Resources

Emergencies

Dial 911 for **medical, fire, and police** emergencies anywhere in New Brunswick.

Hospitals

Chaleur Regional Hospital (✉ 1750 Sunset Dr., Bathurst, ☎ 506/548–8961). **Campbellton Regional Hospital** (✉ 189 Lilly Lake Rd., Campbellton, ☎ 506/789–5000). **Edmundston Regional Hospital** (✉ 275 Hébert Blvd., ☎ 506/739–2211). **Dr. Everett Chalmers Hospital** (✉ Priestman St., Fredericton, ☎ 506/452–5400). **Moncton City Hospital** (✉ 135 MacBeath Ave., Moncton, ☎ 506/857–5111). **Dr. Georges Dumont Hospital** (✉ 330 Archibald St., Moncton, ☎ 506/862–4000). **Saint John Regional Hospital** (✉ Tucker Park Rd., Saint John, ☎ 506/648–6000). **Miramichi Regional Hospital** (✉ 500 Water St., Miramichi, ☎ 506/623–3000).

Outdoor Activities and Sports

Whale-watching, sea kayaking, trail riding, bird-watching, garden tours, river cruising, and fishing are part of the province's day-adventure program, "Adventures Left and Right." The more than 60 packages cover a variety of skill levels and include equipment. All adventures last at least a half day; some are multiday. Get full details at a New Brunswick Adventure Destination Centre (in some information offices, hotels, and attractions), or contact **Tourism New Brunswick** (✉ Box 12345, Fredericton E3B 5C3, ☎ 506/453–2170 or 800/561–0123).

BIKING

B&Bs frequently have bicycles for rent and Tourism New Brunswick has listings and free cycling maps. **Covered Bridge Bicycle Tours** (✉ Dept. F, Box 693, Main Post Office, Saint John E2L 4B3, ☎ 506/849–9028) leads bike trips in the province.

FISHING

New Brunswick Fish and Wildlife (☎ 506/453–2440) can give you information on sporting licenses and tell you where the fish are.

GOLF

Greens fees run about $20–$25, $15 for some nine-hole courses; visitors are generally welcome. For a list of golf courses, contact Tourism New Brunswick (☞ Visitor Information, *below*) or the New Brunswick Golf Association (565 Priestman St, Fredericton, E3B 5X8).

HIKING

For general trail information, contact Eric Hadley at the **New Brunswick Trails Council** (✉ Dept. of Natural Resources and Energy, Box 6000, Fredericton E3B 5H1, ☎ 506/453–2730).

SNOWMOBILING

For information on snowmobiling in New Brunswick contact the **New Brunswick Federation of Snowmobile Clubs** (✉ Box 29, Woodstock E0J 2B0, ☎ 506/325–2625).

Visitor Information

Tourism New Brunswick (✉ Box 12345, Fredericton E3B 5C3, ☎ 506/ 453–2170 or 800/561–0123) can provide information on day adventures, scenic driving routes, accommodations, and the seven provincial tourist bureaus. Also helpful are information services of the cities of **Bathurst** (☎ 506/548–0410), **Campbellton** (☎ 506/789–2700), **Fredericton** (☎ 506/452–9508), **Moncton** (☎ 506/853–3590), and **Saint John** (☎ 506/658–2990).

5 Prince Edward Island

In the Gulf of St. Lawrence north of Nova Scotia and New Brunswick, Prince Edward Island seems too good to be true, with its crisply painted farmhouses, manicured green fields rolling down to sandy beaches, the warmest ocean water north of Florida, lobster boats in trim little harbors, and a vest-pocket capital city, Charlottetown, packed with architectural heritage.

WHEN YOU EXPERIENCE Prince Edward Island, known locally as the Island, you'll understand instantly why Lucy Maud Montgomery's novel of youth and innocence, *Anne of Green Gables,* was framed against this land. What may have been unexpected, however, was how the story burst on the world in 1908 and is still selling untold thousands of copies every year. After potatoes and lobsters, Anne is the Island's most important product.

Updated by
Julie V. Watson

In 1864, Charlottetown, the Island's capital city, hosted one of the most important meetings in Canadian history, which eventually led to the Dominion of Canada in 1867. Initially, Prince Edward Island was reluctant to join, having spent years fighting for the right to an autonomous government. Originally settled by the French in 1603, the Island was handed over to the British under the Treaty of Paris in 1763. Tension ensued as British absentee governors and proprietors failed to take an active interest in the development of the land, and the resulting parliamentary government that was granted islanders proved ineffective for similar reasons. The development of fisheries and agriculture at the turn of the century strengthened the economy. Soon settlement increased and those who were willing to take a chance on the island prospered.

Around the middle of the century, a modern cabinet government was created and relations between tenants and proprietors worsened. At the same time talk of creating a union with other North American colonies began. After much deliberation, and despite the fact that political upheaval had begun to subside, delegates decided that it was in the Island's best economic interest to join the Confederation.

The recent construction of the Confederation Bridge, which connects Borden-Carleton with Cape Tormentine in New Brunswick, physically seals Prince Edward Island's connection with the mainland, and some islanders are fearful that the province's easygoing character will be sacrificed for the widespread development of unseemly tourist attractions. As you explore the landscape—a vast spectrum of colors giving way to crossroads villages and fishing ports—it's not hard to understand why Islanders love their isolation. Outside the tourist mecca of Cavendish, otherwise known as Anne's land, the Island seems like an oasis of peace in a world of turmoil.

Pleasures and Pastimes

The Arts

The arts, particularly theater, are an integral part of the Island. Summer productions and theater festivals are an Island highlight. The grandest is the Charlottetown Festival, which takes place from June through mid-September at the Confederation Centre of the Arts. Theater in Summerside, Georgetown, and Victoria is also good. Live traditional Celtic music, with fiddling and step dancing, can be heard almost any day of the week.

Beaches

Prince Edward Island is ringed by beaches, and few of them are heavily used. Ask a dozen islanders to recommend their favorites. Basin Head Beach, near Souris, says one—miles of singing sands, utterly deserted. West Point, says a second—lifeguards, restaurants nearby, showers at the provincial park. Greenwich, near St. Peter's Bay, another suggests—a half-hour walk through magnificent wandering dunes brings you to an endless empty beach.

Dining

On Prince Edward Island, wholesome, home-cooked fare is a matter of course. Talented chefs ensure fine cuisine in each region. The service is friendly—though a little laid back at times—and the setting is generally informal. Seafood is usually good anywhere on the island, with top honors being given to lobster.

Look for lobster suppers, offered both commercially and by church and civic groups. These meals feature lobster, rolls, salad, and mountains of sweet, home-baked goods. Regular suppers are held daily in New London from mid-May through September. Check the local papers, bulletin boards at local grocery stores, or Visitor Information Centres for other community suppers.

CATEGORY	COST*
$$$$	over $35
$$$	$25–$35
$$	$15–$25
$	under $15

per person, excluding drinks, service, 10% sales tax, and 7% GST.

Lodging

Prince Edward Island offers a variety of accommodations at a variety of prices, from full-service resorts and luxury hotels to moderately priced motels, cottages, and lodges, to farms that take guests. Lodgings in summer should be booked early, especially if you are planning a long stay.

CATEGORY	COST*
$$$$	over $75
$$$	$55–$75
$$	$40–$55
$	under $40

All prices are for a standard double room, excluding 10% provincial sales tax and 7% GST.

Outdoor Activities and Sports

BIKING

Prince Edward Island is popular with bike-touring companies for its moderately hilly roads and stunning scenery. Level areas can be found over most of the island, especially east of Charlottetown to Montague and along the north shore. However, shoulderless, narrow, secondary roads in some areas and summer's car traffic can be challenging for cyclists. A 9-km (5½-mi) path near Cavendish campground loops around marsh, woodland, and farmland. Cycling trips are organized throughout the province, and Prince Edward Island's visitor services can recommend tour operators.

GOLF

Prince Edward Island has several beautiful courses with scenic vistas. Golfing is virtually hassle-free: Tee times are easily booked any day of the week, rates are inexpensive, and courses uncrowded, particularly in the fall.

HIKING

Hiking within the lush scenic areas of Prince Edward Island National Park and provincial parks is encouraged with marked trails. Many of the trails are being upgraded to provide quality surfaces great for walking, hiking, or cycling. One of them is Confederation Trail, a provincial trail system, which will eventually allow outdoors explorers to travel 350 km (217 mi) within the province.

Exploring Prince Edward Island

Prince Edward Island is very irregular in shape, with deep inlets and tidal streams that nearly divide the province into three equal parts, known locally by their county names of Kings, Queens, and Prince (east to west). It is indeed a rich agricultural region surrounded by beautiful sand beaches, delicate dunes, and stunning red sandstone cliffs. The land in the east and central sections consists of gentle hills, creating a rolling landscape that can tax bicyclists. Nevertheless, the land never rises to a height of more than 500 ft above sea level, and you are never more than 15 minutes from a beach or waterway. To the west, from Summerside to North Cape, the land is flatter.

Numbers in the text correspond to numbers in the margin and on the Prince Edward Island and Charlottetown maps.

Great Itineraries

Visitors often tour only the central portion of the Island, taking Confederation Bridge from New Brunswick to Borden-Carleton, and exploring Anne country and the PEI National Park. To more deeply experience the Island's character, stray to the wooded hills of the east—to compact, bustling Montague, straddling its river. Or go west to superb, almost-private beaches, the Acadian parish of Tignish, and the silver-fox country around Summerside. Even if you're in a rush, it won't take long to get off and back on the beaten path: In most places you can cross the Island, north to south, in half an hour or so. The four tours detailed in this chapter are designed to include as many Island essentials as possible; Charlottetown is primarily a walking tour, while the others follow the major scenic highways—Blue Heron Drive, Kings Byway, and Lady Slipper Drive. There are plenty of chances to get out of the car, go fishing, hit the beach, photograph wildflowers, or just watch the sea roll in.

IF YOU HAVE 1 DAY

Leaving ⛴ **Charlottetown** ①–⑨ on Route 2 west, take Route 15 north to **Brackley Beach** ⑪. This puts you onto a 137-km-long (85-mi-long) scenic drive marked with signs depicting a blue heron. Route 6 west will take you to **Cavendish** ⑫, an entryway to **PEI National Park** ⑩. Cavendish is home to the fictional character Anne of Lucy Maud Montgomery's *Anne of Green Gables*. This area has enough attractions for a full day, but if you prefer to keep exploring, continue west on Route 6, where charming museums vie with fishing wharfs and scenic vistas for your attention. Blue Heron Drive joins Route 20, where you'll find the **Anne of Green Gables Museum** at Silver Bush; it offers a glimpse into the life of author Lucy Maud Montgomery in the early 1900s, with a farm, wagon rides, and a family atmosphere. Continue west, then south on Route 20 and rejoin Route 2 south until turning onto Route 1 east and back to Charlottetown.

IF YOU HAVE 2 DAYS

Leaving ⛴ **Charlottetown** ①–⑨ early in the day, follow Highway 1 east to Kings Byway Scenic Drive, marked with signs featuring a king's crown, and on to **Orwell** ⑭, where a period farm re-creates life in the 1800s. Continue on to **Montague** for a seal-watching tour. Overnight in ⛴ **Bay Fortune** ⑮. The next day, a picnic lunch will be the perfect wrap-up to a morning spent at **Basin Head Fisheries Museum** in **Basin Head.** Continue east on Kings Byway to East Point, for a stop at the lighthouse, which marks the most easterly point on the Island. Proceed west along the north shore to the eastern entrance of the **Prince Edward Island National Park** ⑩ and end your tour with a swim or a short hike.

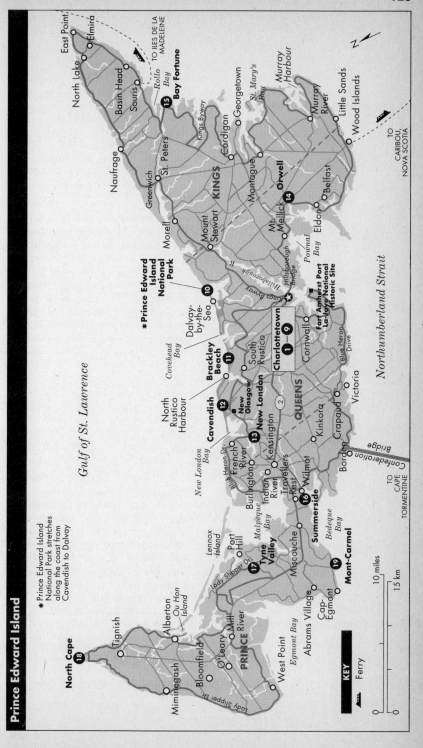

Prince Edward Island

* Prince Edward Island National Park stretches along the coast from Cavendish to Dalvay.

Gulf of St. Lawrence

Northumberland Strait

North Cape

Tignish

Mimmegash

Bloomfield

O'Leary

Alberton

Ou Hon Island

Mill River

Lennox Island

Port Hill

Lady Slipper Dr.

West Point

Egmont Bay

Abrams Village

Cap-Egmont

Mont-Carmel

Lady Slipper Dr.

PRINCE

Bedeque Bay

Miscouche

Tyne Valley

Summerside

Bridge

TO CAPE TORMENTINE

Confederation Bridge

Borden

Malpeque Bay

New London Bay

Blue Heron Dr.

French River

Indian River

Travellers Rest

Wilmot

Burlington

Kensington

Kinkora

Crapaud

Victoria

Cornwall

QUEENS

Charlottetown

Blue Heron Drive

Fort Amherst Port La-Joye National Historic Site

North Rustico Harbour

Covehead Bay

Cavendish

New London

New Glasgow

South Rustico

Brackley Beach

Prince Edward Island National Park

Dalvay-by-the-Sea

Hillsborough R.

Kings Byway

Mount Stewart

Morell

Greenwich

St. Peters

KINGS

Kings Byway

Cardigan

Georgetown

St. Mary's Bay

Naufrage

Souris

Basin Head

Elmira

East Point

North Lake

Bay Fortune

Rollo Bay

TO ILES DE LA MADELEINE

Mt. Mellick

Orwell

Pownal Bay

Hillsborough Bridge

Eldon

Belfast

Mt. Mellick

Montague

Murray River

Little Sands

Wood Islands

Murray Harbour

TO CARIBOU, NOVA SCOTIA

10 miles

15 km

KEY

Ferry

1–9
10
11
12
13
14
15
16
17
18
19

IF YOU HAVE 3 DAYS

From **Charlottetown** ①–⑨, explore the peaceful suburban sprawl of ▣ **Summerside** ⑯ before heading for its bustling waterfront. The relatively undiscovered area west of Summerside is perfect for those who like to pace things slowly. Follow Lady Slipper Drive through Acadian country to the **Acadian Museum of Prince Edward Island** in **Miscouche.** Leave mid-afternoon and take Rte. 12 to ▣ **Tyne Valley** ⑰, a base from which to visit Lennox Island Reserve, where some of the finest crafts on the Island are sold. That evening, dine at **Seasons In Thyme Restaurant,** then take an evening stroll through Green Park in nearby **Port Hill.** On day three, make your way up to **North Cape** ⑱ and explore its reef. Plan to arrive early in the afternoon at ▣ **West Point,** where you can enjoy the beach and walking trails. Finish your time in Prince County with a south shore tour to **Mont-Carmel** ⑲, home to one of the province's best French dinner theaters.

When to Tour Prince Edward Island

While Prince Edward Island is considered a summer destination due to its many seasonal attractions, the "shoulder seasons" should not be overlooked. May, June, September, and October usually have spectacular weather and few visitors. The main lobster season is May through June, while Autumn is an excellent time for hiking and golfing. Migratory birds arrive in vast numbers toward the end of summer, many staying until the snow falls. Winters are unpredictable but offer some of the Island's most overlooked activities: cross-country skiing, snowmobiling, and ice-skating on ponds. Nightlife is limited in cold weather.

CHARLOTTETOWN

On an arm of the Northumberland Strait, Prince Edward Island's oldest city is named for the stylish consort of King George III. This small city, peppered with gingerbread-clad Victorian houses and tree-shaded squares, is the largest community on the Island (population 30,000). It is often called "the Cradle of Confederation," a reference to the 1864 conference that led to the union of Nova Scotia, New Brunswick, Ontario, and Québec in 1867, and eventually, Canada itself.

Charlottetown's main activities center on government, tourism, and private commerce. While new suburbs were springing up around it, the core of Charlottetown remained unchanged, and the waterfront has been restored to recapture the flavor of earlier eras. Today the waterfront includes the Prince Edward Hotel; an area known as Peake's Wharf and Confederation Landing Park, with informal restaurants and handicraft and retail shops; and a marked walking path. Irene Rogers's *Charlottetown: The Life in Its Buildings* gives much detail about the architecture and history of downtown Charlottetown.

Exploring Charlottetown

Historic homes, churches, parks, and the waterfront are among the pleasures of a tour of downtown Charlottetown, and you can see many of the sights on foot.

A Good Tour

Before setting out to explore Charlottetown, brush up on local history at the **Confederation Centre of the Arts** ① on Richmond Street in the heart of downtown. Next door is **Province House National Historic Site** ②, where the first meeting to discuss federal union was held. If you have an interest in churches, turn onto Prince Street where **St. Paul's Anglican Church** ③ stands, then backtrack to Great George Street where you'll be summoned to **St. Dunstan's Basilica** ④ by its towering twin

Gothic spires. Great George Street ends at the waterfront, where the boardwalks of **Confederation Landing Park** ⑤ fronts small eateries and shops.

On the city's west end, the work of Robert Harris, Canada's foremost portrait artist, dons the walls of **St. Peter's Cathedral** ⑥ in Rochford Square, flanked by Rochford and Pownal streets. It's a bit of a walk to get there, but **Victoria Park** ⑦ rewards a grassy respite from heavy footwork. Next, climb to the Belvedere on the top floor of the **Beaconsfield Historic House** ⑧ for panoramic views of Charlottetown Harbour. Leave time to observe a favorite Prince Edward Island pastime—harness racing at **Charlottetown Driving Park** ⑨.

TIMING

You can easily explore the downtown area on foot in a couple of hours, but the wealth of historic sites and harbour views warrants full a day.

Sights to See

⑧ **Beaconsfield Historic House.** Designed by architect W. C. Harris and built in 1877, this gracious Victorian mansion near the entrance to Victoria Park is one of the island's finest residential buildings. On site are a gift shop and bookstore. Special events such as theatrical and musical performances, socials, and lectures are held regularly. Also on the grounds is a carriage house where activities for children are held in summer. ⊠ *2 Kent St.,* ☎ *902/368–6600.* ᐧ *$2.50.* ☉ *June–Labor Day, daily 10–5; Labor Day–June, Tues.–Sun. 1–5.*

⑨ **Charlottetown Driving Park.** Since 1890, this track at the eastern end of the city has been the home of a sport that is dear to the hearts of Islanders—harness racing. Standard-bred horses are raised on farms throughout the island, and harness racing on the ice and on country tracks has been popular for generations. In fact, there are more horses per capita on the Island than in any other Canadian province. August brings **Old Home Week,** when Eastern Canada's best converge for 15 races within an 8-day period. ⊠ *Kensington Rd.,* ☎ *902/892–6823.* ᐧ *$2.* ☉ *Races: June, July, and most of Aug., 3 nights per week; Old Home Week (mid-Aug.), Mon.–Sat. twice daily.*

❶ **Confederation Centre of the Arts.** Set in Charlottetown's historic red-brick core, this modern, concrete structure opened in 1964 as a tribute to the Fathers of Confederation. The Centre houses a 1,100-seat main-stage theater, two 190-seat second-stage theaters with an outdoor amphitheater, a memorial hall, a gift shop with Canadian crafts, a theater shop, an art gallery and museum, a public library with a special Prince Edward Island collection, including first editions of Lucy Maud Montgomery's famous novel, and a restaurant. The **Charlottetown Festival,** which runs from June through September, includes the professional, musical adaption of *Anne of Green Gables.* ⊠ *145 Richmond St.,* ☎ *902/368–1864, 902/566–1267 box office, or 800/565–0278,* FAX *902/566–4648.* ☉ *Year-round, 9–5 daily; hrs extended June–Sept.*

⑤ **Confederation Landing Park.** This waterfront recreation area at the bottom of Great George Street marks the site of the historic landing of the Fathers of Confederation in 1864. Walkways and park benches offer plenty of opportunity to enjoy the activity of the harbour. The adjacent **Peake's Wharf** has small restaurants, crafts shops, and a marina.

NEED A BREAK? The **Merchantman Pub** (⊠ 23 Queen St., ☎ 902/892–9150), in a historic building just steps from the waterfront walking path near Confederation Landing Park, is a cozy spot for burgers, crepes, and fish and chips.

Beaconsfield Historic House, **8**

Charlottetown Driving Park, **9**

Confederation Centre of the Arts, **1**

Confederation Landing Park, **5**

Province House National Historic Site, **2**

St. Dunstan's Basilica, **4**

St. Paul's Anglican Church, **3**

St. Peter's Cathedral, **6**

Victoria Park, **7**

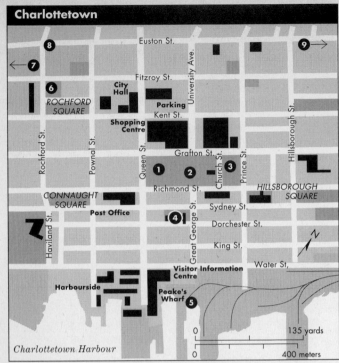

Charlottetown

★ ❷ **Province House National Historic Site.** This three-story sandstone building, completed in 1847 to house the colonial government, has been restored to its mid-19th-century appearance. Visit the many restored rooms including the historic Confederation Chamber, where representatives of the 19th-century colonies met to discuss both the creation of a union and the current legislative chamber. ⊠ *Richmond St.,* ☎ *902/566–7626.* ▣ *Donation accepted.* ☉ *Mid-Oct.–mid-June, weekdays 9–5; mid-June, Sept.–mid-Oct., daily 9–5; July and Aug., daily 9–6.*

❹ **St. Dunstan's Basilica.** One of Canada's largest churches, St. Dunstan's is the seat of the Roman Catholic diocese on the island. It's known for its fine Italian carvings. ⊠ *Great George St.*

❸ **St. Paul's Anglican Church.** This is actually the third church building, erected in 1896, to stand on this site. The first was built in 1747, making this the oldest parish on the island. ⊠ *101 Prince St.*

❻ **St. Peter's Cathedral.** The murals of Robert Harris are found in **All Saints Chapel,** designed in 1888 by his brother W. C. "Willy" Harris, the most celebrated of the island's architects and the designer of many historic homes and buildings. ⊠ *Rochford Sq.*

❼ **Victoria Park.** At the southern tip of the city and overlooking Charlottetown Harbour are 40 beautiful acres that provide the perfect place to stroll, picnic, or watch a baseball game. Next to the park, on a hill between groves of white birches, is the white colonial **Government House,** built in 1835 as the official residence for the province's lieutenant governors. The house is not open to the public. ⊠ *Park, Lower Kent St.* ☉ *Daily sunrise–sunset.*

Dining

$$$$ ✕ **The Selkirk.** With its wing chairs and live piano entertainment, The Selkirk is the Island's most sophisticated dining room. The extensive, imaginative menu concentrates on regional Canadian fare—locally grown potatoes, smoked Atlantic salmon, lobster, mussels, Malpeque oysters, and Canadian beef to name a few. A four-course extravaganza that begins with Cedar Planked Salmon and closes with a Maple Streusel Apple Tart, will satisfy even the largest of appetites. ⊠ *Prince Edward Hotel, 18 Queen St.,* ☎ *902/566–2222 or 800/441–1414. Reservations essential. AE, DC, MC, V.*

$$$ ✕ **Culinary Institute of Canada.** Students at this internationally acclaimed school cook and present lunch and dinner during the school year as part of their training. Here's an opportunity to enjoy excellent food and top service at reasonable prices. Call for schedule and reservations. ⊠ *Kent St.,* ☎ *902/566–9550. Reservations essential. MC, V. Closed May–Sept.*

$$–$$$ ✕ **Claddagh Room Restaurant.** You'll find some of the best seafood in
★ Charlottetown here. The "Galway Bay Delight," one of the Irish owner's specialties, is a savory combination of fresh scallops and shrimp sautéed with onions and mushrooms, flambéed in Irish Mist, and doused with fresh cream. A pub upstairs has live Irish entertainment every night in summer and on weekends in winter. ⊠ *131 Sydney St.,* ☎ *902/892–9661. Reservations essential. AE, DC, MC, V.*

$$ ✕ **Off Broadway.** Popular with Charlottetown's young professional set, this cozy spot began modestly as a crepe-and-soup joint. You can still make a meal of the lobster or chicken crepe and the spinach or Caesar salad that's served with it, but now the restaurant also has a fairly inventive menu of Continental entrées. The old-fashioned private booths won't reveal your indiscretions—including your indulgence in dessert. ⊠ *125 Sydney St.,* ☎ *902/566–4620. Reservations essential. AE, MC, V.*

$ ✕ **Little Christo's.** Hand-tossed gourmet pizzas like cordon bleu with roasted pine nuts and primavera make this the favorite spot in town for a slice. Soup, salad, pasta, and sandwiches round out the menu. ⊠ *411 University Ave.,* ☎ *905/566–4000. MC, V.*

Lodging

$$$$ ⊞ **The Charlottetown.** This five-story, redbrick hotel with white pillars
★ and a circular driveway is just two blocks from the center of Charlottetown. The rooms have the latest amenities but retain the hotel's old-fashioned flavor with antique-reproduction furnishings. The grandeur and charm of the Confederation Dining Room will take you back to the elegance of a previous era. ⊠ *Kent and Pownal Sts., Box 159, C1A 7K4,* ☎ *902/894–7371,* ℻ *902/368–2178. 107 rooms, 2 suites. Bar, dining room, indoor pool, sauna. AE, DC, MC, V.*

$$$$ ⊞ **Prince Edward Hotel.** A member of the Canadian Pacific chain of
★ hotels and resorts, the Prince Edward has all the comforts and luxuries of its first-rate counterparts—from whirlpool baths in some suites to a grand ballroom and conference center. Guest rooms are modern, and two-thirds of the units in this 10-story hotel overlook the developed Charlottetown waterfront. ⊠ *18 Queen St., Box 2170, C1A 8B9,* ☎ *902/566–2222 or 800/441–1414,* ℻ *902/566–2282. 178 rooms, 33 suites. 2 restaurants, bar, indoor pool, sauna, exercise room. AE, DC, MC, V.*

$$$–$$$$ ⊞ **Dundee Arms.** Depending on your mood, you can choose to stay in
★ either a 1960s motel or a 1904 inn. The motel is simple, modern, and neat; the inn is homey and furnished with brass and antiques. The Griffin Room, the inn's dining room, is filled with antiques, copper, and

brass. The French Continental cuisine includes fresh seafood. Specialties include rack of lamb, chateaubriand, and poached or grilled fillet of salmon in a light lime-dill sauce. ⊠ *200 Pownal St., C1A 3.W8,* ☎ *902/892–2496,* 🖷 *902/368–8532. 16 rooms, 2 suites. Restaurant, pub. CP. MC, V.*

$–$$$ 🏠 **Blue Heron Hideaways.** Just 15 minutes from downtown Charlottetown in Blooming Point, the Blue Heron is a small complex of cottages and beach houses. The private beach has sand dunes and wildlife, and it's great for windsurfing. Outboard motorboat and gas barbecues are available for guest use. ⊠ *Meadowbank, R.R. 2, Cornwall C0A 1H0,* ☎ *902/566–2427,* 🖷 *902/368–3798. 1 2-bedroom cottage, 2 3-bedroom cottages, 1 waterfront cottage with bunkhouse, 1 6-bedroom oceanfront house with guest house. Pool, windsurfing, boating. Weekly rentals only early June–mid-Oct. No credit cards.*

$$ 🏠 **Sherwood Motel.** This family-oriented motel is about 5 km (3 mi) north of downtown Charlottetown on Route 15. The friendly owners offer help in reserving tickets for events and planning day trips. Don't be daunted by the Sherwood's proximity to the airport—the motel sees very little traffic. Most rooms have kitchenettes. ⊠ *R.R. 9, Winsloe C1E 1Z3,* ☎ *902/892–1622 or 800/567–1622. 30 rooms. MC, V.*

The Arts

Ceilidhs, or live traditional entertainment combining dancing, fiddling, and comedy, can be found throughout Charlottetown and its environs. **The Benevolent Irish Society Hall** (☎ 902/892–2367) stages concerts on Fridays from mid-May through October.

BLUE HERON DRIVE

From Charlottetown, Blue Heron Drive follows Route 15 north to the north shore, then winds along Route 6 through north-shore fishing villages, the spectacular white-sand beaches of Prince Edward Island National Park, through Anne of Green Gables country, and finally along the south shore, with its red sandstone seascapes and historic sites. The drive takes its name from the great blue heron, a stately water bird that migrates to Prince Edward Island every spring to nest in the shallow bays and marshes. The whole circuit roughly outlines Queens County and covers 190 km (118 mi). It circles some of the Island's most beautiful landscapes and best beaches, but its northern section around picturesque Cavendish and the Green Gables farmhouse is also cluttered with tourist traps. If you're looking for unspoiled beauty, you'll have to look beyond the fast-food outlets, tacky gift shops, and expensive carnival-type attractions and try to keep in your mind's eye the Island's simpler days.

Prince Edward Island National Park

❿ *24 km (15 mi) north of Charlottetown.*

Prince Edward Island National Park stretches for about 40 km (25 mi) along the north shore of the island, from Cavendish to Dalvay, on the Gulf of St. Lawrence. The Park is blessed with nature's broadest brush strokes—sky and sea meet red sandstone cliffs, rolling dunes, and long stretches of sand. Beaches invite you to swim, picnic, or take a quiet walk. Trails lead through woodlands and along streams and ponds. Among more than 200 species of birds are the northern phalarope, Swainson's thrush, and the endangered piping plover. Over 500 campgrounds span the park with varying fees and seasons. In autumn and winter, it's difficult to reach park staff—call the Prince Edward Island

Department of Economic Development and Tourism (☞ Visitor Information *in* Prince Edward Island A to Z, *below*) for exact rates and schedules if you're planning a camping trip ahead of time. Keep in mind that campsites are rented on a first-come, first-served basis; reservations aren't part of the protocol. ☎ 902/672–6350. ⊠ *$3 daily pass, $15 seasonal pass, $2.50 off-season.* ☉ *Year-round.*

Lodging

$$$$ ⊞ **Dalvay-by-the-Sea.** Just within the eastern border of the Prince Edward Island National Park is this Victorian house, built in 1896 as a private summer home. Rooms are furnished with antiques and reproductions. Guests can sip cocktails or tea on the porch while admiring the inn's gardens, Dalvay Lake, or the nearby beach. ⊠ *Rte. 6, Grand Tracadie, near Dalvay Beach; Box 8, York C0A 1P0,* ☎ *902/672–2048. 26 rooms, 4 cottages. Restaurant, bar, driving range, 2 tennis courts, croquet green, boating, gift shop. MAP. AE, MC, V. Closed late Sept.–early June.*

Golf

The 18-hole course at **Stanhope Golf and Country Club** (☎ 902/672–2842) is one of the most challenging and most scenic on the Island. It's a few kilometers west of Dalvay, off Route 6, along beautiful Covehead Bay.

Brackley Beach

➊ *12 km (7½ mi) west of Dalvay.*

Just outside the National Park, Brackley Beach offers a variety of country-style accommodations and eating establishments. Its bays and waterways attract migratory birds and are excellent for canoeing or kayaking and windsurfing.

Dining and Lodging

$$–$$$ ✕ **Dunes Cafe.** This stunning café shares property with a pottery stu-
★   dio, art gallery, artisans outlet (☞ Shopping, *below*), and outdoor gardens. Soaring wood ceilings lend an airy atmosphere inside, while an outside deck overlooks the dunes and marshlands of Covehead Bay. The chef specializes in local seafood and lamb, incorporating locally grown, fresh produce, much of which comes from the café's own gardens. ⊠ *Rte. 15,* ☎ *902/672–2586. Reservations essential. AE, MC, V. Closed Nov.–May. No dinner weekdays June, Sept., or Oct.*

$$$–$$$$ ✕⊞ **Shaw's Hotel and Cottages.** Each room is unique in this 1860s
★   hotel with antique furnishings, floral-print wallpapers, and hardwood floors. Half the cottages have fireplaces. This country elegance doesn't come cheap; Shaw's is one of the more expensive hotels on the Island, but guests have the opportunity to sail (on small vessels) and windsurf. If you'd like, include in your room rate a home-cooked breakfast and dinner in the Shaw's dining room. ⊠ *Rte. 15, Brackley Beach C1E 1Z3,* ☎ *902/672–3000,* ℻ *902/672–6000. 20 rooms, 18 cottages, 2 suites. Restaurant, bar, beach, boating, playground. AE, MC, V. Closed late Sept.–May except for 6 cottages.*

Shopping

The Dunes Studio and Gallery (⊠ Rte. 15, ☎ 902/672–2586) features the work of leading local artists, as well as craftspeople from around the world. The production pottery studio is open for viewing, and a rooftop water garden offers fine views of saltwater bays, sand dunes, rolling hills, and the Gulf of St. Lawrence.

Cavendish

⑫ *21 km (13 mi) west of Brackley.*

Cavendish is the most visited Island community outside of Charlotte-town, due to the heavy influx of visitors to Green Gables, the PEI National Park, and the amusement-park style attractions in the area. Families with children enjoy the entertainment, which ranges from bumper-car rides to water slides to pristine sandy beaches.

Adults will appreciate the **Site of Lucy Maud Montgomery's Cavendish Home,** where the writer lived with her maternal grandparents following the untimely death of her mother. Though the foundation of the home where Montgomery wrote *Anne of Green Gables* and the white picket fence that surrounded it are all that remain, the homestead fields and old apple-tree gardens provide lovely walking grounds. A bookstore and museum are also on the property, which is operated by descendants of the family. ⊠ *Rte. 6,* ☎ *902/963–2231.* ☜ *$2.* ☉ *June–mid-Oct.*

★ **Green Gables House,** ½ km (¼ mi) west of Lucy Maud Montgomery's Cavendish home, is the green-and-white farmhouse that served as the setting for *Anne of Green Gables.* The house, frequently visited by Montgomery, belonged to her cousins. Posted walking trails, the Haunted Wood and Balsam Hollow, re-create the landscape reminiscent of Montgomery's day. The site has been part of Prince Edward Island National Park since 1937. ⊠ *Rte. 6, west of Rte. 13,* ☎ *902/672–6350.* ☜ *$2.75.* ☉ *Mid-May–late June, daily 9–5; late June–Aug., daily 9–8; Sept.–Nov., daily 9–5.*

Dining and Lodging

$$$ ✕▥ **Bay Vista Motor Inn.** This clean, friendly motel caters to families. Parents can sit on the outdoor deck and admire the New London Bay panorama while keeping an eye on their children in the large playground. Fiddles 'n Vittles is a great place to eat with the family. ⊠ *R.R. 1, Breadalbane, Cavendish C0A 1E0; in winter,* ⊠ *R.R. 1, North Wiltshire C0A 1Y0; book reservations at R.R. 2, Hunter River, PEI C0A 1N0,* ☎ *902/963–2225. 28 rooms, 2 efficiencies. Restaurant, pool, boating, fishing, playground. AE, MC, V. Closed late Sept.–mid-June.*

$$$$ ▥ **Kindred Spirits Country Inn and Cottages.** This lovely country estate, a short walk from Green Gables House and golf course, is surrounded by green hills. Relax by its parlour fireplace, and then retreat into a large room or suite, decorated in country-Victorian style with local antiques. ⊠ *Rte. 6, Cavendish C0A 1N0,* ☎ *902/963–2434,* ℻ *902/963–2434. 14 rooms in the Inn, 13 cottages. Restaurant, pool, whirlpool. MC, V. Closed mid-Oct.–mid-May.*

Golf

Green Gables Course (⊠ Rte. 6, ☎ 902/963–2488), part of the Prince Edward Island National Park, is a scenic 18-hole course.

Sea Kayaking

Sea kayaking with **Outside Expeditions** (☎ 800/207–3899), 8 km (5 mi) east of Cavendish in North Rustico, can be geared to suit either the new or experienced paddler. Tours are catered, from light snacks to full-fledged lobster boils, depending on the expedition you choose.

New London

⑬ *11 km (7 mi) southwest of Cavendish.*

This tiny village is best known as the birthplace of Lucy Maud Montgomery. It's also home to several seasonal gift and craft shops, and a tea shop. The wharf area is a great place to stop, rest, and watch as the fishing boats come and go.

The **Lucy Maud Montgomery Birthplace** is the modest white house where the famous author was born in 1874. Among memorabilia on display are her wedding dress and personal scrapbooks. ⊠ *Rte. 6,* ☎ *902/886–2596.* ☞ *$2.* ⊙ *June and Sept.–mid-Oct., daily 9–5; July–Aug., daily 9–7.*

Northwest Corner

12 km (7 mi) from New London.

Some of the most beautiful scenery on the Island is on Blue Heron Drive along the north shore. As the drive follows the coastline south to the other side of the Island, it passes rolling farmland and the shores of Malpeque Bay. Three towns of interest round out this scenic corner of the Island: Burlington, Park Corner, and Indian River.

Woodleigh Replicas and Gardens (⊠ Rte. 234, ☎ 902/836–3401), in Burlington, southwest of New London, is a 45-acre park with 30 scale replicas of Britain's best-known architecture, including the Tower of London and Dunvegan Castle. A medieval maze and 10 acres of English Country gardens are also on the grounds. The models that are large enough to enter are furnished with period antiques.

Park Corner's **Anne of Green Gables Museum at Silver Bush** (⊠ Rte. 20, ☎ 902/886–2884) was once the home of Lucy Maud Montgomery's aunt and uncle. Montgomery herself lived here for a time and was married in the parlor in 1911. Fans will appreciate mementos such as photographs and a quilt the writer worked on.

The Arts

The fine acoustics at **St. Mary's Church** (⊠ Hwy. 104, 5 km (3 mi) south of Park Corner, ☎ 902/836–3733) in Indian River draw visiting artists in July and August.

Borden-Carleton

35 km (22 mi) south of Kensington.

Once home port to the Marine-Atlantic car ferries, Borden-Carleton is now linked to the mainland via the Confederation Bridge. The 13-km (8-mi) behemoth, completed in June of 1997, spans the Northumberland Straight and ends in Cape Tormentine, New Brunswick. **Gateway Village,** at the foot of the bridge near the Borden-Carleton toll booths, has a visitor's center and information on the bridge's construction.

En Route   Prior to the late 1800s (when ferry service began), passengers and mail were taken across the straight in ice boats that were rowed and alternately pushed and pulled across floating ice by a fleet of men attached to leather harnesses. A monument on Route 10 in **Cape Traverse** commemorates their journeys.

Victoria

22 km (14 mi) east of Borden-Carleton.

This picturesque fishing village is filled with antiques, art galleries, and handicraft shops. In summer, thespians flock to historic **Victoria Playhouse** (☎ 902/658–2025) for its celebrated theater program.

Fort Amherst Port-La-Joye National Historic Site

36 km (22 mi) east of Victoria.

The drive from Victoria to Rocky Point passes through the Argyle Shore to Fort Amherst Port-La-Joye National Historic Site, at the mouth of Charlottetown Harbour. In 1720 the French founded the first European settlement on the island, Port-La-Joye; 38 years later it was usurped by the British and renamed Fort Amherst. Take time to stroll around the original earthworks of the fort and enjoy a magnificent panoramic view. The Visitor Centre on the grounds has informative exhibits and an audiovisual presentation. ⊠ *Rte. 19,* ☎ *902/672–6350.* ⌷ *$2.25.* ⊙ *Visitor's Centre: mid-June–Labor Day, daily 10–6; grounds, year-round.*

THE KINGS BYWAY

For 375 km (233 mi), the Kings Byway follows the coastline of green and tranquil Kings County on the eastern end of the island. The route passes wood lots, patchwork-quilt farms, fishing villages, historic sites, and long, uncrowded beaches. In early summer you can see fields of blue, white, pink, and purple wild lupines sloping down to red cliffs and blue sea. To get there from Charlottetown, take Route 1 east and follow Kings Byway counterclockwise.

Orwell

★ ⑭ *27 km (17 mi) west of Charlottetown.*

For those who like the outdoors, Orwell, lined with farms that welcome guests and offer activities, is ideal.

The **Orwell Corner Historic Village** is a living farm museum that re-creates a 19th-century rural settlement by employing methods used by Scottish settlers in the 1800s. The village contains a beautifully restored 1864 farmhouse, school, church, community hall, blacksmith shop, and barns with handsome draft horses. On Wednesdays in summer the village hosts musical evenings (*ceilidhs*) featuring traditional Scottish fiddle music by local musicians. ⊠ *Rte. 1, Orwell Corner,* ☎ *902/ 651–2013.* ⌷ *$3.* ⊙ *Late June–Labor Day, Tues.–Sun. 9–5; mid-May–late June and Labor Day–late Oct., Tues.–Fri. 10–3.*

The **Sir Andrew Macphail Homestead,** a National Historic Site, is a 140-acre farm property that contains an ecological forestry project, gardens, and three walking trails. The restored 1829 house and 19th-century outbuildings commemorate the life of Sir Andrew Macphail (1864–1938), a writer, professor, physician, and soldier. A licensed tea room/restaurant serves traditional Scottish and contemporary fare. ⊠ *Off Rte. 1,* ☎ *902/651–2789.* ⌷ *$3.* ⊙ *June and Sept., Tues.–Sun. 10–5; July–Aug., extended hrs.*

OFF THE   **BEN'S LAKE TROUT FARM –** This is an enjoyable attraction for the whole
BEATEN PATH   family but is especially loved by aspiring young anglers. Not only are
              you almost guaranteed a fish but the staff will clean it and supply the
              barbecue and picnic table for a great meal. ⊠ *Rte. 24 (follow gravel
              road from Sir Andrew Macphail Homestead to Rte. 24; turn right), Belle-
              vue,* ☎ *902/838-2706.* ⌷ *Catch $3.90 per lb.* ⊙ *Apr.–Oct.*

En Route   One of the island's most historic churches, St. John's Presbyterian, is
              in **Belfast,** just off Route 1 on Route 207. This pretty white church,
              on a hill against a backdrop of trees, was built by settlers from the Isle
              of Skye who were brought to the Island in 1803 by Lord Selkirk.

Montague

20 km (12 mi) northeast of Orwell.

The business hub of eastern Prince Edward Island, Montague, a lovely fishing village, is a departure point for seal-watching boat tours. **Cruise Manada** (☎ 902/838–3444 or 800/986–3444) sails past a harbor seal colony and mussel farms. Boats leave from Montague Marina on Route 4 and Brudenell Resort Marina on Route 3 from mid-May through October.

Bay Fortune

⑮ *38 km (24 mi) north of Georgetown.*

Bay Fortune, a little-known scenic village, has been a secret refuge of American vacationers for two generations and is home to the wonderful Inn at Bay Fortune, with its old-time style and panache.

Dining and Lodging

$$$$ ✕▥ **Inn at Bay Fortune.** This enticing, unforgettable getaway, the for-
★ mer summer home of Broadway playwright Elmer Harris, and more recently of actress Colleen Dewhurst, is now a charming inn overlooking Fortune Harbour and Northumberland Straight. You'll find superb dining and a taste of genteel living. Local fresh-caught and -harvested ingredients are served in an ambience reminiscent of a bygone era. A full breakfast is included in room rates. ⊠ *Rte. 310, R.R. 4, C0A 2B0,* ☎ *902/687–3745, 203/633–4930 off-season. 11 rooms. Closed late Oct.–mid-May.*

Souris

14 km (9 mi) north of Bay Fortune.

The Souris area is noted for its fine traditional musicians. An outdoor Scottish concert at **Rollo Bay** in July, with fiddling and step dancing, attracts thousands every year. At Souris a car ferry links Prince Edward Island with the Québec-owned Magdalen Islands.

Basin Head

13 km (8 mi) north of Rollo Bay.

This town is noted for an exquisite silvery beach that stretches northeast for miles, backed by high grassy dunes. Scuff your feet in the sand: It will squeak, squawk, and purr at you. Known locally as the **"singing sands,"** they are a phenomenon found in only a few locations worldwide.

At the **Basin Head Fisheries Museum,** spectacularly located on a bluff overlooking Northumberland Straight, boats, gear, and photographs depict the life of an inshore fisherman. There's an aquarium, a smokehouse, a cannery, and coastal-ecology exhibits. ⊠ *Off Rte. 16,* ☎ *902/357–2966, 902/368–6600 off-season.* ⊠ *$3.* ☉ *June and Sept., weekdays 10–3; July–Aug., daily 10–7.*

En Route Ships from many nations have wrecked on the reef running northeast from the **East Point Lighthouse** (⊠ Off Rte. 16, East Point, ☎ 902/357–2106). Guided tours are offered and numerous detailed books depicting the mysteries and tales of life at sea are available at the gift shop inside the adjacent fog alarm building.

Greenwich

54 km (33 mi) southwest of East Point.

Follow Route 16, the shore road, to Route 2 to St. Peter's Bay and Route 313 to Greenwich. The road ends among sand hills, but from here you can take a half-hour walk through beige dunes to reach the superior beach. These dunes are moving, gradually burying the nearby woods; here and there the bleached skeletons of trees thrust up through the sand like wooden ghosts.

LADY SLIPPER DRIVE

This drive—named for the delicate lady's slipper orchid, the province's official flower—winds along the coast of the narrow, indented western end of the island, known as Prince County, through very old and very small villages, which still adhere to a traditional way of life. Many of these hamlets are inhabited by Acadians, descendants of the original French settlers. The area is known for its oysters and Irish moss, but most famously for its potato farms: The province is a major exporter of seed potatoes worldwide, and half the crop is grown here.

Summerside

16 *71 km (44 mi) west of Charlottetown.*

Summerside, the second-largest city on the Island, has a beautiful waterfront area. A self-guided walking tour arranged by the Eptek National Exhibition Centre (☞ *below*) is a pleasant excursion through the leafy streets lined with large houses. During the third week of July, all of Summerside celebrates the eight-day **Summerside Lobster Carnival,** with livestock exhibitions, harness racing, fiddling contests, and of course, lobster suppers.

Some of the homes in Summerside are known as "fox houses"; silver foxes were first bred in captivity in western Prince Edward Island, and for several decades Summerside was the headquarters of a virtual gold rush based on fox ranching. For more on this unique local history, stop in at the **International Fox Museum and Hall of Fame.** ⊠ *286 Fitzroy St.,* ☎ *902/436–2400 or 902/436–1589.* ☞ *Free.* ☉ *May–Sept., Mon.–Sat. 9–6.*

Eptek National Exhibition Centre and PEI Sports Hall of Fame, on the waterfront, has a spacious main gallery with changing history and fine arts exhibits from all parts of Canada. An adjacent gallery contains the Sports Hall of Fame, a permanent display honoring well-known Island athletes. ⊠ *130 Harbour Dr., Waterfront Properties,* ☎ *902/888–8373,* FAX *902/888–8375.* ☞ *$2.* ☉ *July–Aug., weekdays 10–4, weekends 1–4:30; closed Mon. Sept.–June.*

Spinnaker's Landing, a boardwalk along the peaceful water's edge, is lined with shops and informal eateries. At a boat shed displaying traditional building methods common to the 1800s, you can have your own small ship custom crafted out of wood. ⊠ *130 Waterfront St., Waterfront Properties,* ☎ *902/436–6692.* ☉ *Mid-June–mid-Sept., daily 9:30–9:30.*

Lodging

$$$$ ⊡ **Quality Inn Garden of the Gulf.** Close to downtown Summerside, this clean motel is a convenient place to stay. There's a par-3 golf course on the property slopes to Bedeque Bay. ⊠ *618 Water St. E, C1N 2V5,* ☎ *902/436–2295 or 800/265–5551,* FAX *902/436–6277. 84 rooms.*

Coffee shop, indoor and outdoor pools, 9-hole golf course, gift shop. AE, DC, MC, V.

$$$ ⊞ **Loyalist Country Inn.** A Victorian-street-scene-inspired theme is present throughout this waterfront inn. Ten rooms have whirlpool baths. ⊠ *195 Harbour Dr., C1N 5B2,* ☎ *902/436–3333 or 800/361–2668,* FAX *902/436–4304. 51 rooms. Dining room, tavern, indoor pool, sauna, tennis court, exercise room. AE, DC, MC, V.*

Nightlife and the Arts

The College of Piping and Celtic Performing Arts of Canada (⊠ 619 Water St. E, ☎ 902/436–5377, FAX 902/436–4930) puts on a summer-long Celtic Festival incorporating bagpiping, Highland dancing, step dancing, and fiddling. **The Harbourfront Jubilee Theater** (⊠ 130 Water St., Waterfront Properties, ☎ 902/888–2500 or 800/707–6505) is the Maritimes' newest professional theater. Year-round, the main stage celebrates the tradition and culture of the Maritimes with dramatic and musical productions.

Miscouche

10 km (6 mi) northwest of Summerside.

The **Acadian Museum of Prince Edward Island** (☎ 902/436–6237), on Route 2, has a permanent exhibition on Acadian life as well as an audiovisual presentation depicting the history and culture of Island Acadians. Visitors have access to 30,000 genealogical cards listing Acadian descent. The museum is open year-round.

Port Hill

35 km (22 mi) north of Miscouche.

Follow the Lady Slipper signs from Miscouche to Port Hill on Route 12, where you may visit the **Green Park Shipbuilding Museum and Historic House** (☎ 902/831–2206). The house was originally the home of shipbuilder James Yeo, Jr. This 19th-century mansion is topped by the cupola from which Yeo observed his nearby shipyard through a spyglass. The modern museum building, in what has become a provincial park, details the history of the shipbuilder's craft, brought to life at a re-created shipyard with carpenter and blacksmith shops. The park also provides an opportunity for some welcome R&R, with picnic tables and camping facilities, as well as swimming in the river (there may not be a lifeguard on duty). The house and museum are open mid-June through Labor Day, Tuesday through Sunday 9 to 5.

Tyne Valley

⑰ *8 km (5 mi) south of Port Hill.*

The charming community of Tyne Valley has some of the finest food on Prince Edward Island, as well as an annual Oyster Festival, which takes place the first week in August. The area is home to the famous Malpeque oysters; watch for fishermen standing in flat boats wielding rakes to harvest this famous shellfish.

Dining and Lodging

$$–$$$$ ✕ **Seasons In Thyme.** This casual but charming country restaurant is
★ known for its fresh local ingredients such as quail, pheasant, and duck, and organic vegetables. The owner-chef Stefan Czapalay has 27 potato dishes at his fingertips, allowing him to cater to industry officials visiting to check the quality of the island's famous seed potatoes. In recognition of his varied clientele he utilizes the freshest local ingredients from farm and sea in dishes ranging from the most sophisticated

to the most casual. ✉ *Rte. 178, C0B 2C0,* ☎ *902/831–2124. Reservations essential. AE, MC, V.*

$$ ✕🖫 **Doctor's Inn Bed & Breakfast.** This beautifully landscaped village home is a joy in summer, with its garden of herbs and flowers. In winter cross-country skiers gather 'round the woodstove or fireplace and share good conversation over a warm drink. At the dining room table, the local catch of the day is complemented by produce from the inn's own organic gardens. Dinner is by reservation only. For the horticulturally inclined, there are free tours of the inn's gardens. ✉ *Rte. 167, C0B 2C0,* ☎ *902/831–3057. 3 rooms share bath. CP. MC, V.*

Shopping

At **Shoreline Sweaters** (✉ Rte. 12, ☎ 902/831–2950), sometimes known as Tyne Valley Studio, Lesley Dubey produces sweaters with a unique Fair Isle–style lobster pattern and sells local crafts May through October. An art gallery on premises displays original works by Island artists.

Lennox Island Reserve, one of the largest Mi'Kmaq reserves in the province, has a few shops that sell native crafts. To get there, take Route 12 west to Route 163, and follow the road over the causeway. **Indian Art & Craft of North America** (☎ 902/831–2653) sells sweetgrass baskets, pottery, and beadwork. Earthenware figurines depicting native legends can be found at **Micmac Productions** (☎ 902/831–2277).

O'Leary

37 km (23 mi) northeast of Tyne Valley.

The center of Prince County is composed of a loose network of small towns, many of which are merely a stretch of road. Though quality lodging establishments are hard to find in these parts, O'Leary is host to a resort where opportunities for outdoor activities abound. O'Leary is also a good base from which to visit one of the island's best golf courses and a rare woolen crafts shop.

Lodging

$$$$ 🖫 **Rodd Mill River Resort and Aquaplex.** With activities ranging from night skiing and tobogganing to golfing, this is truly an all-season resort. An international dogsled-racing weekend is a popular winter event. Ask about year-round family weekend packages. ✉ *Box 399, O'Leary C0B 1V0,* ☎ *902/859–3555 or 800/565–7633,* 𝖥𝖠𝖷 *902/859–2486. 87 rooms, 3 suites. 2 bars, dining room, 2 indoor pools, sauna, 18-hole golf course, tennis court, exercise room, squash, windsurfing, boating, bicycles, ice-skating, cross-country skiing, tobogganing, pro shop. AE, MC, V. Closed Nov.–early Dec., Apr.*

Golf

Mill River Provincial Golf Course (☎ 902/859–2238) in Mill River Provincial Park is among the most scenic and challenging courses in eastern Canada.

Shopping

The **Old Mill Craft Company** (✉ Rte. 2, Bloomfield, ☎ 902/859–3508) sells hand-quilted and woolen crafts July through August.

En Route Everything in **Tignish,** a friendly Acadian community on Route 2, 29 km (18 mi) north of Woodstock, seems to be cooperative, including the supermarket, insurance company, seafood plant, service station, and credit union. The imposing parish church of **St. Simon and St. Jude Parish House** (✉ 315 School St., ☎ 902/882–2049), across from Dalton Square, has a superb Tracker pipe organ, one of the finest such instruments in eastern Canada, and is often used for recitals by world-renowned musicians.

North Cape

★ ⑱ *14 km (9 mi) north of Tignish on Route 12.*

As you proceed north on Route 2, the Island narrows to a north-pointing arrow of land at the tip of which is North Cape with its imposing lighthouse. At low tide, one of the longest reefs in the world gives way to tidal pools teeming with marine life. The curious structures near the reef are wind turbines at the **Atlantic Wind Test Site,** set up on this breezy promontory to evaluate the feasibility of electrical generation by wind power. If you feel you are being watched, you probably are: Look offshore to where the seals gather for some prime people-watching. In summer visit the Interpretive Centre and Aquarium for information on North Cape's natural wonders.

The **Interpretive Centre and Aquarium** has information about marine life, local history, and turbines and windmills. ⊠ *End of Rte. 12,* ☎ *902/882–2991.* ⌨ *$2.* ⊙ *July–Aug., daily 9–9; mid-May–June and Sept.–Oct., daily 10–6.*

Dining

$$ ✕ **Wind & Reef.** This restaurant serves good seafood, such as Island clams, mussels, and lobster, as well as steaks, prime rib, and chicken. There's a breathtaking view of the Gulf of St. Lawrence and Northumberland Strait. ⊠ *End of Rte. 12,* ☎ *902/882–3535. MC, V. Closed Oct.–May.*

En Route Near North Cape, just off Lady Slipper Drive on the western side of the island, is the very popular natural rock formation called **"Elephant Rock."** You may also see draft horses in the fields or working in the surf. They are "moss horses," used in harvesting a versatile and valuable sea plant known as Irish moss.

Miminegash

20 km (12 mi) south of North Cape.

Find out everything you wanted to know about Irish Moss, the fan-shaped red alga found in abundance on this coast and used as a thickening agent in foods. Visit the **Irish Moss Interpretive Centre** (☎ 902/882–4313) and find out how much Irish moss there was in your last ice cream cone. Then take time for some Seaweed Pie (made from Irish moss) at the adjacent Seaweed Pie Cafe. The Interpretive Centre is open late June through September, weekdays 9 to 5.

West Point

35 km (22 mi) south of Miminegash.

At the southern tip of the western shore is West Point, with a tiny fishing harbor, campsites, and a supervised beach. **West Point Lighthouse** is more than 120 years old and is the tallest on the island. When the lighthouse was automated, the community took over the building and converted it into an inn (☞ *below*) and museum, with moderately priced restaurant attached. The lighthouse is open daily, late May through late October.

Lodging

$$$–$$$$ ⌂ **West Point Lighthouse.** Few can say they've actually spent the night in a lighthouse. Clam-digging is a central activity at this unusual seaside inn. Rooms, most with ocean views, are furnished with local an-

tiques and handmade quilts. This inn books up so make your reservations early. Ask the innkeeper about the region's folklore—buried treasure is reputed to be nearby. ⊠ *Rte. 14,* ☎ *902/859–3605 or 800/764–6854. 9 rooms. Restaurant, beach, fishing, bicycles. AE, MC, V. Closed Oct.–May.*

En Route   Lady Slipper Drive meanders from West Point back to Summerside through **Région Évangéline,** the main Acadian district of the island. At **Cape-Egmont,** stop for a look at the **Bottle Houses,** two tiny houses and a chapel built by a retired carpenter entirely out of glass bottles mortared together like bricks.

Mont-Carmel

⑲   *84 km (52 mi) southeast of West Point.*

This community has a magnificent brick church overlooking Northumberland Strait. **Acadian Pioneer Village,** a reproduction of an 1820s French settlement, has a church, school, blacksmith shop, store, restaurant (where you can sample authentic Acadian dishes), and modern accommodations. ⊠ *Rte. 11,* ☎ *902/854–2227.* ☜ *$2.* ☉ *Mid-June–mid-Sept., daily 9–7.*

The Arts
La Cuisine à Mémé (⊠ Rte. 11, ☎ 902/854–2227), a French dinner theater, serves a buffet and has typical Acadian entertainment, such as step dancing and fiddle music.

PRINCE EDWARD ISLAND A TO Z

Arriving and Departing

By Car
The 13-km (8-mi) Confederation Bridge now connects Borden-Carleton, Prince Edward Island, with Cape Tormentine in New Brunswick. The bridge replaces the services of the Marine Atlantic ferries, shortening travel time to a mere 10 minutes. The round-trip cost is $35 per car, $40 for a recreational vehicle.

By Ferry
Northumberland Ferries (☎ 902/566–3838, 800/565–0201 in the Maritimes) sails between Caribou, Nova Scotia, and Wood Islands, from May to mid-December. The crossing takes about 75 minutes, and the round-trip costs approximately $28.25 per automobile and $8.75 per adult. This ferry service will continue after the bridge opens. Reservations are not accepted, and no fares are collected inbound; you pay only on leaving the island.

By Plane
Charlottetown Airport is 5 km (3 mi) north of town. **Air Canada/Air Nova** (☎ 902/892–1007 or 800/776–3000) and **Canadian Airlines International/Air Atlantic** (☎ 902/892–4581 or 800/665–1177) offer daily service to major cities in eastern Canada and the United States via Halifax. **Prince Edward Air** (☎ 902/566-4488) is available for private charters.

Getting Around

By Car
With no public transportation on the Island, your own vehicle is almost a necessity. **Ed's Taxi** (☎ 902/892–6561) can be booked for tours by the hour or day. There are more than 3,700 km (2,300 mi)

of paved road in the province, including the three scenic coastal drives called Lady Slipper Drive, Blue Heron Drive, and Kings Byway. The adventurous will enjoy exploring the designated "Heritage Roads," which consist of red clay, the native soil base. These unpaved roads meander through undeveloped areas of rural Prince Edward Island, where you're likely to see lots of wildflowers and birds. A four-wheel-drive vehicle is not necessary, but in spring and inclement weather the mud can get quite deep and the narrow roads become impassable. Keep an eye open for bicycles, motorcycles, and pedestrians.

Contacts and Resources

Emergencies
Police and **fire,** dial 0.

Golf
For a publication listing courses, contact **Golf Prince Edward Island** (⊠ Box 2653, Charlottetown C1A 8C3, ☎ 800/463–4734).

Guided Tours
The Island has about 20 sightseeing tours, including double-decker bus tours, taxi tours, cycling tours, harbor cruises, and walking tours. Most tour companies are based in Charlottetown and offer excursions around the city and to the beaches. For a listing of current tour companies, contact **Tourism PEI** (⊠ Box 940, Charlottetown C1A 7M5, ☎ 800/463–4734, FAX 902/368–4438).

Hiking
Island Nature Trust and Island Trails (⊠ Ravenwood, Box 265, Charlottetown C1A 7K4, ☎ 902/894–7535, FAX 902/628–6331) publishes a nature trail map of the island, available for $4.50.

Hospital
Queen Elizabeth Hospital (⊠ Riverside Dr., Charlottetown, ☎ 902/566–6200).

Shopping
Information on crafts outlets is provided by the **Prince Edward Island Crafts Council** (⊠ 156 Richmond St., Charlottetown C1A 1H9, ☎ 902/892–5152).

Visitor Information
The **Prince Edward Island Department of Economic Development & Tourism** (⊠ Quality Service Division, Box 940, Charlottetown C1A 7M5, ☎ 902/368–4444 or 800/463–4734, FAX 902/629–2428) publishes an excellent annual "Visitor's Guide" and maintains eight **Visitor Information Centres** (VICs) on the island. The main VIC is in Charlottetown (⊠ 178 Water St., Box 940, Charlottetown C1A 7M5, ☎ 902/368–4444 or 902/463–4623, FAX 902/929–2428) and is open mid-May–October, daily; November–mid-May, weekdays.

6 Newfoundland and Labrador

Canada's easternmost province consists of the island of Newfoundland and Labrador on the mainland. In summer, Newfoundland's stark cliffs, bogs, and meadows become a riot of wildflowers and greenery, and the sea is dotted with boats and buoys. Mountains, lakes, and rivers provide further opportunities for first-class adventures from wildlife viewing to kayaking and fishing. St. John's, the capital, is a classic harbor city offering a lively arts scene and warm hospitality.

NEWFOUNDLAND WAS THE FIRST PLACE explorers John Cabot (1497) and Gaspar Corte-Real (1500) touched down in the New World. Exactly where they went no one knows, for neither survived a second voyage. But while he was here, Cabot reported that he saw fish in the water so thick you could dip your basket in anywhere and catch as much as you wanted. Within a decade of the explorers' discovery, St. John's had become a crowded harbor. Fishing boats from France, England, Spain, and Portugal vied for a chance to catch Newfoundland's lucrative cod, which was to subsequently shape the province's history and geography.

Updated by
Ed Kirby

At one time there were 700 hard-working settlements or "outports" dotting Newfoundland's coast, most devoted to catching, salting, and drying the world's most plentiful fish. Today, only about 400 of these settlements survive. Newfoundland's most famous resource has become so scarce that a partial fishing moratorium was declared in 1992 and extended in 1993. While the province waits for the cod to return, some 25,000 fishers and processors are going to school or looking for other work instead of fishing. The discovery of perhaps the largest nickel deposit in the world at Voisey's Bay in northern Labrador, near Nain, may bring some relief. A mine and mill are expected to begin production in 1999. In addition, a number of offshore oil fields are expected to go into operation between late 1997 and the turn of the century.

Newfoundland and Labrador became part of Canada in 1949. For almost 400 years before this, however, the people had survived the vagaries of a fishing economy on their own, until the Great Depression forced the economy to go belly-up. After almost 50 years of Confederation with Canada, the economy of the province has improved considerably, but the people are still of independent mind: Newfoundlanders regard themselves as North America's first separatists and maintain a unique language and lifestyle as well as their own customs. E. Annie Proulx's Pulitzer Prize–winning novel, *The Shipping News*, brought the attention of many readers to this part of the world.

Visitors to Newfoundland find themselves straddling the centuries. Old accents and customs are common in small towns and outports, yet the major cities of St. John's on the east coast and Corner Brook on the west coast of the island of Newfoundland are very much part of the 20th century. Regardless of where you visit—an isolated outport or lively Duckworth Street—you're sure to interact with some of the warmest, wittiest people in North America. Strangers have always been welcome in Newfoundland, since the days when locals brought visitors in from out of the cold, warmed them by the fire, and charmingly interrogated them for news of events outside the province.

Before you can shoot the breeze, though, you'll have to acclimate yourself to the strong provincial dialects. Newfoundland is one of two provinces with their own dictionaries. Prince Edward Island is the other, but its book has only 873 entries. The *Dictionary of Newfoundland English* has more than 5,000 words, mostly having to do with fishery, weather, and scenery. To get started, you can practice the name of the province—it's *New'fund'land*, with the accent on "land." However, only "livyers" ever get the pronunciation exactly right.

Pleasures and Pastimes

Dining

John Cabot and Sir Humphrey Gilbert raved about "waters teeming with fish." Today, despite the fishing moratorium, seafood is still an excellent value in Newfoundland and Labrador. Many restaurants offer seasonal specialties with a wide variety of traditional wild and cultured species. Although cod may still be available, it may not be locally harvested. It will still, however, be traditionally prepared—pan-fried, baked, or poached. Aquaculture species like steelhead trout, salmon, mussels, and sea scallops are available in better restaurants. Cold-water shrimp, snow crab, lobster, redfish, grenadier, halibut, and turbot are also good seafood choices.

Two other foods you shouldn't leave without trying are partridgeberries and bakeapples. Partridgeberries are a small, lush-tasting berry, called the mountain cranberry in the United States, and locally they are used for just about everything—pies, jams, cakes, pancakes, and even as a sauce for turkey and game. Bakeapples in the wild are a low-growing berry that looks like a yellow raspberry—you'll see them ripening in bogs in August throughout the province. Enterprising pickers sell them by the side of the road in jars. If the ones you buy are hard, wait a few days and they'll ripen into rich-tasting fruit. The berries are popular on ice cream or spread on fresh homemade bread. In Scandinavia they're known as cloudberries and are made into a liqueur.

You may also hear Newfoundlanders talk about the herb they call summer savory. Newfoundlanders are so partial to this peppery herb that they slip it into most stuffings and stews. Growers in the province ship the product all over the world, and Newfoundlanders visiting relatives living outside the province are usually asked to "bring the savory."

Only the large urban centers, especially St. John's and Corner Brook, have gourmet restaurants. Fish is a safe dish to order just about everywhere—even in the lowliest take-out. You'll be surprised by the quality of the meals along the Trans-Canada Highway: Restaurants in the Irving Gas Station chain, for example, have thick homemade soups with dumplings and Sunday dinners that draw in local customers for miles around. Don't be shy about trying some of the excellent meals offered in the province's expanding network of "hospitality homes," where home cooking goes hand in hand with a warm welcome.

CATEGORY	COST*
$$$$	over $50
$$$	$35–$50
$$	$20–$35
$	under $20

*per person, excluding drinks, service, and 15% Harmonized Sales Tax (HST).

Festivals and Performing Arts Events
From the Folk Festival main stage in St. John's to the front parlor, Newfoundland and Labrador are filled with music of all kinds. Festivals around the province draw performers and fans from near and far. Newfoundlanders love a party, and from the cities to the smallest towns they celebrate their history and unique culture with events throughout the summer, whether it's music and recitations at a World War II artillery bunker near Cape Spear or a Shakespeare-by-the-Sea event.

Fishing
Newfoundland has over 200 salmon rivers—60% of all salmon rivers in North America—and thousands of trout streams. Angling in these unpolluted waters is a fisherman's dream. The feisty Atlantic salmon is king of the game fish. Top salmon rivers in Newfoundland include the Gander, Humber, and Exploits, while Labrador's top-producing waters are the Sandhill, Michaels, Flowers, and Eagle rivers. Lake trout, brook trout, and landlocked salmon are other favorite species. In Labrador, northern pike and Arctic char can be added to that list.

Hiking

Many provincial and both national parks in Newfoundland and Labrador have hiking and nature trails. Coastal and woods trails radiate from most small communities. However, you can never be sure how far the trail will go unless you ask a local. Be careful: Landmarks are few, the weather is changeable, and it is surprisingly easy to get lost. Many small communities now also have formal walking trails.

Lodging

Newfoundland and Labrador offer lodgings that range from modestly priced "hospitality homes," which you can find through local tourist offices, to luxury accommodations. In between, you can choose from affordable, basic lodging and mid-priced hotels. In remote areas, be prepared to find very basic lodgings. However, the lack of amenities is usually made up for by the home-cooked meals and great hospitality.

CATEGORY	COST*
$$$$	over $110
$$$	$85–$110
$$	$60–$85
$	under $60

All prices are for a standard double room, excluding 15% harmonized sales tax (HST).

Exploring Newfoundland and Labrador

This chapter divides the province into the island of Newfoundland, beginning with St. John's and the Avalon Peninsula and moving west. Labrador is considered as a whole, with suggested driving and train excursions for a number of areas.

Numbers in the text correspond to numbers in the margin and on the Newfoundland and Labrador map.

Great Itineraries

IF YOU HAVE 3 DAYS

Pick either the west or east coast of Newfoundland. On the west coast, after arriving by ferry at **Port aux Basques** ㉜, drive through the Codroy Valley, heading north to the **Gros Morne National Park** ㉓ and its fjords, and overnight in 🏨 **Rocky Harbour** ㉖ or 🏨 **Woody Point** ㉔. The next day, visit **L'Anse aux Meadows National Historic Site** ㉘, where the Vikings built a village a thousand years ago; here there are reconstructions of the dwellings, plus a Viking boat tour. Then overnight in 🏨 **St. Anthony** ㉙ or nearby.

On the east coast, the ferry docks at Argentia. Explore the Avalon Peninsula beginning in 🏨 **St. John's** ②, where you should spend your first night. The next day, visit **Cape Spear** ①, the most easterly point in North America, and the **Witless Bay Ecological Reserve** ③ for seabirds, whales, and icebergs. Overnight in 🏨 **Placentia** ⑨ and spend your third day at **Cape St. Mary's Ecological Reserve** ⑪, known for its gannets.

IF YOU HAVE 6 DAYS

On Newfoundland's west coast, add southern Labrador to your list. A ferry takes you from St. Barbe to Blanc Sablon on the Québec-Labrador border. Drive 60 mi to **Red Bay** ㉟ to explore the remains of a 17th-century Basque whaling station; then head to **L'Anse Amour** ㉞ to see Canada's second-tallest lighthouse. Overnight at 🏨 **L'Anse au Clair** ㉝. Return through Gros Morne National Park and explore 🏨 **Corner Brook** ㉚, where you should stay overnight. The next day, travel west of **Stephenville** ㉛ to explore the Port au Port Peninsula, home of Newfoundland's French-speaking population.

Newfoundland and Labrador

QUEBEC

L'Anse
au Loup **L'Anse** **Red Bay** Cape Onion
Forteau **Amour** Cook's Har. **28** **L'Anse aux**
L'Anse au Clair **33** **34** Raleigh **National H**
Blanc Sablon Strait of Belle **29**
Isle **436**
430 Flowers **St. Anthony**
Cove Hare Bay
Brig Bay **St. Barbe** St. Julien's
Bartlett's Har. Groais I.
Port au Choix Roddickton
Bell I.
Hawke's Bay
430 TO GOOSE BAY
(Labrador)
Bellburns Harbour Deep
Portland Creek Fleur de Lys
Arches Provincial Park **27**
Cow Head Baie Verte
St. Pauls Jackson Arm La Scie
Rocky Harbour 410
Bonne Bay **26** **Gros Morne** Rattling **Nipper's** **Twillingate**
Woody Point **24** **Nat'l Park** Brook Har. Notre Dame
23 Springdale Bay
Trout River **25** Richard
431 Squires South **Boyd'**
Memorial Brook **Cov**
430 Park Sandy 1
Lake 340
Cox's Lake Millertown 1 Lew
Bay York Harbour **22** Cove **Deer** Junction Badger Botwood
of Islands **Lake**
Corner Brook **30** Marble Mountain **Grand Falls-**
Humbermouth **Windsor**
Black Duck Lewis Hills Buchans 370 G
Brook Grand
Mainland Port Au Lake Red 360
Peninsula Port Point au Mal Indian
St. Teresa Prov. Park Lake **NEWFOUNDLAND**
Stephenville **31**
Meelpaeg Round
Jeffery's St. George's Bay Lake Lake
404
Codroy R. 480
Cape N. Branch St. Albans
Anguille
406 1 Terrence
407 **Port**
aux Basques 360
32 Rose Burgeo Harbour
Blanche Breton Marystown
Burin
Grand Peninsula Salt
Bank Pond **18**
Gr. Miquelon I. Fortune **16** **Buri**
TO NORTH SYDNEY **Miquelon** St. Lawrenc
(Nova Scotia) **(France)** **17** 220
Lit. Miquelon I. **St-Pierre**

Gulf of St. Lawrence

Long Range Mountains

White Bay

Long Range Mountains

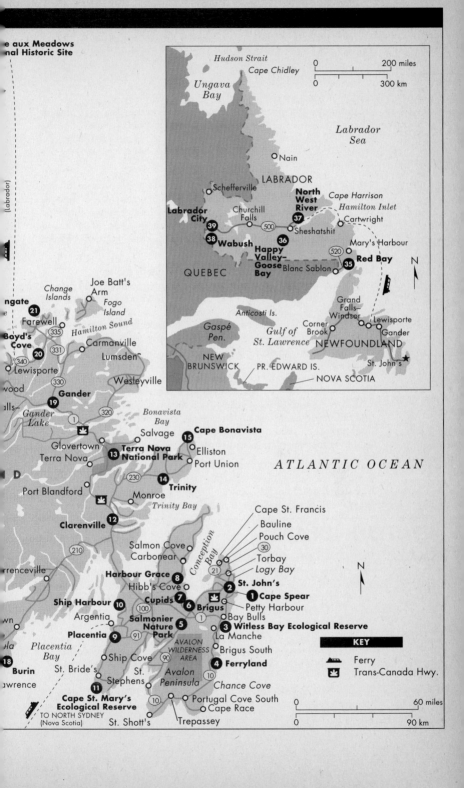

On the east coast add ▦ **Trinity** ⑭ to your must-see list, and overnight there or in ▦ **Clarenville** ⑫. The north shore of Conception Bay is where you will find many picturesque villages, including ▦ **Cupids** ⑦ or ▦ **Harbour Grace** ⑧. Several half-day, full-day, and two-day excursions are possible from St. John's, and in each direction a different personality of the region unfolds.

IF YOU HAVE 9 DAYS

In addition to the places already mentioned on the west coast, take a drive into central Newfoundland and visit the lovely villages of Notre Dame Bay. Overnight in ▦ **Twillingate** ㉑. Catch a ferry to offshore islands like ▦ **Fogo** or the ▦ **Change Islands.** Accommodations are available in both towns, but book ahead.

On the east coast add the Burin Peninsula and a trip to France to your itinerary. Yes, France. You can reach the French territory of ▦ **St-Pierre and Miquelon** ⑰ by passenger ferry from Fortune. Explore romantic **Grand Bank** ⑯, named for the famous fishing area just offshore, and climb Cook's Lookout in ▦ **Burin** ⑱, where Captain James Cook kept a lookout for smugglers from St-Pierre.

When to Tour Newfoundland and Labrador

Depending on the time of year you visit, your experiences will be dramatically different. In spring icebergs float down from the north, and fin, pilot, minke, and humpback whales hunt for food along the coast. Their preferred cuisine is capelin, a small, smeltlike fish that moves in schools and spawns on Newfoundland's many pebble beaches. During the summer, temperate days turn Newfoundland's stark cliffs, bogs, and meadows into a riot of wildflowers and greenery; and the sea is dotted with boats and buoys marking traps and nets. Fall is a favored season: The weather is usually fine; cliffs and meadows are loaded with berries; and the woods are alive with moose, caribou, partridges, and rabbits, to name just a few residents. In the winter, the forest trails hum with the sound of snowmobiles and ATVs hauling wood home or taking the fishers to their favorite lodges and lakes.

The tourist season runs from June through September, when the province is awash with festivals, fairs, concerts, plays, and crafts shows. The temperature hovers between 75° and 85°, and gently cools off in the evening, providing a good night's sleep.

NEWFOUNDLAND

The rocky coasts and peninsulas of the island of Newfoundland present much dramatic beauty and many opportunities for exploring. Seaport and fishing towns such as St. John's and Grand Bank tell a fascinating history, and parks from Terra Nova National Park on the eastern side of the island and Gros Morne National Park on the west have impressive landscapes. The Avalon Peninsula includes the provincial capital of St. John's as well as the Cape Shore on its west. The Bonavista Peninsula and the Burin Peninsula and Notre Dame Bay have some intriguing sights, from Cape Bonavista, associated with John Cabot's landing, to pretty towns around Notre Dame Bay such as Twillingate. The Great Northern Peninsula on the western side of Newfoundland holds a historic site with the remains of Viking sod houses; the west coast has Corner Brook, a good base for exploring the mountains, as well as farming and fishing communities.

St. John's

When Sir Humphrey Gilbert sailed into St. John's to establish British colonial rule for Queen Elizabeth in 1583, he found Spanish, French, and Portuguese fishermen actively working the harbor. As early as 1627, the merchants of Water Street—then known as "the lower path"—were doing a thriving business buying fish, selling goods, and supplying booze to soldiers and sailors. Today St. John's still encircles the snug, punch-bowl harbor that helped establish its reputation.

This old seaport town, the province's capital, mixes English and Irish influences, Victorian architecture and modern convenience, and traditional music and rock and roll into a heady brew that finds expression in a lively arts scene and a relaxed pace—all in a setting that has the ocean on one side and unexpected greenery on the other.

★ ❶ True early birds can begin a tour of the area at daybreak by filling up a thermos of coffee, getting some muffins, and driving on Route 11 to **Cape Spear,** so you can be among the first to watch the sun come up over North America. This is the easternmost point of land on the continent. Songbirds begin their chirping in the dim light of dawn, and whales feed directly below the cliffs, providing an unforgettable start to the day. In May and June you may well see icebergs floating by.

Cape Spear Lighthouse (☎ 709/772–5367), Newfoundland's oldest such beacon, has been lovingly restored to its original form and furnishings and is open to visitors, daily 10–6 from early June through Labor Day. Admission is $2.25.

❷ You can begin exploring **St. John's** on the waterfront, site of the Tourist Chalet. This is a converted railway caboose, staffed from May through October; you can pick up maps with some good walking tours. ✉ *Harbour Dr.,* ☎ *709/576–8514.* ◷ *May–Oct., daily 9–7.*

Whichever way you look on the harbor, you'll see the always-fascinating array of ships that tie up along **Harbour Drive.** Walk the harbor front, a favorite route in St. John's, east to the **Battery,** a tiny, still-active fishing village perched precariously at the base of steep cliffs between hill and harbor. The walk is about 1 km (½ mi)

On downtown streets such as **Water Street,** where longtime businesses sit cheek-by-jowl with vacant storefronts, you'll notice the diversity of architectural styles due to two major fires in 1846 and 1892. The 1892 fire stopped where George and Water streets intersect, at **Yellowbelly Corner.** This junction was so-named because in the 19th century it was a gathering spot for Irish immigrants from Wexford who wore yellow sashes to distinguish themselves from their Waterford rivals.

Look west on Water Street, where the block still resembles a typical Irish market town of the 1840s. To the east, Victorian-style architecture predominates, with curved mansard roofs typical of the Second Empire style. After the 1892 fire the city's elite moved to **Circular Road,** in the center of the city, out of reach of future fires, and built a string of highly ornamented Victorian mansions, which bear witness to the sizable fortunes made from the humble cod.

Be sure to take a walk on **Duckworth Street,** which hums with a lively and changing mix of crafts shops, coffee bars, and restaurants. The **Newfoundland Museum** has displays on the province's cultural and natural history, along with changing exhibits from other museums. ✉ *285 Duckworth St.,* ☎ *709/729–0916.* ▱ *Free.* ◷ *Daily.*

While you're downtown, take a look at the **churches of St. John's,** rich in architectural history; many usually schedule summer tours. The

Basilica Cathedral of St. John the Baptist (✉ Military Rd., ☎ 709/754–2170), with a commanding position above Military Road, overlooks the older section of the city and the harbor. The land was granted to the church by young Queen Victoria, and the edifice was built with stones from both Ireland and Newfoundland. The **Anglican Cathedral of St. John the Baptist** (✉ 22 Church Hill, ☎ 709/726–5677) is one of the finest examples of Gothic Revival architecture in North America. The imposing **Gower Street United Church** (✉ Gower St., ☎ 709/753–7286) has redbrick facade and green turrets. The **St. Thomas (Old Garrison) Church** (✉ Bottom of Military Rd., adjacent to Hotel Newfoundland, ☎ 709/576–6632) is where the English soldiers used to worship during the early and mid-1800s.

The **Commissariat House,** just around the corner from St. Thomas church, has been restored to the way it appeared when it was the residence and office of the British garrison's supply officer in the 1830s. Interpreters dress in period costume. ✉ *King's Bridge Rd.,* ☎ *709/729–6730.* ▣ *Free.* ☉ *June–mid-Oct., daily 10–5:30.*

★   You can either walk or drive from the Battery to **Signal Hill National Historic Site,** with excellent views of the city to the west. To walk, take the well-maintained 1¾-km (1-mi) walking path that leads along the cliff edge, through the Narrows, and zigzags through the park. To drive, take steep Signal Hill Road. In spite of its height, Signal Hill was difficult to defend: Throughout the 1600s and 1700s it changed hands with every attacking French, English, and Dutch force. A wooden palisade encircles the summit of the hill, indicating the boundaries of the old fortifications. En route to the hill is the **Park Interpretation Centre,** with exhibits describing St. John's history. **Gibbet Hill,** the rocky knob immediately to the west of the Interpretation Centre, got its name—a gibbet is a post with a projecting arm for hanging—because a miscreant was once hanged there and left dangling as a deterrent to other would-be lawbreakers. From the top of the hill it's a 500-ft drop to the narrow harbor entrance below. **Cabot Tower,** at the summit of Signal Hill, was constructed in 1897 to commemorate the 400th anniversary of Cabot's landing in Newfoundland. ✉ *Cabot Tower,* ☎ *709/772–5367.* ▣ *Free.* ☉ *Labor Day–early June, daily 9–5; mid-June–Labor Day, daily 8:30–8, guides available on summer weekends.*

Quidi Vidi Village is an authentic fishing community whose history goes back to the beginning of St. John's. If you're driving here from Signal Hill, go down from Signal Hill, make a right turn at Quidi Vidi Road, and continue to the right, down Forest Road. If you are walking, paths lead from the summit and the Interpretation Centre to the village. **Quidi Vidi Battery** is a small redoubt that has been restored to the way it appeared in 1812 and is staffed by costumed interpreters who will tell you about the hard, unromantic life of a soldier of the empire. ✉ *Near entrance to Quidi Vidi harbor,* ☎ *709/729–2460 or 709/729–2977.* ▣ *Free.* ☉ *July–early Sept., daily 10–5:30.*

Quidi Vidi Lake, to the west of Quidi Vidi Village, is encircled by a leisurely path, popular with walkers and joggers. It's the site of the **Royal St. John's Regatta,** the oldest continuing sporting event in North America, which has taken place since at least 1826. Weather permitting, the regatta takes place on the first Wednesday in August.

The **Newfoundland Freshwater Resource Center** has the only public fluvarium in North America; underwater windows let you view a brook. Here you can observe spawning brown and brook trout in their natural habitat. Feeding time for the fish, frogs, and eels is 4 PM daily. If you want to walk here from Quidi Vidi Lake, follow the Rennies

River Trail (4½ km, or 3 mi) that cuts through the city along a wooded stream. ⊠ *Pippy Park,* ☎ *709/754–3474.* 🖾 *$2.75.* ☉ *July–Aug., daily 9–5; guided tours at 11, 1, and 3; Sept.–June, Mon.–Tues. and Thurs.–Sat. 9–4:30; Sun. noon–4:30.*

The **Memorial University Botanical Garden** is a 110-acre garden and natural area at Oxen Pond with four pleasant walking trails and many gardens, including rock gardens and scree, a Newfoundland heritage-plants bed, ericaceous borders, peat and woodland beds, a wildlife garden, an alpine house, wildfire cottage and vegetable gardens, an herb wall, and native plant collections. The environmental education programs include seasonal indoor exhibits, and wildflower and bird-watching walks. ⊠ *306 Mt. Scio Rd., Pippy Park,* ☎ *709/737–8590.* 🖾 *$1.* ☉ *May–June and Sept.–Nov., Wed.–Sun. 10–5; July–Aug., Fri.–Mon. and Wed. 10–5, Tues. and Thurs. 10–8.*

Bowring Park, an expansive Victorian park west of downtown, was donated to the city by the wealthy Bowring family in 1911. It resembles the famous inner city parks of London, after which it was modeled. Dotting the grounds are ponds and rustic bridges; there's also a statue of Peter Pan. ⊠ *Waterford Bridge Rd.* 🖾 *Free.*

Dining and Lodging

$$$ ✕ **The Cellar.** This restaurant, in a historic building on the waterfront,
★ gets rave reviews for its innovative Continental cuisine featuring the best local ingredients. Menu selections include blackened fish dishes and tiramisu for dessert. ⊠ *Baird's Cove, between Harbour and Water Sts.,* ☎ *709/579–8900. Reservations essential. AE, MC, V.*

$$$ ✕ **Stone House.** In one of St. John's most historic buildings, a restored
★ 19th-century stone cottage, this dining room serves imported game and Newfoundland specialties. ⊠ *8 Kenna's Hill,* ☎ *709/753–2380. AE, DC, MC, V.*

$$–$$$ ✕ **Hungry Fishermen.** Salmon, scallops, halibut, mussels, cod, and shrimp top the menu here. Nonfish eaters can choose veal, chicken, or the five-onion soup. This restaurant in a 19th-century historic building overlooking a courtyard has great sauces; desserts change daily and are homemade. ⊠ *Murray Premises, 5 Beck's Cove, off Water St.,* ☎ *709/726–5790. AE, D, DC, MC, V.*

$$$$ ✕🖾 **Delta St. John's.** In this convention hotel in downtown St. John's,
★ rooms overlook the harbor and the city. The restaurant, Brazil Square, is known for its breakfast and noon buffets. ⊠ *120 New Gower St., A1C 6K4,* ☎ *709/739–6404,* 🖾 *709/570–1622. 276 rooms, 9 suites. Restaurant. AE, DC, MC, V.*

$$$$ ✕🖾 **Hotel Newfoundland.** St. John's residents gather at this comfort-
★ able modern hotel for special occasions. It's noted for its Sunday and evening buffets, charming rooms that overlook St. John's harbor, atrium, and the fine cuisine of the Cabot Club. ⊠ *Box 5637, Cavendish Sq., A1C 5W8,* ☎ *709/726–4980,* 🖾 *709/726–2025. 267 rooms, 20 suites. Restaurant. AE, DC, MC, V.*

$$$ 🖾 **Quality Hotel by Journey's End Motel.** This hotel overlooks St. John's harbor. Like other properties in the chain, it offers clean, comfortable rooms at a reasonable price. The hotel's restaurant, Rumplestiltskins, has a splendid view and an unpretentious menu. ⊠ *Hill O'Chips, A1C 6B1,* ☎ *709/754–7788,* 🖾 *709/754–5209. 162 rooms. Restaurant. AE, DC, MC, V.*

$$ 🖾 **Compton House Bed & Breakfast.** In a charming, restored historic
★ St. John's residence in the west end of the city, this inn is professionally run and beautifully decorated. Twelve-foot ceilings and wide halls

give the place a majestic feeling, and rooms done in pastels and chintzes add an air of coziness. The location, within walking distance of downtown St. John's, is ideal. ⊠ *26 Waterford Bridge Rd., A1E 1C6,* ☎ *709/739–5789. 4 rooms, 2 suites. AE, MC, V.*

$$ 🖬 **Gower Street House Bed & Breakfast.** This gracious former home of the late photographer Elsie Holloway has been designated by the Newfoundland Historic Trust as a point of interest. It's also an ideal setting for paintings by prominent local artists. The location is within walking distance of all the city's main attractions. A full breakfast is included in the room rate. ⊠ *180 Gower St., A1C 1P9,* ☎ *709/754–0047 or 800/563–3959,* FAX *709/754–0047. 4 rooms. MC, V.*

$$ 🖬 **Prescott Inn.** Local art decorates the walls of this house, the city's
★ most popular bed-and-breakfast. The inn has been modernized, tastefully blending the new and the old. It's central to shopping and downtown attractions. ⊠ *17–21 Military Rd., A1C 2C3,* ☎ *709/753–7733,* FAX *709/753–6036. 15 rooms, 7 suites. MC, V.*

Nightlife and the Arts

THE ARTS

St. John's has a lively and, for its size, large arts community. Drop into the **Ship Inn** (☎ 709/753–3870), a pub in Solomon's Lane between Duckworth and Water streets that serves as the local arts watering hole. Actors, musicians, painters, writers, poets, artisans, and their fans and friends hang out here. It's unpretentious and a good place to find out what's happening.

The **Resource Centre for the Arts** (⊠ LSPU Hall, 3 Victoria St., ☎ 709/753–4531, FAX 709/753–4537) is one of the country's oldest and most innovative experimental theaters. In addition to a busy fall and winter season, the center has a busy summer, with cabarets, outdoor concerts, plays, and alternative concerts.

The **Newfoundland and Labrador Folk Festival** (☎ 709/576–8508), held in St. John's in early August, is the province's best-known traditional music festival. **The Newfoundland International Irish Festival** (☎ 709/754–0700), held in Mount Pearl (south of St. John's) each July, features international performers and a Leprechaun Festival for the kids. **Shakespeare by the Sea** (☎ 709/576–0980) summer performances use the ocean as a backdrop.

NIGHTLIFE

It has been a long-standing claim (since at least the 1700s) that St. John's has more bars per mile than any city in North America. Each establishment has its own personality. **Erin's Pub** (⊠ 186 Water St., ☎ 709/722–1916) is famous for its Irish music. The **Blarney Stone** (⊠ 342 Water St., 2nd floor, ☎ 709/754–1798) also has Irish music. **George Street,** downtown, a beautifully restored street of pubs and restaurants, often has open-air concerts.

Shopping

ANTIQUES

Murray's Antiques (⊠ 414 Blackmarsh Rd., ☎ 709/579–7344) is renowned for silver, china, and fine mahogany and walnut furniture. **Livyers** (⊠ 202 Duckworth St., ☎ 709/726–5650) carries locally crafted furniture and is a great spot for digging through books, prints, and maps.

ART GALLERIES

St. John's has a dozen commercial and public art galleries, nearly all of which carry works by local artists. Newfoundland's unique landscape, portrayed realistically or more experimentally, is a favorite subject. **The Art Gallery of Newfoundland and Labrador** (⊠ Allandale Rd.

and Prince Philip Dr., ☎ 709/737–8209) is the province's largest public gallery and exhibits historical and contemporary Canadian arts and crafts with an emphasis on Newfoundland and Labrador artists and artisans. The gallery is closed Monday. The **Emma Butler Gallery** (✉ 111 George St., ☎ 709/739–7111) sells a large selection of Newfoundland art including works by David Blackwood and Christopher Pratt. **Christina Parker Fine Art** (✉ 7 Plank Rd., ☎ 709/753–0580) represents local and national artists in all media, including painting, sculpture, drawing, and fine art prints.

BOOKS

Most bookstores have a prominent section devoted to local history, fiction, and memoirs. **Word Play** (✉ 221 Duckworth St., ☎ 709/726–9193 or 800/563–9100) carries a wide selection of magazines and books of general interest to visitors.

HANDICRAFTS

St. John's has more than its fair share of fine crafts shops. **NONIA** (Newfoundland Outport Nurses Industrial Association, ✉ 286 Water St., ☎ 709/753–8062) was founded in 1920 to give Newfoundland women in the outports an opportunity to earn money to support nursing services in these remote communities. Their reputation for fierce independence was as colorful as their reputation for turning homespun wool into exquisite clothing. Today the shop continues to sell these fine homespun articles as well as lighter and more modern handmade items. **The Salt Box** (✉ 194 Duckworth St., ☎ 709/753–0622) sells local crafts and specializes in pottery. **The Cod Jigger** (✉ 245 Duckworth St., ☎ 709/726–7422) carries handmade wool sweaters, socks, and mitts as well as Newfoundland's unique Grenfell coats. **The Devon House Craft Gallery** (✉ 59 Duckworth St., ☎ 709/753–2749) is owned by the Newfoundland and Labrador Crafts Development Association and carries only juried crafts. **The Newfoundland Weavery** (✉ 177 Water St., ☎ 709/753–0496) sells rugs, prints, lamps, books, crafts, and other gifts.

MUSIC

Fred's Records (✉ 198 Duckworth St., ☎ 709/753–9191) has the best selection of local recordings, as well as other music.

Avalon Peninsula

On the southern half of the peninsula are small Irish hamlets separated by large tracts of wilderness. You can travel part of the peninsula's southern coast in one or two days, depending on how much time you have. Quaint coastal towns line the road, and the natural sites are beautiful. La Manche and Chance Cove—both now-abandoned communities turned provincial parks—attest to the bounty of natural resources of the region. At the intersection of Routes 90 and 91, in Salmonier, you need to decide whether to continue north toward Salmonier Nature Park and on to the towns on Conception Bay, or to head west and then south to Route 100 to Cape St. Mary's Ecological Reserve (☞ Route 100: The Cape Shore, *below*). Each option takes about three hours. On the former route, stop in Harbor Grace; if you plan to travel on to Bay de Verde, at the northern tip of the peninsula, and down the other side of the peninsula on Route 80 along Trinity Bay, consider turning in for the night in the Harbour Grace–Carbonear area. Otherwise turn around and follow the same route back to Route 1.

Witless Bay Ecological Reserve

❸ *29 km (18 mi) south of St. John's.*

The wildness of the peninsula's eastern coast is usually what's most striking to visitors, as evidenced at the Witless Bay Ecological Reserve

(⊠ Rte. 10), a strip of water and four offshore islands between Bay Bulls and Tors Cove. Sometimes referred to as "the Serengeti of the northwest Atlantic," the reserve is the summer home of millions of seabirds—puffins, murres, kittiwakes, razorbills, and guillemots—that nest on the islands. The birds, and the humpback and minke whales that tarry here before continuing north to the summer grounds in the Arctic, feed on the billions of capelin that swarm inshore to spawn. Here, too, is an excellent place to see icebergs; the best views are from tour boats that operate in the reserve. For information, contact the **Parks and Natural Areas Division** (☎ 709/729–2421).

OUTDOOR ACTIVITIES AND SPORTS
O'Brien's Bird Island Charters (☎ 709/753–4850 or 709/334–2355, FAX 709/753–3140) offers popular two-hour excursions featuring whale-, iceberg-, and seabird-watching as well as cod jigging. **Gather-all's Puffin and Whale Watch** (☎ 709/334–2887 or 800/41WHALE) has trips for viewing wildlife in the reserve.

En Route   Although a visit to many of the hamlets along the way from Witless Bay to Ferryland on **Route 10** will fulfill any search for prettiness, a few favorites are exceptional. La Manche and Brigus South have especially attractive settings and strong traditional flavors.

Ferryland
❹ *43½ km (27 mi) south of Witless Bay Ecological Reserve.*

This seaside town has a long history, some of which is described in its small community museum. A major ongoing **archaeological dig** at Ferryland has uncovered the early 17th-century colony of Lord Baltimore, who abandoned the Colony of Avalon after a decade for the warmer climes of Maryland. The site includes an archaeology laboratory and exhibit center. ⊠ *Rte. 10, The Pool (seasonal),* ☎ *709/432–3200.* ⌑ *Free.* ☉ *June–Oct., daily 9–8.*

En Route   In springtime, between Chance Cove and Portugal Cove South, in a stretch of land about 58 km (36 mi) long, hundreds of **caribou** and their calves gather on the barrens near Route 10. Although the animals are there at other times of the year, their numbers are few and it's hard to spot them because they blend in so well with the scenery.

Salmonier Nature Park
❺ *88 km (55 mi) from Ferryland, 14½ km (9 mi) north of the intersection of Rtes. 90 and 91.*

You can see many of the animal species indigenous to the province here. The park is a 3,000-acre wilderness reserve area and has an enclosed 100-acre exhibit that allows up-close viewing. ⊠ *Salmonier Line, Rte. 90,* ☎ *709/729–6974.* ⌑ *Free.* ☉ *June 5–Canadian Thanksgiving (mid-Oct.), daily noon–7; other times by appointment.*

En Route   From Salmonier Nature Park to Brigus, take Route 90, which passes through the scenic **Hawke Hills** before meeting up with the Trans-Canada Highway (Route 1). Turn off at the Holyrood Junction (Route 62) and follow Route 70, which skirts Conception Bay.

Brigus
❻ *19 km (12 mi) off Rte. 1 and Rte. 70.*

This beautiful village on Conception Bay has a wonderful public garden, winding lanes, and a teahouse. Brigus is best known as the birthplace of Captain Bob Bartlett, the famed Arctic explorer who accompanied Admiral Peary on polar expeditions during the first decade of this century. **Hawthorne Cottage,** the home of Captain Bartlett, is one of the few surviving examples of the picturesque cottage style, with a veranda decorated with ornamental wooden fretwork. It dates from 1830 and is a National Historic Site. ⊠ *Irishtown Rd.,* ☎ *709/753–9262; in summer, 709/528–4004.* ☜ *$2.25.* ☉ *Early June–mid-Oct., daily 10–8 (shorter hours in fall; call ahead).*

Ye Old Stone Barn Museum displays photos and artifacts of the town's history, especially its connection with the fishery. ⊠ *4 Magistrate's Hill,* ☎ *709/528–3298.* ☜ *$1.* ☉ *Mid-June–Labor Day, daily 10–5; Sept.–Canadian Thanksgiving (mid-Oct.), weekends 10–5.*

Cupids
❼ *5 km (3 mi) north of Brigus.*

Cupids is the oldest English colony in Canada, founded in 1610 by John Guy, to whom the town erected a monument. In 1995 archaeologists began unearthing the long-lost site of the original colony here, and some of these artifacts are on display in the community museum, **Cupids Archaeological Site.** ⊠ *United Church Hall, Main Rd.,* ☎ *709/528–3477.* ☜ *Free.* ☉ *June–Aug., daily 9–4:30.*

Harbour Grace
❽ *21 km (13 mi) north of Cupids.*

Harbour Grace was once the headquarters of Peter Easton, a 17th-century pirate. Beginning in 1919, this town was the departure point for many attempts to fly the Atlantic. Amelia Earhart left Harbour Grace in 1932 to become the first woman to fly solo across the Atlantic. Several handsome stone churches and buildings remain as evidence of the town's pride.

Route 100: The Cape Shore

You can reach the Cape Shore on the western side of the Avalon Peninsula from Route 1, at its intersection with Route 100. The ferry from Nova Scotia docks in Argentia, near Placentia. Besides the coastal towns, a highlight of the area is the outstanding seabird colony at Cape St. Mary's.

Placentia
❾ *48 km (30 mi) south of Route 1.*

Placentia was the French capital of Newfoundland in the 1600s. Trust the French to select a beautiful place for a capital! **Castle Hill National Historic Site,** just north of town, is on what remains of the French fortifications. The visitor's center has a "life at Plaisance" exhibit that shows the life and hardships endured by early English and French settlers. ⊠ *Off Rte. 100,* ☎ *709/227–2401.* ☜ *$2.25.* ☉ *June–Labor Day, daily 8:30–8; Labor Day–May, daily 8:30–4:30.*

Ship Harbour
❿ *34 km (21 mi) north of Placentia.*

An isolated, edge-of-the-world place, Ship Harbour has historic significance. Off Route 102, amid the splendor of Placentia Bay, an unpaved road leads to a monument marking the Atlantic Charter. It was on a ship in these waters where, in 1941, Franklin Roosevelt and Winston Churchill signed the charter and formally announced the "Four Freedoms," which still shape the politics of the world's most successful democracies: freedom of speech, freedom of worship, freedom from want, and freedom from fear.

Cape St. Mary's Ecological Reserve

★ ⓫ *65 km (40 mi) south of Placentia.*

Cape St. Mary's Ecological Reserve is the most southerly nesting site in the world for gannets and common and thick-billed murres. A paved road takes you within a mile of the seabird colony. Visit the interpretation center—guides are on site during the summer—then walk to within 100 ft of the colony of nesting gannets, murres, black-billed kittiwakes, and razorbills. You'll also be able to enjoy some of the most dramatic coastal scenery in Newfoundland. For information, contact the **Parks and Natural Areas Division** (☎ 709/729–2431).

Cape St. Mary's Charters and Boat Tours (☎ 709/337–2660 or 709/337–2614) gives passengers a look at this famous gannet colony from the ocean.

Clarenville and the Bonavista Peninsula

Clarenville, about two hours northwest of St. John's via the Trans-Canada Highway (Route 1), is the departure point for two different excursions in the Bonavista Peninsula: the Discovery Trail and Terra Nova National Park.

Clarenville

⓬ *189 km (117 mi) northwest of St. John's.*

★ If history and quaint towns appeal to you, this is the starting point for Route 230A—the **Discovery Trail.** The route goes as far north as the town of Bonavista, one of John Cabot's reputed landing spots in 1497.

LODGING

$$$ 🏨 **Clarenville Inn.** This property was renovated in 1996; rooms are standard. ⊠ *Rte. 1, Box 967, A0E 1J0,* ☎ *709/466–7911,* FAX *709/466–3854. 64 rooms. Restaurant, bar. AE, DC, MC, V.*

Terra Nova National Park

⓭ *24 km (15 mi) northwest of Clarenville.*

If you're interested in rugged terrain, golf, fishing, and camping, Terra Nova National Park, on the exposed coastline that adjoins Bonavista Bay, is the place to be. If you are a golfer, you can play on one of the most beautiful courses in Canada, at the Terra Nova Park Lodge in the park at Port Blandford. It's the only one where a salmon river cuts through the 18-hole course. Call 709/543–2626 for a reservation; fees run between $24 and $30 per person, depending on the season. The park also has a new Marine Interpretation Center, attractive campsites, whale-watching tours, and nature walks. ⊠ *Trans-Canada Hwy., Glovertown,* ☎ *709/533–2801 or 709/533–2802,* FAX *709/533–2706.* 🎟 *Park and vehicle permit $6 daily, 4-day pass $18, seasonal pass $30 ($20 before June 22).* ☉ *June–Aug., daily 10–9; Sept.–May, weekdays 8–4:30.*

Trinity

⓮ *71 km (44 mi) northeast of Clarenville.*

Trinity is one of the jewels of Newfoundland. The village's picturesque views, winding lanes, and snug houses are the main attraction, and several homes have been turned into museums and inns. In the 1700s Trinity competed with St. John's as a center of culture and wealth. Its more contemporary claim to fame, however, is that its intricate harbor was a favorite anchorage for the British navy, and it was here that the smallpox vaccine was introduced to North America by a local rector. An information center with costumed interpreters is open daily from July through September. To get here, take Route 230 to Route 239.

The **Lester-Garland Premises** (✉ Rte. 239, ☎ 800/563–6353 at press time) is a re-creation of a fish merchant's house that was once one of the most prominent 18th-century homes in Newfoundland. The original was torn down in the 1960s, but the new house was set to open in summer 1997.

Rising Tide Theatre (☎ 709/738–3256,) conducts The New-Founde-Land Trinity Pageant walking tours (Wednesday, Saturday, and Sunday at 2) of the town that are more theater than tour, led by actors in period costumes.

THE ARTS

Rising Tide Theatre (☎ 709/738–3256) stages the **Summer in the Bight** festival. Outdoor Shakespeare productions, dinner theater, and back-porch dramas and comedies fill the bill.

WHALE-WATCHING

Ocean Contact Limited (☎ 709/464–3269) is an established specialist in whale-watching and whale research. Dr. Peter Beamish's book, *Dancing with Whales,* documents their interesting findings.

Cape Bonavista

🟤 *16 km (10 mi) north of Port Union.*

Cape Bonavista is a popular destination because of its association with Cabot's landing in 1497. The **Ryan Premises National Historic Site** on the waterfront, opened in 1997, depicts the almost 500-year history of the commercial cod fishery in a restored fish merchant's properties. ✉ *Off Rte. 230,* ☎ *709/772–5364.* 🎫 *Free.* ☉ *Mid-June–mid-Oct., daily 10–6.*

The **lighthouse** on the point, about 1 km (½ mi) outside town, has been restored to its condition in 1870. The **Mockbeggar Property** teaches about the life of an outport merchant in the years immediately before Confederation. ✉ *Off Rte. 230,* ☎ *709/729–2460 or 709/468–7300/7444.* 🎫 *Free.* ☉ *Late June–early Sept., daily 10–5:30.*

Burin Peninsula, Gander, and Notre Dame Bay

The journey down to the Burin Peninsula is a three- to four-hour drive from the intersection of Routes 230 and 1 through the craggy coastal landscapes along Route 210. The peninsula's history is tied to the rich fishing grounds of the Grand Banks, which established this area as a center for European fishery as early as the 1500s. By the early 1900s, one of the world's largest fishing fleets was based on the Burin Peninsula. Today its inhabitants hope for a recovery of the fish stocks that have sustained their economy for centuries. Marystown is the peninsula's commercial center.

Gander, in east-central Newfoundland, is famous for its airport. North of it is Notre Dame Bay, an area of rugged coastline and equally rugged islands that was once the domain of the now-extinct Beothuk tribe. Only the larger islands are now inhabited. Before English settlers moved into the area in the late 18th and early 19th centuries, it was seasonally occupied by French fishermen. Local dialects preserve centuries-old words that have vanished elsewhere. The bay is swept by the cool Labrador Current that carries icebergs south through Iceberg Alley; the coast is also a good whale-watching area.

Grand Bank

🔵 *53 km (33 mi) southwest of Marystown on Rte. 220.*

One of the loveliest communities in Newfoundland, Grand Bank has a fascinating history as an important fishing center. Because of trade patterns, the architecture here was influenced more by Halifax, Boston, and Bar Harbor than by the rest of Newfoundland. For details about the town's past visit the **Southern Newfoundland Seamen's Museum,** in a sail-shape building. ⊠ *Marine Dr.,* ☎ *709/832–1484.* ⊑ *Free.* ☉ *May–Oct., weekdays 9–5, weekends 2–5.*

St-Pierre and Miquelon
⑰ *55-min. ferry ride from Fortune.*

The islands of St-Pierre and Miquelon are France's only territory in North America. A ferry trip to these islands is a great idea if you crave French cuisine or a bottle of perfume. Shopping and eating are both popular pastimes. Visitors traveling to the islands should carry proof of citizenship; people from outside the United States and Canada will have to show valid visas and passports. Because of the ferry schedule, a trip to St-Pierre means an overnight stay in a modern hotel such as Hotel Robert (☎ 011–508/412419) or a pension, the French equivalent of a bed-and-breakfast. Call the St-Pierre tourist board (☎ 011–508/412222 or 800/565–5118) for information about accommodations.

A passenger ferry operated by **Lloyd G. Lake Ltd.** (☎ 709/832–2006) leaves Fortune (south of Grand Bank) daily at 2:15 PM from mid-June to late September; the crossing takes 70 minutes. The ferry leaves St-Pierre at 1 PM daily; round-trip is $55. The ferry operated by **St-Pierre Tours** (☎ 709/722–4103 or 709/832–0429) crosses daily from Fortune to St-Pierre from May through September, and weekly from October to early December. The ferry leaves Fortune at 2:45 PM, Newfoundland time, and departs St-Pierre at 1:30 PM, St-Pierre (Atlantic) time. Round-trip fare is $59.95. The trip takes 70 minutes.

Burin
⑱ *62 km (38 mi) from Grand Bank.*

Following Route 220 south and east from Grand Bank will take you around the peninsula to the old town of Burin, a community built amid intricate cliffs and coves. This was an ideal setting for pirates and privateers who used to lure ships into the rocky, dead-end areas in order to plunder them. Captain Cook was among those who watched for smugglers from "Cook's Lookout" on a hill that still bears his name.

The **Heritage House and Heritage II** museums, considered two of the best community museums in Newfoundland, give you a sense of what life was like in the past. Heritage II has a display on the 1929 tidal wave that struck Burin. ⊠ *Square off Rte. 221,* ☎ *709/891–2217.* ⊑ *Free.* ☉ *May–Oct., Mon.–Tues. 9–5, Wed.–Sun. 9–9.*

Gander
⑲ *170 km (105 mi) northwest of Goobies.*

A busy town with 12,000 people, Gander is notable for its aviation history. It also has many lodgings and makes a good base for your travels in this part of the province. During World War II, **Gander International Airport** was chosen by the Canadian and U.S. Air Forces as a major strategic air base because of its favorable weather and secure location. After the war, the airport became an international hub for civilian travel; today it is a major air traffic control center. The **Aviation Exhibition** in the airport's domestic passengers' lounge (☎ 709/256–3905 or 709/651–2656) traces Newfoundland's role in the history of air travel. It's open 24 hours, 7 days a week.

The **North Atlantic Aviation Museum,** opened in 1996, gives an expansive view of Gander's and Newfoundland's roles in aviation. In addition to viewing the expected models and photographs, you can climb into the cockpit of a real DC-3 parked outside next to a World War II Hudson bomber and a Canadian jet fighter, or take a helicopter ride in summer. ⊠ *On Rte. 1, between hospital and visitor information center,* ☎ *709/256–2923.* ☒ *$3.* ☉ *Daily 9–5.*

DINING AND LODGING

$$ ✕☷ **Albatross Motel.** This motel has a deserved reputation as an at-
★ tractive place to stop off for a meal. Try the cod au gratin—you won't find it this good anywhere else. Rooms are basic and clean. ⊠ *Rte. 1, Box 450, A1V 1W8,* ☎ *709/256–3956 or 800/563–4900,* ℻ *709/651–2692. 103 rooms, 4 suites. Restaurant. AE, DC, MC, V.*

Boyd's Cove
⑳ *66 km (41 mi) north of Gander.*

The coastline in and near Boyd's Cove is somewhat sheltered by Twillingate Island and New World Island, and it's from this area that short causeways link the shore to the islands.

The **Boyd's Cove Beothuk Interpretation Centre** offers a fresh look at the lives of the Beothuks, an extinct aboriginal people who succumbed in the early 19th century to a combination of disease and battle with European settlers. Opened in 1995, the center uses traditional Beothuk building forms and adjoins an archaeological site that was inhabited from about 1650 to 1720, when pressure from settlers drove the Beothuk from this part of the coast. ⊠ *Rte. 340,* ☎ *709/656–3114 or 709/729–2460.* ☒ *Free.* ☉ *Summer, daily 10–5:30.*

Twillingate
㉑ *31 km (19 mi) north of Boyd's Cove.*

The inhabitants of this scenic old fishing village make their living from the sea and have been doing so for nearly two centuries. Colorful houses, rocky waterfront cliffs, a local museum, and a nearby lighthouse add to the town's appeal. Every year on the last weekend in July, the town hosts the **Fish, Fun and Folk Festival,** where fish are cooked every kind of way. Twillingate is one of the best places on the island to see **icebergs,** and is known to the locals as "Iceberg Alley." These majestic and dangerous mountains of ice are awe-inspiring to see while they're grounded in early summer.

Twillingate Island Boat Tours (☎ 709/884–2242 or 709/882–2317) specializes in iceberg photography in the waters around Twillingate. There is an iceberg interpretation center right on the dock.

OFF THE **CHANGE ISLANDS AND FOGO ISLAND –** You can take a ferry (☎ 709/
BEATEN PATH 627-3448) from Farewell to either Change Islands or Fogo Island. To get to Farewell, take Route 340 to Route 335, which takes you through scenic coastal communities. These islands give you the impression of a place frozen in time. Clapboard homes are precariously perched on rocks or built on small lots surrounded by vegetable gardens. As you walk the roads, watch for moose and herds of wild Newfoundland ponies who spend their summers grazing and enjoying the warm breeze off the ocean.

The Great Northern Peninsula

The Great Northern Peninsula is the most northern visible extension of the Appalachian Mountains. Its eastern side is rugged and sparsely populated. The Viking Trail—Route 430 and its side roads, and Route 510 in southern Labrador—snakes along its western coast through a national park, fjords, sand dunes, and communities that have relied on the lobstery fishery for generations. At the tip of the peninsula, the Vikings established the first European settlement in North America. For thousands of years before their arrival, however, the area was home to native peoples who hunted, fished, and gathered berries and wild herbs.

Deer Lake

② *208 km (129 mi) west of Grand Falls-Windsor.*

Deer Lake was once just another small town on the Trans-Canada Highway, but the opening of Gros Morne National Park in the early '70s and a first-class paved highway passing right through to St. Anthony changed all that. Today, with an airport and car rentals available, Deer Lake is a good starting point for a fly-drive vacation.

LODGING

$$ ☒ **Deer Lake Motel.** The guest rooms here are clean and comfortable, and the food in the café is basic, home-cooked fare. You'll find the seafood dishes exceptionally well prepared. ⊠ *Box 820, A0K 2E0,* ☎ *709/635–2108,* 𝖥𝖠𝖷 *709/635–3842. 54 rooms, 2 suites. Café. AE, DC, MC, V.*

OFF THE BEATEN PATH   **SIR RICHARD SQUIRES MEMORIAL PARK –** From Deer Lake take Route 430 to Route 422 north to this park. Natural and unspoiled, it contains one of the most interesting salmon fishing areas in Newfoundland. This drive will also take you through Cormack, a farming region.

Gros Morne National Park

★ ㉓ *46 km (29 mi) north of Deer Lake on Rte. 430.*

Because of its geological uniqueness and immense splendor, this park has been named a UNESCO World Heritage Site. Among the more breathtaking visions are the expanses of wild orchids in springtime. There is an excellent **interpretation center** (☎ 709/458–2417) in Rocky Harbour, which has displays and videos about the park, plus an interactive vacation planner. Camping and hiking are popular recreations, and boat tours are available. It takes at least two days to see Gros Morne properly. Scenic **Bonne Bay,** a deep, mountainous fjord, divides the park in two. You can drive around the perimeter of the fjord on Route 430 going north.

㉔ In the south of the park, on Route 431, is **Woody Point,** a charming community of old houses and imported Lombardy poplars. Until it was bypassed by the now-defunct railway, the community was the commercial capital of Newfoundland's west coast. The **Tablelands,** rising behind Woody Point, are a unique rock massif that was once an ancient seabed. Its rocks, which were raised from the earth's mantle through tectonic upheaval, are toxic to most plant life, and Ice Age conditions linger in the form of persistent snow and moving rock glaciers.

㉕ The once-isolated small community of **Trout River** is at the western end of Route 431 on the Gulf of St. Lawrence. You pass the scenic **Trout River Pond** along the way. The **Green Gardens Trail,** a four- to five-hour hike, is also nearby, and it's one you'll remember for your lifetime, but be prepared to do a bit of climbing on your return journey. The trail passes through the Tablelands barrens and descends sharply down to a fairy-tale coastline of eroded cliffs and green meadows.

㉖ On the northern side of the park, along coastal Route 430, is **Rocky Harbour,** with a wide range of services and a luxurious indoor public pool—the perfect thing to soothe tired limbs after a strenuous day.

The most popular attraction in the northern portion of Gros Morne is the boat tour of **Western Brook Pond** (☞ Outdoor Activities and Sports, *below*). You park at a lot on Route 430 and take a 45-minute walk to the boat dock through an interesting mix of bog and woods. Cliffs rise 2,000 ft on both sides of the gorge, and high waterfalls tumble over ancient rocks. If you have strong legs and are in good shape, another natural attraction is the 10-mi hike up **Gros Morne Mountain,** at 2,644 ft the second-highest peak in Newfoundland. Weather permitting, your labor will be rewarded by a unique arctic landscape and spectacular views. The park's **northern coast** has an unusual mix of sand beaches, rock pools, and trails through tangled dwarf forests known locally as "tuckamore." Sunsets, seen from **Lobster Point Lighthouse,** are spectacular. Keep an eye out for whales and visit the lighthouse museum, devoted to the history of the area. ⊠ *Gros Morne National Park, via the Viking Trail (Rte. 430),* ☎ *709/458–2417.* 🎫 *Daily $3, 4 days $9.* ☉ *Summer, daily 9 AM–10 PM; winter, daily 9–4.*

LODGING

$$–$$$$ 🏨 **Sugar Hill Inn.** This small hostelry in Gros Morne National Park has quickly developed a reputation for fine wining and dining because of host Vince McCarthy's culinary talents and educated palate. You can take guided cross-country skiing and snowmobiling treks here. ⊠ *Box 100, Norris Point, A0K 3V0,* ☎ FAX *709/458–2147. 4 rooms. Hot tub, sauna. MC, V.*

OUTDOOR ACTIVITIES AND SPORTS

Gros Morne Adventure Guides (☎ 709/458–2722 or 709/686–2241) has sea kayaking up the fjords and land-locked ponds of Gros Morne National Park, as well as a variety of hikes and adventures in the area.

Bontours (☎ 709/458–2730) runs the best-known of the sightseeing trips on the west coast of Newfoundland—up Western Brook Pond in Gros Morne National Park—and another tour of Bonne Bay. **Table-land Boat Tours** (☎ 709/451–2101 or 709/451–5146) leads tours up Trout River Pond near the southern boundary of Gros Morne National Park. **Seal Island Boat Tours** (☎ 709/243–2376 or 709/243–2278) explores St. Paul's Inlet, an area of Gros Morne National Park rich in seals, terns, and other marine and shore life.

Arches Provincial Park

㉗ *20 km (12 mi) north of Gros Morne National Park.*

Arches Provincial Park is a geological curiosity where the action of undersea current millions of years ago cut a succession of caves through a bed of dolomite that was later raised above sea level by tectonic upheaval.

En Route Continuing north on Route 430, parallel to the Gulf of St. Lawrence, you'll find yourself refreshingly close to the ocean and the wave-tossed beaches: Stop to breathe the fresh sea air and listen to the breakers. The **Long Range Mountains** to your right reminded Jacques Cartier, who saw them in 1534, of the long, rectangular-shape farm buildings of his home village in France. Small villages are interspersed with rivers where salmon and trout grow to be "liar-size."

The remains of the Maritime Archaic Indians and Dorset Eskimos have been found in abundance along this coast, and **Port au Choix** has an interesting interpretation center (☎ 709/623–2608; 🎫 $1).

L'Anse aux Meadows National Historic Site

★ ❷ *210 km (130 mi) northeast of Arches Provincial Park.*

A UNESCO World Heritage Site, L'Anse aux Meadows was discovered in 1960 by a Norwegian team, Helge and Anne Stine Ingstad. Most believe the remains of the long sod houses here were built around 1000 as the site of Norseman Leif Eriksson's colony in the New World. The Canadian Parks Service has established a fine **visitor center** and has meticulously reconstructed some of the sod huts to give you a sense of centuries past. ✉ *Rte. 436,* ☎ *709/623−2608.* ☜ *$2.50* ☉ *Mid-June−Labor Day, daily 9−8.*

DINING AND LODGING

$ ✕⊟ **Tickle Inn at Cape Onion.** This refurbished, century-old fisherman's house on the beach is probably the most northerly residence on the island of Newfoundland. You can relax around the Franklin stove in the parlor after a day of exploring the area meadows, hills, and coast, or taking a trip to the Viking settlement at L'Anse aux Meadows (about 45 km, or 28 mi, away). ✉ *R.R. 1, Box 62, Cape Onion, A0K 4J0,* ☎ *709/452−4321 June−Sept., 709/739−5503 Oct.−May. 4 rooms share bath. Dining room. CP, MAP available. MC, V.*

$ ⊟ **Valhalla Lodge Bed & Breakfast.** Comfortable and inviting, the Valhalla is 10 km (6 mi) from L'Anse aux Meadows. Note the interesting fossils in the rock fireplace in the dining room. Hot breakfasts are available, and other meals can be had on request. E. Annie Proulx, author of *The Shipping News,* stayed here when she was writing the novel. ✉ *Gunner's Cove, Griquet A0K 2X0,* ☎ *709/623−2018 in summer, 709/896−5519 in winter. 6 rooms. V.*

OUTDOOR ACTIVITIES AND SPORTS

In nearby St. Lunaire you can take a tour boat modeled after a Viking trading vessel and see the coast from the ocean. **Viking Boat Tours** (☎ 709/623−2100) visits the site at the tip of the Great Northern Peninsula where Vikings landed 1,000 years ago.

St. Anthony

❷ *16 km (10 mi) south of L'Anse aux Meadows.*

The northern part of the Great Northern Peninsula served as the model for *The Shipping News,* E. Annie Proulx's Pulitzer-winning novel. St. Anthony, which has a number of attractions, is built around a natural harbor on the eastern side of the Great Northern Peninsula, near its tip. Take a trip out to the **lighthouse**—you may see an iceberg or two floating by.

The **Grenfell Mission,** founded by Sir Wilfred Grenfell, a British medical missionary who established nursing stations and cooperatives and provided medical services to the scattered villages of northern Newfoundland and the south coast of Labrador in the early 1900s, remains the town's main employer. The main foyer of the **Charles S. Curtis Memorial Hospital** has a decorative tile mural that's worth a visit. **Grenfell House,** the home of Sir Wilfred and Lady Grenfell, has been restored to period condition and can be visited. ✉ *On west side of town on hill overlooking harbor,* ☎ *709/454−8596.* ☜ *$2.* ☉ *June−Sept., daily 10− 8; winter, by appointment.*

Don't leave without visiting the **Grenfell Handicrafts** store (☎ 709/454− 3576). Training villagers to become self-sufficient in a harsh environment was one of Grenfell's aims. A windproof cloth that villagers turned into well-made parkas came to be known as Grenfell cloth. Beautiful clothes fashioned out of Grenfell cloth have a unique quality and style and are available for sale here.

The West Coast

Western Newfoundland is known for the unlikely combination of world-class Atlantic salmon fishing and papermaking at two newsprint mills. This area includes Corner Brook, a major center of the west coast. To the south, the Port au Prince Peninsula west of Stephenville shows the French influence in Newfoundland; the farming valleys of the southwest were settled by Scots. A ferry from Nova Scotia docks at Port aux Basques in the far southwest corner.

Corner Brook

30 *50 km (31 mi) southwest of Deer Lake.*

Corner Brook is Newfoundland's second-largest city and the hub of the west coast of the island. Mountains fringe three sides of the city, and there are beautiful views of the harbor and the Bay of Islands. Corner Brook is also home to one of the largest paper mills in the world; you may smell it. Captain James Cook, the British explorer, charted the coast in the 1760s, and a memorial to him overlooks the bay.

If you plan to explore the west coast, Corner Brook is a convenient hub and point of departure. It is only three hours from the Port aux Basques ferry from Nova Scotia and is an attractive, active city. The town enjoys more clearly defined seasons than most of the rest of the island, and in summer there are many pretty gardens. In addition, the nearby Humber River is the best-known salmon river in the province.

The north and south shores of the **Bay of Islands** have fine paved roads—Route 440 on the north shore and Route 450 on the south—and both are a scenic half-day drive from Corner Brook. On both roads, farming and fishing communities exist side by side. Take a camera with you—the scenery is breathtaking, with farms, mountains, and pockets of brilliant wildflowers.

DINING AND LODGING

$$ ✕⊞ **Best Western Mamateek Inn.** Rooms are more modern than at the
★ Glynmill Inn (☞ *below*). The dining room, which serves good Newfoundland home-cooked food, is known for its exquisite view of the city. Sunsets seen from here are remarkable. ⊠ *Rte. 1, Box 787, A2H 6G7,* ☎ *709/639–8901 or 800/563–8600,* FAX *709/639–7567. 55 rooms. Restaurant. AE, MC, V.*

$$ ✕⊞ **Glynmill Inn.** This charming inn, refurbished in 1994, has the feel
★ of old England. It was once the staff house for the visiting top brass of the paper mill. Rooms are cozy and the dining room serves basic and well-prepared Newfoundland seafood, soups, and specialty desserts made with partridgeberries. There's also a popular steak house in the basement. ⊠ *1 Cobb La., Box 550, A2H 6E6,* ☎ *709/634–5181, 800/563–4400 in Canada,* FAX *709/634–5106. 57 rooms, 24 suites. 2 restaurants. AE, MC, V.*

$$ ⊞ **Comfort Inn by Journey's End Motel.** This is a comfortable, modern motel with an attractive interior (the dominating colors are dusty rose and blue) and beautiful views of either the city or the Bay Islands. ⊠ *41 Maple Valley Rd., Box 1142, A2H 6T2,* ☎ *709/639–1980,* FAX *709/639–1549. 81 rooms. Restaurant. AE, DC, MC, V.*

$$ ⊞ **Holiday Inn.** There's nothing extraordinary here, aside from the convenience of being located right in town. The outdoor pool is heated and some of the rooms have minibars. The restaurant is average, aside from good seasonal fish dishes. ⊠ *48 West St., A2H 2Z2,* ☎ *709/634–*

5381, FAX *709/634–1723. 103 rooms. Restaurant, lobby lounge, pool. AE, DC, MC, V.*

Strawberry Hill Resort (☎ 709/634–0066, FAX 709/634–7604) in Little Rapids, 12 km (7 mi) east of Corner Brook on Route 1, was once an exclusive retreat for the owner of the Corner Brook mill. Guests here can enjoy Newfoundland's finest sport salmon fishing.

The **Marble Mountain Ski Resort** (☎ 709/637–7600), just east of the city, has the highest slopes and the most snowfall in eastern North America and is growing rapidly. There are 27 downhill runs, as well as a large day lodge, ski shop, day-care center, and restaurant at the mountain summit.

Stephenville

③ *77 km (48 mi) south of Corner Brook.*

The former Harmon Air Force Base is in Stephenville, which is best known for its summer festival (☞ *below*). It also has a large modern paper mill. To the west of town is the Port au Port Peninsula, which was largely settled by the French, who brought their way of life and language to this small corner of Newfoundland.

The **Stephenville Festival** (☎ 709/643–5756) is held mid-July to mid-August. The festival is the province's major annual summer theatrical event and presents a mix of light musicals and serious drama.

En Route   As you travel down the Trans-Canada Highway toward Port aux Basques, Routes 404, 405, 406, and 407 will bring you into the small Scottish communities of the **Codroy Valley.** Nestled in the valley are some of the finest salmon rivers and most productive farms in the province, all of this against the backdrop of the Long Range Mountains and the Lewis Hills, from which gales strong enough to stop traffic hurl off the plateau and down to the coast.

Port aux Basques

③ *70 km (43 mi) south of Stephenville.*

Port aux Basques was one of seven Basque ports along Newfoundland's west coast and in southern Labrador during the 1500s and early 1600s, and was given its name by the town's French successors. It is now the main ferry port connecting the island to Nova Scotia. In **J. T. Cheeseman Provincial Park** (15 km, or 9 mi) north of town on the Trans-Canada Highway and at **Grand Bay West** you can catch sight of the endangered piping plover, which nests in the sand dunes along this part of the coast.

$$ ⊞ **St. Christopher's Hotel.** This clean, comfortable hotel has quiet, air-conditioned rooms and good food. Rooms have satellite TV. ✉ *Box 2049, Caribou Rd., Port aux Basques, A0M 1C0,* ☎ *709/695–7034 or 800/563–4779,* FAX *709/695–9841. 54 rooms, 3 suites. Restaurant, meeting room. AE, DC, MC, V.*

LABRADOR

Isolated from the rest of the continent, Labrador has remained one of the world's truly wild places, and yet its two main centers of Labrador City–Wabush and Happy Valley–Goose Bay offer all the amenities available in larger urban areas. Labrador is steeped in history, a place where the past invades the present and life evolves as it did many years ago—

a composite of natural phenomena, wilderness adventure, history, and culture. This vast landscape—293,347 square km (113,204 square mi) of land and 8,000 km (5,000 mi) of coastline—is home to 30,000 people. The small but richly diverse population has a history that in some cases stretches back thousands of years; in other cases—the mining towns of Labrador West, for example—the history goes back less than four decades.

The Straits

The Straits in southeastern Labrador were a rich hunting-and-gathering ground for the continent's earliest peoples. In the area is the oldest industrial site in the New World, the 16th-century Basque whaling station at Red Bay.

L'Anse au Clair

33 *5 km (3 mi) from Blanc Sablon, Québec (ferry from St. Barbe, Newfoundland, docks in Blanc Sablon).*

In L'Anse au Clair, anglers can try their luck for trout and salmon on the scenic Forteau and Pinware rivers. You can also walk the "Doctor's Path," where long ago Dr. Marcoux searched out herbs and medicinal plants in the days when hospitals and nursing stations were few and far between.

L'Anse Amour

34 *19 km (12 mi) east of L'Anse au Clair.*

The elaborate **Maritime Archaic Indian burial site** discovered near L'Anse Amour is 7,500 years old. A plaque marks a site that is the oldest known aboriginal funeral monument in North America. The L'Anse Amour **lighthouse** was constructed in 1857 and is the second-tallest lighthouse in Canada.

En Route The **Labrador Straits Museum** provides a glimpse into the history and lifestyle of the area. ⊠ *Rte. 510 between Forteau and L'Anse au Loup,* ☎ *709/927–5659 or 709/931–2067.* ⊠ *$1.50.* ☉ *Summer, daily.*

Red Bay

★ **35** *35 km (22 mi) from L'Anse Amour.*

You must drive to the very end of Route 510 to visit the area's main attraction: Red Bay, the site of a 16th-century Basque whaling station and a National Historic Site. Basque whalers began harpooning migrating whales from flimsy boats in frigid waters a few years after Cabot's discovery of the coast in 1497. Between 1550 and 1600 Red Bay was the world's whaling capital. A **visitor center** (☎ 709/920–2197) interprets the Basque heritage through film and artifact. It's open mid-June–September, Monday–Saturday 8–8 and Sunday noon–8. From June through October, a boat will take you on a five-minute journey over to the site of excavations on Saddle Island.

Coastal Labrador

This area is almost as isolated today as it was a century ago. Along the southern coast, most villages are inhabited by descendants of Europeans, while farther north they are mostly native. Over the years the European settlers have adopted native skills and survival strategies, and the natives have adopted many European technologies. In summer the ice retreats and a coastal steamer delivers goods. In winter small airplanes and snowmobiles are the only ways in and out.

You can tour central coastal Labrador aboard Marine Atlantic's car ferry from Lewisporte, Newfoundland (☞ Getting Around *in* Newfoundland and Labrador A to Z, *below*). A second vessel, a coastal freighter, travels from St. Anthony, Newfoundland, to Nain, Labrador's northernmost settlement. This trip takes two weeks to complete. Both vessels carry all sorts of food and goods for people living along the coast. On the coastal freighter you'll stop at a number of summer fishing stations and coastal communities. Reservations are required.

Battle Harbour National Historic Site
12 km (7 mi) from Mary's Harbour by boat.

This island site has the only remaining outport fishing merchant's premises that remains intact in the province. Battle Harbour was settled in the 18th century; it was the main fishing port in Labrador until the first half of the 20th century when, after fires destroyed some of the community, the people moved to nearby Mary's Harbour. The site also contains the oldest Anglican church in Labrador. ⊠ *Southern Labrador coast, accessible by boat from Mary's Harbour,* ☎ *709/921–6216, 709/497–8805 off-season.* ☉ *June–Sept.*

Happy Valley–Goose Bay
36 *525 km (326 mi) from Labrador City.*

Happy Valley–Goose Bay is the chief service center for coastal Labrador. If you've come to Labrador to fish, you'll probably pass through here. The town was founded in the 1940s as a top-secret air base used to ferry fleets of North American–manufactured aircraft to Europe. It is still used as a low-level flying training base by the British, Dutch, and German air forces.

SKIING

Ski Mount Shana (☎ 709/896–8162 or 709/896–8068), with 10 downhill runs, is between Happy Valley–Goose Bay and North West River.

North West River
37 *20 km (12 mi) northeast of Happy Valley–Goose Bay.*

North West River, which retains its frontier charm, was founded as a Hudson's Bay trading post and is the former Labrador headquarters of the International Grenfell Association.

Labrador West

Labrador West's subarctic landscape is challenging and unforgettable. Here are some of the world's best angling and wilderness adventure opportunities. The best way to see this area is to ride the **Québec North Shore and Labrador Railway** (☎ 418/968–7805 or 709/944–8205), which leaves Sept Isles, Québec, three times a week in summer and twice a week in the winter. The seven- to eight-hour trip to Schefferville takes you through nearly 600 km (372 mi) of virgin forest, spectacular waterfalls, and majestic mountains.

Wabush
38 *525 km (326 mi) west of Happy Valley–Goose Bay.*

The modern town of Wabush has all the amenities of larger centers, including accommodations, sports and recreational facilities, good shopping, live theater, and some of the finest hospitality you will find anywhere.

SKIING

The **Smokey Mountain Alpine Skiing Center** (☎ 709/944–3505), west of Wabush, is open mid-November to late April and has trails and slopes for both beginners and advanced skiers.

Labrador City

39 *525 km (326 mi) west of Happy Valley–Goose Bay.*

Labrador City has all the facilities of nearby Wabush (☞ *above*). Each March Labrador City and Wabush play host to a 645-km (400-mi) dogsled race, the longest such race in eastern North America.

NEWFOUNDLAND AND LABRADOR A TO Z

Arriving and Departing

By Car Ferry
Marine Atlantic (✉ Box 250, North Sydney, Nova Scotia B2A 3M3, ☎ 902/794–5700 or 709/772–7701, TTY 902/794–8109, FAX 902/564–7480) operates a car ferry from North Sydney, Nova Scotia, to Port aux Basques, Newfoundland (crossing time is six hours); and, from June through October, from North Sydney to Argentia, twice a week (crossing time 12–14 hours). In all cases, reservations are required.

By Plane
The province's main airport for connections from all major North American and European destinations is in St. John's. Other airports in Newfoundland are at Stephenville, Deer Lake, St. Anthony, and Gander; airports in Labrador are in Happy Valley–Goose Bay, Wabush, and Churchill Falls. **Air Canada** (☎ 800/776–3000; in Canada, 800/422–6232) flies into Newfoundland. **Royal Airlines** flies to Newfoundland from Ireland once a week; see your travel agent. **Air Club/Air Transat** flies from Great Britain to Newfoundland once a week (☎ 31–70–35–88–300). The following are **regional connectors:** Air Nova (☎ 800/776–3000; in Newfoundland, 800/563–5151); Air Atlantic (☎ 800/426–7000); Interprovincial Airlines (☎ 709/576–1666; in Newfoundland 800/563–2800); Air Labrador (☎ 709/896–3387; in Newfoundland, 800/563–3042); Air Alliance (Québec to Wabush) (☎ 800/363–7050).

By Train
Iron Ore Canada's Québec North Shore and Labrador Railway (☎ 418/962–9411) has service between Sept Isles, Québec, and Labrador City and Schefferville in Labrador.

Getting Around

In winter some highways may close during and after severe snowstorms. For winter road conditions on the west coast and in Labrador, call the **Department of Works, Services, and Transportation** (in Deer Lake, ☎ 709/635–2162; in Grand Falls–Windsor and Central Newfoundland, 709/292–4300; in Clarenville, 709/466–7953; in St. John's, 709/729–2391).

Labrador
From the island of Newfoundland, you can fly to Labrador via St. John's, Gander, Deer Lake, or Stephenville. Route 500 links Labrador City with Happy Valley–Goose Bay via Churchill Falls. Conditions on this 526-km (326-mi) unpaved wilderness road are best between June and October. If you plan on doing any extensive driving in any part of Labrador, you should contact the **Department of Tourism, Culture and Recreation** (☎ 709/729–2830 or 800/563–6353) for advice on the best routes and road conditions.

To explore the south coast of Labrador, catch the **ferry** at St. Barbe on Route 430 in Newfoundland to Blanc Sablon, Québec. From here you can drive to Red Bay along Route 510.

Summer travel is possible by car ferry through **Marine Atlantic** (☎ 800/ 341–7981; in Lewisporte, Newfoundland, ☎ 709/535–6876; in Happy Valley–Goose Bay, Labrador, 709/896–0041). The ship travels from Lewisporte in Newfoundland to Cartwright, on the coast of Labrador, and then through the Hamilton inlet to Happy Valley–Goose Bay. Reservations are required. The trip takes 33 hours one-way, and two regularly scheduled return trips are made weekly.

Newfoundland

DRL Coachlines (☎ 709/738–8088) runs a trans-island bus service. Buses leave at 8 AM from St. John's and Port aux Basques. Small buses known as outport taxis connect the major centers with surrounding communities.

Newfoundland has an excellent **highway system,** and all but a handful of secondary roads are paved. The province's roads are generally uncrowded, adding to the pleasure of driving. Travel time along the Trans-Canada Highway (Route 1) from Port aux Basques to St. John's is about 13 hours, with time out for a meal in either Gander or Grand Falls–Windsor. The trip from Corner Brook to St. Anthony at the northernmost tip of the island is about five hours. The drive from St. John's to Grand Bank on the Burin Peninsula takes about four hours.

From St. John's to the north coast of the Avalon Peninsula, take Route 30 (Logy Bay Road) to Marine Drive. If you're heading for the southern coast, pick up Route 10 just south of St. John's and follow it toward Trepassey. Locals call this trip "going up the shore," even though it looks like you're traveling down on a map.

Contacts and Resources

Emergencies
Dial **911** for medical emergencies and police.

Fishing
Seasonal and regulatory fishing information can be obtained from the **Department of Tourism, Culture and Recreation** (☎ 800/563–6353).

Guided Tours
ADVENTURE TOURS
Adventure travel in Newfoundland and Labrador is growing rapidly. Local operators offer sea kayaking, ocean diving, canoeing, wildlife viewing, mountain biking, white-water rafting, heli-hiking, and interpretive walks in summer. In winter, snowmobiling, heli-skiing, and caribou- and seal-watching expeditions are popular. Before choosing an operator it's advisable to contact the Department of Tourism, Culture and Recreation to make sure you're calling an established outfit.

Eastern Edge Outfitters (☎ 709/782–1465) leads east-coast sea-kayaking tours and gives white-water kayaking instruction. **Tuckamore Wilderness Lodge** (☎ 709/865–6361 or 709/865–4371) in Main Brook uses its luxurious lodge on the Great Northern Peninsula as a base for viewing caribou, seabird colonies, whales, and icebergs. **Labrador Scenic Ltd.** (☎ 709/497–8326) in North West River organizes tours through central and northern Labrador with an emphasis on wildlife and Labrador's spectacular coast. **Wildland Tours** (☎ 709/ 722–3123) in St. John's, winner of the Governor-General's Award for

Conservation, has weeklong tours to view wildlife and visit historically and culturally significant sites across Newfoundland.

BUS TOURS

McCarthy's Party (☎ 709/781–2244 or 709/781–2266) in St. John's offers guided bus tours across Newfoundland (May–October) in addition to a variety of charter services. **Fleetline Motorcoach Tours** (☎ 709/722–2608 or 709/229–7600) in Holyrood runs island-wide tours. Local tours are available for Port aux Basques, the Codroy Valley, Corner Brook, the Bay of Islands, Gros Morne National Park, the Great Northern Peninsula, and St. John's.

Hospitals

St. Clare's Mercy Hospital (⊠ 154 Le Marchant Rd., St. John's, ☎ 709/778–3111). **Grace Hospital** (⊠ 241 Le Marchant Rd., St. John's, ☎ 709/778–6222). **General Hospital** (⊠ 300 Prince Philip Dr., St. John's, ☎ 709/737–6300). **George B. Cross Hospital** (⊠ Manitoba Dr., Clarenville, ☎ 709/466–3411). **James Paton** (⊠ 125 Trans-Canada Hwy., Gander, ☎ 709/651–2500). **Western Memorial** (⊠ Brookfield Ave., Corner Brook, ☎ 709/637–5000). **Charles S. Curtis Memorial Hospital** (⊠ West St., St. Anthony, ☎ 709/454–3333). **Captain William Jackman Hospital** (⊠ 410 Booth Ave., Labrador City, ☎ 709/944–2632).

Visitor Information

The Department of Tourism, Culture and Recreation (⊠ Box 8730, St. John's A1B 4K2, ☎ 709/729–2830) distributes brochures and maps from its offices in the Confederation Building, West Block, St. John's. The province maintains a **tourist information line** (☎ 800/563–6353), which operates year-round, 24 hours a day.

From June until Labor Day, a network of **Visitor Information Centres,** open daily 9–9, dots the province. These centers carry information on events, accommodations, shopping, and crafts stores in their area. There are in-season visitor information booths at the airports in Gander and St. John's. The city of St. John's operates an information center in a restored railway carriage next to the harbor.

FRENCH VOCABULARY

One of the trickiest French sounds to pronounce is the nasal final *n* sound (whether or not the *n* is actually the last letter of the word). You should try to pronounce it as a sort of nasal grunt—as in "huh." The vowel that precedes the *n* will govern the vowel sound of the word, and in this list we precede the final *n* with an *h* to remind you to be nasal.

Another problem sound is the ubiquitous but untransliterable *eu*, as in *bleu* (blue) or *deux* (two), and the very similar sound in *je* (I), *ce* (this), and *de* (of). The closest equivalent might be the vowel sound of "stood."

English	French	Pronunciation
Basics		
Yes/no	Oui/non	wee/nohn
Please	S'il vous plaît	seel voo play
Thank you	Merci	mair-**see**
You're welcome	De rien	deh ree-**ehn**
That's all right	Il n'y a pas de quoi	eel nee ah pah de kwah
Excuse me, sorry	Pardon	pahr-**dohn**
Sorry!	Désolé(e)	day-zoh-**lay**
Good morning/ afternoon	Bonjour	bohn-**zhoor**
Good evening	Bonsoir	bohn-**swahr**
Goodbye	Au revoir	o ruh-**vwahr**
Mr. (Sir)	Monsieur	muh-**syuh**
Mrs. (Ma'am)	Madame	ma-**dam**
Miss	Mademoiselle	mad-mwa-**zel**
Pleased to meet you	Enchanté(e)	ohn-shahn-**tay**
How are you?	Comment allez-vous?	kuh-mahn-tahl-ay-**voo**
Very well, thanks	Très bien, merci	tray bee-ehn, mair-**see**
And you?	Et vous?	ay voo?
Numbers		
one	un	uhn
two	deux	deuh
three	trois	twah
four	quatre	**kaht**-ruh
five	cinq	sank
six	six	seess
seven	sept	set
eight	huit	wheat
nine	neuf	nuf
ten	dix	deess
eleven	onze	ohnz
twelve	douze	dooz

thirteen	treize	trehz
fourteen	quatorze	kah-**torz**
fifteen	quinze	kanz
sixteen	seize	sez
seventeen	dix-sept	deez-**set**
eighteen	dix-huit	deez-**wheat**
nineteen	dix-neuf	deez-**nuf**
twenty	vingt	vehn
twenty-one	vingt-et-un	vehnt-ay-**uhn**
thirty	trente	trahnt
forty	quarante	ka-**rahnt**
fifty	cinquante	sang-**kahnt**
sixty	soixante	swa-**sahnt**
seventy	soixante-dix	swa-sahnt-**deess**
eighty	quatre-vingts	kaht-ruh-**vehn**
ninety	quatre-vingt-dix	kaht-ruh-vehn-**deess**
one-hundred	cent	sahn
one-thousand	mille	meel

Colors

black	noir	nwahr
blue	bleu	bleuh
brown	brun/marron	bruhn/mar-**rohn**
green	vert	vair
orange	orange	o-**rahnj**
pink	rose	rose
red	rouge	rouge
violet	violette	vee-o-**let**
white	blanc	blahnk
yellow	jaune	zhone

Days of the Week

Sunday	dimanche	dee-**mahnsh**
Monday	lundi	luhn-**dee**
Tuesday	mardi	mahr-**dee**
Wednesday	mercredi	mair-kruh-**dee**
Thursday	jeudi	zhuh-**dee**
Friday	vendredi	vawn-druh-**dee**
Saturday	samedi	sahm-**dee**

Months

January	janvier	zhahn-vee-**ay**
February	février	feh-vree-**ay**
March	mars	marce
April	avril	a-**vreel**
May	mai	meh
June	juin	zhwehn
July	juillet	zhwee-**ay**
August	août	ah-**oo**
September	septembre	sep-**tahm**-bruh
October	octobre	awk-**to**-bruh
November	novembre	no-**vahm**-bruh
December	décembre	day-**sahm**-bruh

Useful Phrases

Do you speak English?	Parlez-vous anglais?	par-lay **voo** ahn-**glay**
I don't speak French	Je ne parle pas français	zhuh nuh parl pah frahn-**say**
I don't understand	Je ne comprends pas	zhuh nuh kohm-**prahn** pah
I understand	Je comprends	zhuh kohm-**prahn**
I don't know	Je ne sais pas	zhuh nuh say **pah**
I'm American/ British	Je suis américain/ anglais	zhuh sweez a-may-ree-**kehn**/ahn-**glay**
What's your name?	Comment vous appelez-vous?	ko-mahn voo za-pell-ay-**voo**
My name is . . .	Je m'appelle . . .	zhuh ma-**pell** . . .
What time is it?	Quelle heure est-il?	kel air eh-**teel**
How?	Comment?	ko-**mahn**
When?	Quand?	kahn
Yesterday	Hier	yair
Today	Aujourd'hui	o-zhoor-**dwee**
Tomorrow	Demain	duh-**mehn**
This morning/ afternoon	Ce matin/cet après-midi	suh ma-**tehn**/set ah-pray-mee-**dee**
Tonight	Ce soir	suh **swahr**
What?	Quoi?	kwah
What is it?	Qu'est-ce que c'est?	kess-kuh-**say**
Why?	Pourquoi?	poor-**kwa**
Who?	Qui?	kee
Where is . . .	Où est . . .	oo ay
the train station?	la gare?	la gar
the subway station?	la station de métro?	la sta-**syon** duh may-**tro**
the bus stop?	l'arrêt de bus?	la-**ray** duh **booss**
the terminal (airport)?	l'aérogare?	lay-ro-**gar**
the post office?	la poste?	la post
the bank?	la banque?	la bahnk
the . . . hotel?	l'hôtel . . .?	lo-**tel**
the store?	le magasin?	luh ma-ga-**zehn**
the cashier?	la caisse?	la **kess**
the . . . museum?	le musée . . .?	luh mew-**zay**
the hospital?	l'hôpital?	lo-pee-**tahl**
the elevator?	l'ascenseur?	la-sahn-**seuhr**
the telephone?	le téléphone?	luh tay-lay-**phone**
Where are the restrooms?	Où sont les toilettes?	oo sohn lay twah-**let**
Here/there	Ici/là	ee-**see**/la
Left/right	A gauche/à droite	a goash/a drwaht

Straight ahead	Tout droit	too drwah
Is it near/far?	C'est près/loin?	say pray/lwehn
I'd like . . .	Je voudrais . . .	zhuh voo-**dray**
a room	une chambre	ewn **shahm**-bruh
the key	la clé	la clay
a newspaper	un journal	uhn zhoor-**nahl**
a stamp	un timbre	uhn **tam**-bruh
I'd like to buy . . .	Je voudrais acheter . . .	zhuh voo-**dray** ahsh-**tay**
a cigar	un cigare	uhn see-**gar**
cigarettes	des cigarettes	day see-ga-**ret**
matches	des allumettes	days a-loo-**met**
dictionary	un dictionnaire	uhn deek-see-oh-**nare**
soap	du savon	dew sah-**vohn**
city plan	un plan de ville	uhn plahn de **veel**
road map	une carte routière	ewn cart roo-tee-**air**
magazine	une revue	ewn reh-**vu**
envelopes	des enveloppes	dayz ahn-veh-**lope**
writing paper	du papier à lettres	dew pa-pee-**ay** a **let**-ruh
airmail writing paper	du papier avion	dew pa-pee-**ay** a-vee-**ohn**
postcard	une carte postale	ewn cart pos-**tal**
How much is it?	C'est combien?	say comb-bee-**ehn**
It's expensive/cheap	C'est cher/pas cher	say share/pa share
A little/a lot	Un peu/beaucoup	uhn peuh/bo-**koo**
More/less	Plus/moins	plu/mwehn
Enough/too (much)	Assez/trop	a-say/tro
I am ill/sick	Je suis malade	zhuh swee ma-**lahd**
Call a doctor	Appelez un docteur	a-play uhn dohk-**tehr**
Help!	Au secours!	o suh-**koor**
Stop!	Arrêtez!	a-reh-**tay**
Fire!	Au feu!	o fuh
Caution!/Look out!	Attention!	a-tahn-see-**ohn**

Dining Out

A bottle of . . .	une bouteille de . . .	ewn boo-**tay** duh
A cup of . . .	une tasse de . . .	ewn tass duh
A glass of . . .	un verre de . . .	uhn vair duh
Ashtray	un cendrier	uhn sahn-dree-**ay**
Bill/check	l'addition	la-dee-see-**ohn**
Bread	du pain	dew pan
Breakfast	le petit-déjeuner	luh puh-**tee** day-zhuh-**nay**
Butter	du beurre	dew burr

Cheers!	A votre santé!	ah vo-truh sahn-**tay**
Cocktail/aperitif	un apéritif	uhn ah-pay-ree-**teef**
Dinner	le dîner	luh dee-**nay**
Dish of the day	le plat du jour	luh plah dew **zhoor**
Enjoy!	Bon appétit!	bohn a-pay-**tee**
Fixed-price menu	le menu	luh may-**new**
Fork	une fourchette	ewn four-**shet**
I am diabetic	Je suis diabétique	zhuh swee dee-ah-bay-**teek**
I am on a diet	Je suis au régime	zhuh sweez o ray-**jeem**
I am vegetarian	Je suis végétarien(ne)	zhuh swee vay-zhay-ta-ree-**en**
I cannot eat . . .	Je ne peux pas manger de . . .	zhuh nuh **puh** pah mahn-**jay** deh
I'd like to order	Je voudrais commander	zhuh voo-**dray** ko-mahn-**day**
I'm hungry/thirsty	J'ai faim/soif	zhay fahm/swahf
Is service/the tip included?	Est-ce que le service est compris?	ess kuh luh sair-**veess** ay comb-**pree**
It's good/bad	C'est bon/mauvais	say bohn/mo-**vay**
It's hot/cold	C'est chaud/froid	say sho/frwah
Knife	un couteau	uhn koo-**toe**
Lunch	le déjeuner	luh day-zhuh-**nay**
Menu	la carte	la cart
Napkin	une serviette	ewn sair-vee-**et**
Pepper	du poivre	dew **pwah**-vruh
Plate	une assiette	ewn a-see-**et**
Please give me . . .	Donnez-moi . . .	doe-nay-**mwah**
Salt	du sel	dew sell
Spoon	une cuillère	ewn kwee-**air**
Sugar	du sucre	dew **sook**-ruh
Waiter!/Waitress!	Monsieur!/ Mademoiselle!	muh-**syuh**/ mad-mwa-**zel**
Wine list	la carte des vins	la cart day **van**

INDEX

NOTES

NOTES

Know Before You Go

Wendy Perrin's
Secrets Every Smart
Traveler Should Know

"A lively and useful guide."

—*The Washington Post*

How should you pick a travel agent? How do you get a room at a sold-out hotel? Wendy Perrin of *Condé Nast Traveler* tells how to avoid travel snafus and what to do if the unexpected happens.

$15.00 ($21.00 Canada) ISBN: 0-679-03351-3
At bookstores, or call 1-800-533-6478.
www.fodors.com/

Fodor's *The name that means smart travel.*™

Fodor's Travel Publications

Available at bookstores everywhere, or call 1–800–533–6478, 24 hours a day.

Gold Guides

U.S.

Alaska

Arizona

Boston

California

Cape Cod, Martha's
Vineyard, Nantucket

The Carolinas &
Georgia

Chicago

Colorado

Florida

Hawai'i

Las Vegas, Reno,
Tahoe

Los Angeles

Maine, Vermont,
New Hampshire

Maui & Lāna'i

Miami & the Keys

New England

New Orleans

New York City

Pacific North Coast

Philadelphia & the
Pennsylvania Dutch
Country

The Rockies

San Diego

San Francisco

Santa Fe, Taos,
Albuquerque

Seattle & Vancouver

The South

U.S. & British Virgin
Islands

USA

Virginia & Maryland

Walt Disney World,
Universal Studios
and Orlando

Washington, D.C.

Foreign

Australia

Austria

The Bahamas

Belize & Guatemala

Bermuda

Canada

Cancún, Cozumel,
Yucatán Peninsula

Caribbean

China

Costa Rica

Cuba

The Czech Republic
& Slovakia

Eastern &
Central Europe

Europe

Florence, Tuscany
& Umbria

France

Germany

Great Britain

Greece

Hong Kong

India

Ireland

Israel

Italy

Japan

London

Madrid & Barcelona

Mexico

Montréal &
Québec City

Moscow, St.
Petersburg, Kiev

The Netherlands,
Belgium &
Luxembourg

New Zealand

Norway

Nova Scotia, New
Brunswick, Prince
Edward Island

Paris

Portugal

Provence &
the Riviera

Scandinavia

Scotland

Singapore

South Africa

South America

Southeast Asia

Spain

Sweden

Switzerland

Thailand

Toronto

Turkey

Vienna & the Danube
Valley

Special-Interest Guides

Adventures to Imagine

Alaska Ports of Call

Ballpark Vacations

Caribbean Ports
of Call

The Complete Guide
to America's
National Parks

Disney Like a Pro

Europe Ports of Call

Family Adventures

Fodor's Gay Guide
to the USA

Fodor's How to Pack

Great American
Learning Vacations

Great American
Sports & Adventure
Vacations

Great American
Vacations

Great American
Vacations for
Travelers with
Disabilities

Halliday's New
Orleans Food
Explorer

Healthy Escapes

Kodak Guide to
Shooting Great
Travel Pictures

National Parks and
Seashores of the East

National Parks of
the West

Nights to Imagine

Rock & Roll Traveler
Great Britain and
Ireland

Rock & Roll Traveler
USA

Sunday in
San Francisco

Walt Disney World
for Adults

Weekends in New
York

Wendy Perrin's
Secrets Every Smart
Traveler Should
Know

Worldwide Cruises
and Ports of Call

Fodor's Special Series

Fodor's Best Bed & Breakfasts

America

California

The Mid-Atlantic

New England

The Pacific Northwest

The South

The Southwest

The Upper Great Lakes

Compass American Guides

Alaska

Arizona

Boston

Chicago

Colorado

Hawaii

Idaho

Hollywood

Las Vegas

Maine

Manhattan

Minnesota

Montana

New Mexico

New Orleans

Oregon

Pacific Northwest

San Francisco

Santa Fe

South Carolina

South Dakota

Southwest

Texas

Utah

Virginia

Washington

Wine Country

Wisconsin

Wyoming

Citypacks

Amsterdam

Atlanta

Berlin

Chicago

Florence

Hong Kong

London

Los Angeles

Montréal

New York City

Paris

Prague

Rome

San Francisco

Tokyo

Venice

Washington, D.C.

Exploring Guides

Australia

Boston & New England

Britain

California

Canada

Caribbean

China

Costa Rica

Egypt

Florence & Tuscany

Florida

France

Germany

Greek Islands

Hawaii

Ireland

Israel

Italy

Japan

London

Mexico

Moscow & St. Petersburg

New York City

Paris

Prague

Provence

Rome

San Francisco

Scotland

Singapore & Malaysia

South Africa

Spain

Thailand

Turkey

Venice

Flashmaps

Boston

New York

San Francisco

Washington, D.C.

Fodor's Gay Guides

Los Angeles & Southern California

New York City

Pacific Northwest

San Francisco and the Bay Area

South Florida

USA

Pocket Guides

Acapulco

Aruba

Atlanta

Barbados

Budapest

Jamaica

London

New York City

Paris

Prague

Puerto Rico

Rome

San Francisco

Washington, D.C.

Languages for Travelers (Cassette & Phrasebook)

French

German

Italian

Spanish

Mobil Travel Guides

America's Best Hotels & Restaurants

California and the West

Major Cities

Great Lakes

Mid-Atlantic

Northeast

Northwest and Great Plains

Southeast

Southwest and South Central

Rivages Guides

Bed and Breakfasts of Character and Charm in France

Hotels and Country Inns of Character and Charm in France

Hotels and Country Inns of Character and Charm in Italy

Hotels and Country Inns of Character and Charm in Paris

Hotels and Country Inns of Character and Charm in Portugal

Hotels and Country Inns of Character and Charm in Spain

Short Escapes

Britain

France

New England

Near New York City

Fodor's Sports

Golf Digest's Places to Play

Skiing USA

USA Today The Complete Four Sport Stadium Guide

WHEREVER YOU TRAVEL, *H*ELP IS NEVER FAR AWAY.

From planning your trip to

providing travel assistance along

the way, American Express®

Travel Service Offices are

always there to help

you do more.

American Express Travel Service
Offices are found in central locations
throughout Canada.

http://www.americanexpress.com/travel